Western Europe
phrasebook

Chris Andrews
Rob van Driesum
James Jenkin
Isabel Moutinho
Seán Ó Riain
Javi Pascual Otalora
Wally Thompson

Western Europe Phrasebook
   1st edition

Published by
   Lonely Planet Publications
   Head Office: PO Box 617, Hawthorn, Vic 3122, Australia
   Branches: 155 Filbert St, Suite 251, Oakland, CA 94607, USA
                        10 Barley Mow Passage, Chiswick, London W4 4PH, UK
                        71 bis rue du Cardinal Lemoine, 75005 Paris, France

Printed by
   Colorcraft, Hong Kong

Published
   November 1992

National Library of Australia Cataloguing in Publication Data

Western Europe phrasebook

   Includes Index.
   ISBN 0 86442 152 4

   1. Europe – Languages – Conversation and phrase books –
   I. Thompson, R.W., 1922- . (Series: Language survival kit)

418

© Lonely Planet Publications Pty Ltd, 1992

Contents

Basque..10

Introduction.........................10 Small Talk............................14
Pronunciation......................12 Food.....................................15
Greetings & Civilities 13

Catalan..18

Introduction.........................18 Small Talk............................21
Pronunciation......................19 Food.....................................22
Greetings & Civilities 20

Dutch..26

Introduction.........................26 Around Town 58
Pronunciation......................27 In the Country 65
Greetings & Civilities ....29 Food.....................................66
Small Talk............................30 Shopping..............................80
Signs....................................37 Health..................................87
Emergencies........................38 Time & Dates 91
Paperwork............................40 Numbers & Amounts............94
Getting Around....................41 Abbreviations 96
Accommodation...................52

French..98

Introduction.........................98 Paperwork..........................113
Pronunciation....................100 Getting Around 114
Greetings & Civilities ....102 Accommodation 125
Small Talk..........................103 Around Town 133
Signs..................................110 In the Country 139
Emergencies......................110 Food...................................141

Shopping 152
Health 159
Time & Dates 164

Numbers & Amounts 167
Abbreviations 169

German 172

Introduction......................172
Pronunciation 173
Greetings & Civilities 176
Small Talk.........................177
Signs..............................184
Emergencies.......................185
Paperwork 188
Getting Around....................189
Accommodation...................201

Around Town 208
In the Country 214
Food...............................216
Shopping..........................224
Health.............................230
Time & Dates 235
Numbers & Amounts 238
Abbreviations 240

Irish 242

Introduction......................242
Pronunciation.....................244
Greetings & Civilities 245

Small Talk.........................246
Food...............................248

Portuguese 252

Introduction......................252
Pronunciation 253
Greetings & Civilities 257
Small Talk 258
Signs..............................264
Emergencies.......................264
Paperwork 267
Getting Around....................268

Accommodation 277
Around Town 282
In the Country 287
Health.............................303
Time & Dates 307
Numbers & Amounts 310
Abbreviations 311

Spanish 314

Introduction......................314
Pronunciation.....................315
Greetings & Civilities 318

Small Talk.........................319
Signs..............................325
Emergencies.......................326

Paperwork 329
Getting Around....................330
Accommodation..................343
Around Town......................350
In the Country 357
Food 359

Shopping...........................367
Health................................374
Time & Dates 380
Numbers & Amounts..........383
Abbreviations 385

Index **387**

Acknowledgements

The Basque section was written by Kalegana, Bilbao, in collaboration with SUA Edizioak, Bilbao. Wally Thompson wrote the Catalan section. Dutch was written by Rob van Driesum, with thanks to Doekes Lulofs, and Chris Andrews wrote the French chapter. James Jenkin wrote the German chapter, with assistance from Edward and Alex Scharaschkin. Dr Seán Ó Riain is the author of the Irish section. Isabel Moutinho wrote the Portuguese and Spanish chapters.

The editor of this book is Sally Steward, and Tamsin Wilson was responsible for design and illustrations. Thanks to Dan Levin for computer assistance.

From the Publisher

In this book Lonely Planet uses a simplified phonetic translation, based on the International Phonetic Alphabet. While this can only approximate the exact sounds of each language, it serves as the most useful guide for readers attempting to speak the various words and phrases. As you spend time in a country, listening to native speakers and following the rules offered here in the pronunciation sections, you should be able to read directly from the language itself.

All the languages in this book have masculine, feminine and sometimes neuter, forms of words. The different forms are separated in the text by slashes and/or the bracketed letters (m), (f) and (neut), when appropriate. Many words share the same form, so no indication of gender is required.

Several of the languages in this book have both formal and informal ways of speech, which means that for one word in English you may find two in the other language, one being the polite, formal, word and the other being more casual, informal. For the purposes of this book the formal way of speech has been adopted throughout, as this will ensure that at least you will not offend anyone by using the more intimate speech. In instances where the informal is commonly used, we have included it, indicated with the letters (inf).

Basque

Basque

Introduction

The Basque language is one of the oldest languages in the world, and one of the keys to primitive Europe. It's the only pre-Indo-European language that survives in Europe, apart from Hungarian and Finnish, languages that arrived in Europe considerably later. In fact, it's quite difficult to understand how this language has survived up to now in a land that has known many different settlements (Celts, Romans, Visigoths and Vandals, amongst others).

In a territory situated between two states (France and Spain), and divided by the Pyrenees, the Basque language is spoken by 800,000 people among the 2.4 million who live in the Basque Country, *Euskal Herria*.

The Basque language is spoken in the seven historical territories of Euskal Herria: south of the Pyrenees (Spanish state) it is spoken in the north of Nafarroa (Navarra), Gipuzkoa, Bizkaia and Araba, although the language is almost completely lost in this last territory; north of the Pyrenees (French state) it is spoken in Lapurdi, Behenafarroa and Zuberoa.

According to researchers who have studied the history of the Basque language, the biggest extension of this language took place about 2,000 years ago, when the Romans started to occupy this land. At that time the Basque language was spoken in the southeast of France, and from Aragon to Burgos in Spain.

The regression of the language to current limits has happened since the 13th century, when Spanish and the other Romance languages appeared and replaced Latin in public administration.

The Bourbons resolved the Spanish language as the only language of the area in the 18th century.

Nowadays the situation of the Basque language is in trouble because it is a minor language in its own territory (only 25% of the population are Basque speakers) and because the weight of the Spanish and French languages, having more legal resources, is getting heavier day by day in all areas of life. This is considered by the groups and organisations that work for the Basque language as a clear situation of linguistic oppression.

Since 1960, in spite of the dictator Franco's persecution (1939–1975), a popular movement for the recuperation of the Basque language has arisen. Nowadays it has moved forward a little bit: the Basque language, as well as the Spanish one, has its own place at school, and even a TV channel.

However, the lack of real and lasting help from the Basque administration, and the misgivings, lack of appraisement and a kind of margination and hidden persecution by the Spanish and French administrations, have jeopardised the survival of this old language into the 21st century. The awareness and feelings of the Basque people not to lose the language, and to make it their method of daily communication, is the only solution to avoiding this disaster.

At present, at the same time as the *bertsolarismo* (improvised poems in public), Basque has arisen as an important literature, and it has begun to be translated into different languages. In spite of the lack of institutional support there are groups of theatre, musicians, and other forms of entertainment, who use the Basque language only, as a way of transmission of their messages. All this popular and cultural Basque movement is as much at risk as the language itself. The future will either see the survival of the Basque nation with its culture and language intact, or its absorption by another, different, culture and language. Some attempt by visitors to speak this language, with this little conversation guide, will be well appreciated and deeply thanked by the Basque people.

Pronunciation

An English speaker shouldn't have many difficulties with Basque pronunciation. There are no written accents, and stress is flexible. Vowels are always pronounced in the same way. There are two distinct 'r' sounds to be aware of: one, much as the English 'r' at the beginning or middle of a word; and the other, like a cross between the Scottish 'r' and the growl of a two-stroke motorbike: 'r-r-r-r-r-r'. Here is a list of particular sounds to remember – other letters are approximately the same as in English.

b	as in 'box' (there is no 'v' sound)
k	as in English
g	always hard (rendered as *gh* in our pronunciation guide)
h	dropped, Cockney-style
j	as the 'j' in 'jaw'
r	as in English
rr	the 'growly' r
x	as in 'pleasure' (*zh* in our pronunciation guide)
tx	as the 'ch' in 'chew'
tz	as the 'tz' in 'tzetze'
ts	as the 'sh' in 'ship'

Greetings & Civilities
Greetings
Hi!
  kaai-zho! Kaixo!
Good morning.
  e-ghu-non Egunon.
Good night.
  gha-bon Gabon.
How are you?
  zer mo-duz? Zer moduz?
What's new?
  zer be-rri? Zer berri?
Very well, thanks.
  oso on-ghi, es-kerr-ik as-ko! Oso ongi, eskerrik asko!

Goodbyes
Goodbye.
  ah-ghurr Agur.
See you later.
  ghe-ro arr-te Gero arte.
Take care.
  on-do i-bi-li Ondo ibili.

Important Civilities
Please.
  me-se-dez Mesedez.
Thank you.
  es-kerr-ik as-ko Eskerrik asko.

I'd like to introduce you
to …
   aurr-kez-tu naai di-z ut …   Aurkeztu nahi dizut …
I'm pleased to meet you.
   poz-ten naiz zu ezaghu-tseaz   Pozten naiz zu ezagutzeaz.

Forms of Address
Mr/Mrs (middle-aged man or
woman)
   aai-zu!   Aizu!
young man
   aai-zak mu-til!   Aizak mutil!
young woman
   aai-zan nes-ka   Aizan neska!
friend
   laa-ghun   Lagun

Small Talk
Where are you from?
   non gho-a za-rah?   Nongoa zara?

I'm from …
   ni … naiz   Ni … naiz.

Australia	*austra-liaa-koa*	Australiakoa
England	*ingala-terra-koa*	Ingalaterrakoa
Ireland	*ir-lan-da-koa*	Irlandakoa
New Zealand	*ze-laan-da berr-i-koa*	Zelanda Berrikoa
Scotland	*eskozia-koa*	Eskoziakoa
the USA	*a-mer-i-kanoa*	Amerikanoa
Wales	*galesekoa*	Galesekoa

What's your name?
no-lah du-zu i-ze-naa?   Nola duzu izena?
I'm called John.
ni-re i-ze-naa jon dah   Nire izena Jon da.

Some Useful Phrases

How do you say that in
Basque?
no-lah e-saa-ten da   Nola esaten da hori eus-
o-ri eus-ka-raz?   karaz?
Excuse me.
parr-kaa-tu   Parkatu.
Where's the toilet, please?
non da-gho ko-mu-nah,   Non dago komuna,
me-se-dez?   mesedez?
At the end.
aaz-ke-ne-an   Azkenean.
On the left.
ez-kerre-taa-ra   Ezkerretara.
On the right.
es-kuine-taa-ra   Eskuinetara.

Food

Waiter!
aai-zan!   Aizan! (f)
aai-zak!   Aizak! (m)
A little bread, please.
o-ghi pizh-ka bat, me-se-dez   Ogi piska bat, mesedez.
A bottle of wine.
bo-ti-la bat aar-do   Botila bat ardo.

salad	*en-shah-la-da*	entsalada
fish	*arraai-na*	arraina
beefsteak with chips (French fries)	*zherr-ah pa-ta-ta fri-ji-tue-kin*	xerra patata frijituekin
a beer	*gha-rah-gar-do bat*	garagardo bat
mineral water	*me-taa-lu-ra*	metalura
water	*u-ra*	ura

Specific Dishes

The gastronomy of the Basque Country is very famous, and if you'd like to taste some typical dishes and drinks, try any of the following.

Makailoa bizkaitar erara.	Codfish à la Bizkai.
Legatza euskal erara.	Hake à la Basque.
Indaba gorriak.	Red beans.
Arrozesnea.	Creamed rice.
Sagardoa.	Cider.
Errioxako ardoa.	Wine from La Rioja.

Catalan

Catalan

Introduction

Catalan is one of the Romance, or neo-Latin, languages, like French, Italian, Portuguese, Romanian and Spanish. It is not a dialect of any other language and its nearest relative is Occitan, spoken in southern France. It is the mother tongue of up to seven million people, most of whom also speak at least one other language. It is spoken in Catalonia proper, coastal Valencia, the Balearic Islands, north-eastern Aragon, Andorra, Roussillon (in France), and in and around Alguer (Alghero) in Sardinia. The varieties heard in all these areas are mutually intelligible, but learners are advised to attempt to acquire the educated speech of Barcelona, which owes much to the literary tradition of the language and whose acquisition is well supported by text-books, cassettes and excellent video courses.

In Barcelona, Spanish (Castilian) is widely spoken, and English is studied in a myriad of language academies. Still, Catalans usually appreciate it when visitors attempt to communicate, if even in rudimentary fashion, in the Catalan language. Catalan, in written form, first appears in glosses or marginal comments in texts of the 9th century, but from the 12th century onwards, right up to the present day, it has been the vehicle of a rich and vigorous literature. Even during periods of eclipse, as in the 16th century when the unification of the crowns of Castile and Aragon led to the primacy of Spanish as the language of administration, the burgesses of Barcelona continued to cultivate their traditional language, particularly in its spoken form. After its banning and persecution in the 18th century by the Bourbons, it was to see a new birth, or *Renaixença*, in the 19th century, with the publication of important work in prose and verse. Even during the dictatorships of Primo de Rivera (1923–1930) and Francisco Franco (1939–1975), the literary language continued to flourish, underground, of course, since outward manifestations were often severely persecuted and punished.

Contemporary Catalan literature, in the novel, poetry and drama, has universal appeal and has been translated into many languages, including English. A case in point is the work of Mercè Rodoreda whose magnificent novel, *Plaça del Diamant (Diamond Square)*, has enjoyed as much popularity in the English-speaking world as in Catalonia itself.

Pronunciation

There are no very difficult sounds in Catalan for an English-speaker. Learners should, however, note that vowels will vary according to whether they occur in stressed or unstressed syllables. You should be aware that there are two distinct 'r'-sounds: one, much as English 'r' at the beginning or middle of a word; and the other, like a cross between the Scottish 'r' and the growl of a two-stroke motorbike: 'r-r-r-r-r-r'.

a	stressed, as the 'a' in 'father'. Unstressed, as in 'about'.
b	pronounced 'p' at the end of a word
c	hard before **a**, **o** and **u**. Soft before **e** and **i**.
ç	like 'ss'
d	pronounced 't' at the end of a word
g	hard before **a**, **o** and **u**. Before **e** and **i**, like the 's' in measure.
h	dropped, Cockney-style
i	like the 'i' in machine

j	like the 's' in pleasure
o	stressed, as in 'pot'. Unstressed, like the 'oo' in 'zoo'.
r	as in English, in the middle of a word. Silent at the end.
rr	the 'growly' 'r', at the beginning of a word, or 'rr' in the middle of a word.
s	as in English at the beginning of a word. In the middle, as 'z'.
v	as the 'b' in Barcelona. Pronounced 'v' in some other areas.
x	mostly as in English but sometimes 'sh'

Other letters are approximately as in English. There are a few odd combinations:

ll	like 'll' in million
l.l	repeat the 'l'
tx	like 'ch'
gu	a hard 'g'
qu	like 'k'

Following the above pronunciation guide, you should find most sounds quite straightforward. Where any tricky words crop up, you'll find a guide to pronunciation in brackets.

Greetings & Civilities

Hi!	Hola!
Good morning/Goodbye.	Bon dia.
Good afternoon.	Bona tarda.
Good night.	Bona nit.
How are you?	Com esteu? *(ess-tay-oo)*
What's new?	Què hi ha?
Very well, thanks.	Molt bé *(moll bay)*, gràcies.

Goodbyes

Goodbye.	Adeu-siau.
	(ah-day-oo see-ow)
See you later.	A reveure.
	(ah rah-vay-oo rah)
Take care.	Passi-ho bé.

Important Civilities

Please.	Sisplau. *(seess plow)*
Thank you.	Gràcies.
Thank you very much.	Moltes gràcies.
No worries, mate. You're welcome.	De res, company. *(coom-pan)*
I'd like to present you to …	Li presento …
I'm pleased to meet you.	Molt de gust de coneixe-lo. *(conesha-loo)*
Delighted!	Incantat (m)/Incantada. (f)

Forms of Address

Mr, Sir (important in Catalan)	Senyor ('e' sounds like 'ah')
Mrs, Madame	Senyora
young woman (polite)	senyoreta
friend	amic (m)/amiga (f)
mate	compagn ('n' as in French *campagne*)

Small Talk

Where are you from?	Don és?
I'm from the UK, USA, New Zealand, Australia.	Soc de Anglaterra, América, Nova Zelanda, Austràlia.
What's your name?	Com es diu? *(az-dyu)*
I'm called …	Em dic … *(ah'm dik …)*

More Useful Phrases

How do you say that in Catalan?	Com es diu això (*ah-shaw*) en català?
Excuse me.	Perdoni.
Where's the toilet, please?	On és el lavabo (*labaabu*), sisplau?
At the end.	Al fons.
on the left	a mà esquerra
on the right	a la dreta
I like …	M'agrada …

Food

Instead of asking for garlic bread, ask for tomato-bread: *pa amb tomàquet*. As a first dish you might try an *escalivada*, a dish of grilled vegetables (no meat). For flavour add *allioli*, a classical sauce made from oil and garlic, with egg-yolk often added.

L'escudella i carn d'olla is a kind of broth containing many kinds of meat. After the broth is consumed, the meat is eaten as a special course. You know *paella* already. It is originally a dish from Valencia, but try it anywhere in Spain.

Waiter!	Cambrer!
A little bread, please.	Una mica de pa, sisplau.
A drop of wine. (No byo here!)	Un glop de vi.
A bottle.	Una ampolla.
A beer.	Una cervesa.
I'm vegetarian.	Soc vegetarià. (*vaj-ha-tari-aa*)

barbecued rabbit	conill a la plancha
	(coo-niy a la plansha)
a Catalan salad	'na amanada
chips (French fries)	patates frites
fish	peix *(pesh)*
mineral water	aigua mineral
	(aay-wa mee-na-raal)
pavlova	Pavlova
water	aigua

If you are not inspired by the rich cuisine of Catalonia, Valencia or the Balearics, you can always ask for 'Feesh an Cheeps', bacon and eggs, and apple pie (just like mother makes), as these dishes are well-known all along the Mediterranean coast of Spain.

Dutch

Dutch

Introduction

Most English speakers use the term 'Dutch' to describe the language spoken in the Netherlands, and 'Flemish' for that spoken in the northern half of Belgium and a tiny north-western corner of France. Both are, in fact, the same language, the correct term for which is Netherlandic, *Nederlands*, a West Germanic language that is spoken by about 25 million people worldwide.

The differences between Dutch and Flemish are similar to those between British and North American English: despite some differences they're very much the same language, with a shared literature.

Netherlandic is also spoken in Surinam in South America, in the Netherlands Antilles in the Caribbean, and among a dwindling group of colonially educated elders in Indonesia. Afrikaans, spoken in southern Africa, is a descendant of 18th century Netherlandic. In North American history, the term 'Dutch' referred to the sizeable group of German immigrants, the 'Pennsylvania Dutch'. The term was a corruption of *Deutsch*, which means 'German'. The Dutch resent being confused with Germans, and the two languages, despite common roots which make it relatively easy for a speaker of one to learn the other, are as different today as Spanish and Portuguese.

When travelling in the Netherlands and Flemish-speaking Belgium, you'll find that virtually everyone speaks English to some degree, and will use it. Don't let that put you off. Like almost anywhere else in the world, an effort to speak the local tongue will always be met with goodwill. If they still insist on speaking English, it's because they want to ease communication rather than deny you the chance of speaking their language.

The Netherlandic pronunciation used here is based on *Algemeen Beschaafd Nederlands* (ABN), or 'General Cultured Netherlandic', the Dutch/Flemish equivalent of 'BBC English'. This is used in education and generally in the media, and is understood, if not always used, by everyone.

Like many other languages, Netherlandic gives its nouns genders. There are three: masculine, feminine and neuter. When talking about people, you'll often find masculine and feminine versions. For example, 'student' is a male student, 'studente' a female student. These versions are rendered in the text here with the masculine first. When a noun is preceded by a definite article ('the'), masculine and feminine forms take the article **de**, pronounced *der*, while neutral forms use **het**, *ert*. The indefinite article ('a/an') is **een**, *ern*.

Netherlandic also has a formal and an informal version of the English 'you'. The formal is 'U' (written with a capital letter and pronounced *ü*); the informal is 'je' (pronounced *yer*). Netherlandic has become less formal in recent years and 'U' is no longer commonly used to address people the same age as you, let alone younger, whether you know them or not. But people who are older, especially if you don't know them, should still be addressed with 'U'. Flemish tends to be slightly more formal than Dutch.

Pronunciation
Vowels
Single vowels are pretty straightforward, with long and short sounds for each vowel. Here are some sounds peculiar to Dutch:

DUTCH

Letter/s	Pronunciation Guide	Sounds
a	*ah*	short, as the 'u' in 'cut'
a, aa	*aa*	long, as the 'a' in 'father'
au, ou	*ow*	both are pronounced the same, somewhere between the 'ow' in 'how' and the 'ow' in 'glow'
e	*eh, er*	short, as the 'e' in 'bet', or as the 'er' in 'fern'
e, ee	*ay*	long, as the 'ay' in 'day'
ei, ij	*ey*	as the 'ey' in 'they'
eu	*er*	this combination sounds the way the British queen would pronounce the 'o' in 'over' if she were exaggerating.
i	*i*	short, as the 'i' in 'in'
i, ie	*ee*	long, as the 'ee' in 'see'
o	*o*	short, as in 'pot'
o, oo	*oh*	long, as the 'o' in 'note'
oe	*oo*	as the 'oo' in 'zoo'
u	*er*	short, similar to the 'er' in 'fern', or the French *de*
u, uu	*ü*	long, like the 'u' in German *über*
ui	*er*	there's no equivalent sound in English. For those who speak French, the *eui* in *fauteuil* comes pretty close, so long as you leave out the slide towards the *l*.

Consonants

ch & g	in the north, a hard 'kh' sound as in the Scottish *loch*. In the south, a softer, lisping sound.
j	a 'y' sound. Occasionally, especially with borrowed words, a 'j' or 'zh' sound, as in 'jam' or 'pleasure'.

r	in the south, a trilled sound. In the north it varies, often occurring as a back-of-the-throat sound as in French or German.
s	usually the 's' in 'sample'. Sometimes a 'zh' sound as in 'pleasure'.
w	a clipped sound, almost like a 'v', when at the beginning or middle of a word. At the end of a word it is like the English 'w'.

Greetings & Civilities
Top Useful Phrases

Hello.
> *dahkh/hah-loh* Dag/Hallo.

Goodbye.
> *dahkh* Dag.

Yes./No.
> *yaa/nay* Ja./Nee.

Excuse me.
> *pahr-don* Pardon.

May I? Do you mind?
> *mahkh ik? vint ü/vint yer heht ehrkh?* Mag ik? Vindt U/vind je het erg?

Sorry. (excuse me, forgive me)
> *so-ree* Sorry.

Please.
> *ahls-tü-bleeft/ahls-yer-bleeft* Alstublieft./Alsjeblieft.

Thank you.
> *dahnk ü/yer (wehl)* Dank U/je (wel).

Many thanks.
> *vayl dahnk* Veel dank.

DUTCH

That's fine. You're welcome.
daht is khoed. khayn dahnk · Dat is goed. Geen dank.

Greetings
Good morning.
khoo-der mor-khern Goede morgen.
Good afternoon.
khoo-der mid-dahkh Goede middag.
Good evening/night.
khoo-dern aa-vont/khoo-der nahkht Goeden avond./Goede nacht.
How are you?
hoo khaat heht meht ü/yer? Hoe gaat het met U/je?
Well, thanks.
khoot, dahnk ü/yer Goed, dank U/je.

Forms of Address
Madam/Mrs	*mer-vrow*	Mevrouw/Mevr
Sir/Mr	*mer-near*	Meneer/Mr
Miss	*yer-frow*	Juffrouw
companion	*reys-kher-noht*	reisgenoot (m)
	reys-kher-noht-er	reisgenote (f)
friend	*vreent*	vriend (m)
	vreend-in	vriendin (f)

Small Talk
Meeting People
What is your name?
hoo hayt ü/yer? Hoe heet U/je?
My name is ...
ik hayt ... Ik heet ...

I'd like to introduce you to …
mahkh ik ü/yer vor-stehl-   Mag ik U/je voorstellen
lern aan …   aan …
I'm pleased to meet you.
aan-kher-naam   Aangenaam.

Nationalities

Where are you from?
waar komt ü/kom yer   Waar komt U/kom je
vahn-daan?   vandaan?

I am from …
ik kom ert …   Ik kom uit …

Australia	*oh-straa-lee-yer*	Australië
Belgium	*behl-khee-yer*	België
Canada	*kah-naa-daa*	Canada
England	*ehng-er-lahnt*	Engeland
Flanders	*vlaan-der-ern*	Vlaanderen
Holland,	*hol-lahnt, nay-der-*	Holland,
Netherlands	*lahnt*	Nederland
Ireland	*eer-lahnt*	Ierland
New Zealand	*neeoo zay-lahnt*	Nieuw Zeeland
Scotland	*skhot-lahnt*	Schotland
the USA	*ver-ay-nikh-der*	Verenigde Staten
	staa-tern	
Wales	*wayls*	Wales

Age

How old are you?
hoo owt behnt ü/behn yer?   Hoe oud bent U/ben je?
I am … years old.
ik behn … yaar owt   Ik ben … jaar oud.

DUTCH

Occupations

What (work) do you do?

waht doot ü/doo yer (vor wehrk)?	Wat doet U/doe je (voor werk)?

I am a/an …
ik behn ern …   Ik ben een …

artist	*kern-ster-naar*	kunstenaar
business person	*zaa-kern-mahn*	zakenman (m)
	zaa-kern-vrow	zakenvrouw (f)
doctor	*dok-ter*	dokter
engineer	*in-zhin-yer*	ingenieur
farmer	*booer*	boer
journalist	*zhoor-nah-list*	journalist (m)
	zhoor-nah-list-er	journalister (f)
lawyer	*aht-voh-kaat*	advocaat (m)
	aht-voh-kaat-er	advocate (f)
manual worker	*ahr-bey-der*	arbeider (m)
	ahr-beyd-ster	arbeidster (f)
mechanic	*mon-ter*	monteur
nurse	*ver-playkh-er*	verpleger (m)
	ver-playkh-ster	verpleegster (f)
office worker	*kahn-tor-wehr-ker*	kantoorwerker
scientist	*way-tern-skhahp-per*	wetenschapper
student	*stü-dehnt*	student (m)
	stü-dehnt-er	studente (f)
teacher	*lear-aar*	leraar (m)
	lear-aar-ehs	lerares (f)
waiter	*oh-ber*	ober (m)
	sehr-vear-ster	serveerster (f)
writer	*skhrey-ver*	schrijver (m)
	skhreyf-ster	schrijfster (f)

Religion

What is your religion?
*waht is üoo/yer **khots-deenst**?*

Wat is Uw/je godsdienst?

I am not religious.
*ik behn neet ray-lee-**khee-ers***

Ik ben niet religieus.

I am ...
ik behn ...

Ik ben ...

Buddhist	boo-**dist**	boeddhist
Catholic	kah-toh-**leek**	katholiek
Christian	**kris**-tern	christen
Hindu	**hin**-doo	hindoe
Jewish	yohts	joods
Muslim	**mos**-lim	moslim

Family

Are you married?
*behnt ü/behn yer **kher-trowt**?*

Bent U/ben je getrouwd?

I am single.
*ik behn on-**kher-trowt***

Ik ben ongetrouwd.

I am married.
*ik behn **kher-trowt***

Ik ben getrouwd.

How many children do you have?
*hoo-**vehl kin-der-ern** hayft ü/hehp yer?*

Hoeveel kinderen heeft U/heb je?

I don't have any children.
*ik hehp khayn **kin-der-ern***

Ik heb geen kinderen.

I have a daughter/a son.
*ik hehp ern **dokh**-ter/ern zohn*
Ik heb een dochter/een zoon.

How many brothers/sisters do you have?
***hoo**-vayl brooers/**zer**-sters hayft ü/hehp yer?*
Hoeveel broers/zusters heeft U/heb je?

Is your husband/wife here?
is üoo/yer mahn/vrow heer?
Is Uw/je man/vrouw hier?

Do you have a boyfriend/girlfriend?
*hayft ü/hehp yer ern vreend/vreend-**in**?*
Heeft U/heb je een vriend/vriendin?

brother	*brooer*	broer
children	***kin**-der-ern*	kinderen
daughter	***dokh**-ter*	dochter
family	*faa-**mee**-lee*	familie
father	***vaa**-der*	vader
grandfather	***khroht**-vaa-der, oh-**paa***	grootvader, opa
grandmother	***khroht**-moo-der, oh-**maa***	grootmoeder, oma
husband	*mahn*	man
mother	***moo**-der*	moeder
sister	***zer**-ster*	zuster
son	*zohn*	zoon
wife	*vrow*	vrouw

Feelings

I (don't) like …
ik howt (neet) vahn … | Ik houd (niet) van …
I am well.
heht khaat khoot meht mey | Het gaat goed met mij.
I am sorry. (condolences)
heht speyt mer | Het spijt me.
I am grateful.
ik behn ü/yer dahnk-baar | Ik ben U/je dankbaar.

I am …
ik hehp … | Ik heb …

cold/hot	*heht kowt/wahrm*	het koud/warm
hungry/thirsty	*hong-er/dorst*	honger/dorst
in a hurry	*haast*	haast
right	*kher-leyk*	gelijk
sleepy	*slaap*	slaap

I am …
ik behn … | Ik ben …

angry	*bohs*	boos
happy/sad	*bley/ver-dree-terkh*	blij/verdrietig
tired	*moo*	moe
worried	*on-khe-rerst*	ongerust

Language Difficulties

Do you speak English?
spraykt ü/sprayk yer ehng-erls? | Spreekt U/spreek je Engels?

DUTCH

Does anyone speak English?
spraykt ee-mahnt   Spreekt iemand Engels?
ehng-erls?

I speak a little …
ik sprayk ern bay-tyer …   Ik spreek een beetje …

I don't speak …
ik sprayk khayn …   Ik spreek geen …

I (don't) understand.
ik ber-khreyp heht (neet)   Ik begrijp het (niet).

Could you speak more slowly please?
kernt ü ahls-tü-bleeft/kern   Kunt U alstublieft/kun je
yer ahls-yer-bleeft lahng-   alsjeblieft langzamer
zaamer spray-kern?   spreken?

Could you repeat that?
kernt ü/kern yer daht   Kunt U/kun je dat herhalen?
hehr-haa-lern?

How do you say …?
hoo zehkht ü/zehkh yer …?   Hoe zegt U/zeg je …?

What does … mean?
waht ber-tay-kernt …?   Wat betekent …?

I speak …
ik sprayk …   Ik spreek …

English	*ehng-erls*	Engels
French	*frahns*	Frans
German	*derts*	Duits
Netherlandic,	*nay-der-lahnts,*	Nederlands,
Flemish,	*vlaams, hol-lahnts*	Vlaams, Hollands
'Hollandic'		

Some Useful Phrases

Sure.
zay-ker   Zeker.

Just a minute.
ern oh-khern-blik-yer   Een ogenblikje.

It's (not) important.
heht is (neet) ber-lahng-reyk   Het is (niet) belangrijk.

It's (not) possible.
heht is (neet) moh-kher-lerk   Het is (niet) mogelijk.

Wait!
wahkht!   Wacht!

Good luck!
(vayl) sük-sehs!   (Veel) succes!

Signs

BAGGAGE COUNTER	BAGAGEBALIE
CHECK-IN COUNTER	INCHECK BALIE
CUSTOMS	DOUANE
EMERGENCY EXIT	NOODUITGANG
ENTRANCE	INGANG
EXIT	UITGANG
FREE ADMISSION	GRATIS TOEGANG
HOT/COLD	WARM/KOUD
INFORMATION	INFORMATIE, INLICHTINGEN
NO ENTRY	VERBODEN TOEGANG
NO SMOKING	VERBODEN TE ROKEN
OPEN/CLOSED	OPEN/GESLOTEN
PROHIBITED	VERBODEN
RESERVED	GERESERVEERD

DUTCH

| TELEPHONE | TELEFOON |
| TOILETS | WC's/TOILETTEN |

Emergencies

| POLICE | POLITIE |
| POLICE STATION | POLITIEBUREAU |

Help!
help!
Help!

It's an emergency!
heht is ern noht-kher-vahl!
Het is een noodgeval!

There's been an accident!
ehr is ern orn-kher-lerk kher-bert!
Er is een ongeluk gebeurd!

Call a doctor!
haal ern dok-ter!
Haal een dokter!

Call an ambulance!
haal ern zee-kern-oh-toh!
Haal een ziekenauto!

I've been raped.
ik behn aan-kher-rahnd
Ik ben aangerand.

I've been robbed!
ik behn ber-rohft!
Ik ben beroofd!

Call the police!
haal der poh-leet-see!
Haal de politie!

Where is the police station?
waar is heht poh-leet-see-bü-roh?
Waar is het politiebureau?

Go away!
khaa wehkh!
Ga weg!

I'll call the police!
ik roop der poh-leet-see!
Ik roep de politie!

Thief!
deef!
Dief!

I am ill.
ik behn zeek
Ik ben ziek.

My friend is ill.
meyn vreend/vreend-in is zeek
Mijn vriend (m)/vriendin (f) is ziek.

I am lost.
ik behn der wehkh kweyt
Ik ben de weg kwijt.

Where are the toilets?
waar zeyn de twah-leht-tern/way-says?
Waar zijn de toiletten/WC's?

Could you help me please?
kernt ü mey ahls-tü-bleeft/ kern yer mey ahls-yer-bleeft hehl-pern?
Kunt U mij alstublieft/ kun je mij alsjeblieft helpen?

Could I please use the telephone?
zow ik moh-khern behl-lern?
Zou ik mogen bellen?

I'm sorry. (I apologise)
heht speyt mer/so-ree
Het spijt me./Sorry.

I didn't realise I was doing anything wrong.
ik haht neet in der khaa-tern daht ik eets ver-kearts dayt
Ik had niet in de gaten dat ik iets verkeerds deed.

I didn't do it.
ik hehp heht neet kher-daan
Ik heb het niet gedaan.

I wish to contact my embassy/consulate.

*ik wil kon-**tahkt** op-nay-mern meht meyn ahm-bah-**saa**-der/kon-sü-**laat*** — Ik wil kontakt opnemen met mijn ambassade/consulaat.

I speak English.

*ik sprayk **ehng**-erls* — Ik spreek Engels.

I have medical insurance.

*ik behn **may**-dees ver-**zay**-kert* — Ik ben medisch verzekerd.

My luggage is insured.

*meyn baa-**khaa**-zher is ver-**zay**-kert* — Mijn bagage is verzekerd.

My ... was stolen.

*meyn ... is kher-**stoh**-lern!* — Mijn ... is gestolen!

I've lost my ...

*ik behn meyn ... ver-**lor**-ern* — Ik ben mijn ... verloren.

bags	**tahs**-sern	tassen
handbag	**hahnd**-tahs	handtas
money	khehlt	geld
travellers' cheques	**reys**-shehks/travellers' cheques	reischeques/travellers' cheques
passport	**pahs**-port	paspoort

Paperwork

name	naam	naam
address	ah-**drehs**	adres
date of birth	kher-**bor**-ter-**daa**-term	geboortedatum
place of birth	kher-**bor**-ter-plaats	geboorteplaats
age	**layf**-teyt	leeftijd

sex	*kher-slahkht*	geslacht
nationality	*nahts-joh-naa-lee-teyt*	nationaliteit
religion	*khots-deenst*	godsdienst
reason for visit	*ray-dern vor ber-zook*	reden voor bezoek
profession	*be-roop*	beroep
marital status	*hü-wer-lerk-ser staat*	huwelijkse staat
passport	*pahs-port*	paspoort
passport number	*pahs-port-ner-mer*	paspoortnummer
visa	*vee-serm*	visum
tourist card	*too-rist-ern-kaart*	toeristenkaart
identification	*lay-khee-tee-maat-see*	legitimatie
birth certificate	*kher-bor-ter-ber-weys*	geboortebewijs
driver's licence	*rey-ber-weys*	rijbewijs
car owner's title	*kehn-tay-kern-ber-weys*	kentekenbewijs
car registration	*kehn-tay-kern*	kenteken
customs	*doo-aa-ner*	douane
immigration	*im-mee-khraat-see*	immigratie
border	*khrehns*	grens

DUTCH

Getting Around

ARRIVALS	AANKOMST
BUS STOP	BUSHALTE
DEPARTURES	VERTREK
STATION	STATION
SUBWAY	METRO
TICKET OFFICE	KAARTVERKOOP
TIMETABLE	VERTREKTIJDEN
TRAIN STATION	TREINSTATION

DUTCH

What time does … leave/
arrive?
   hoo laat ver-trehkt/   Hoe laat vertrekt/
   ah-ree-veart …?   arriveert …?

the (air)plane	*heht vleekg-terkh*	het vliegtuig
the boat	*der boht*	de boot
the bus	*der bers*	de bus
the train	*der treyn*	de trein
the tram	*der trehm*	de tram

Directions

Where is …?
   waar is …?   Waar is …?
How do I get to …?
   hoo kom ik in …?   Hoe kom ik in …?
Is it far from/near here?
   is heht vehr/dikht-bey?   Is het ver/dichtbij?
Can I walk there?
   is heht ter loh-pern?   Is het te lopen?
Can you show me (on the map)?
   kernt ü/kern yer heht (op   Kunt U/kun je het (op de
   der kaart) aan-wey-zern?   kaart) aanwijzen?
Are there other means of get-
ting there?
   kahn ik ehr op ern ahn-   Kan ik er op een andere
   derer mah-neer koh-mern?   manier komen?
I want to go to …
   ik vil naar … khaan   Ik wil naar … gaan.

| Go straight ahead. | *khaa rehkht-dor* | Ga rechtdoor. |
| Turn left … | *khaa links-ahf …* | Ga linksaf … |

Turn right ...	*khaa rehkhts-ahf ...*	Ga rechtsaf ...
at the next corner	*bey der **vol-khern-dehr** hook*	bij de volgende hoek
at the traffic lights	*bey heht **stop**-likht*	bij het stoplicht
behind	***ahkh**-ter*	achter
far	*vehr*	ver
in front of	*vor*	voor
near	*dikht-bey*	dichtbij
opposite	*tay-khern-**oh**-ver*	tegenover

Booking Tickets

Excuse me, where is the ticket office?

*pahr-**don**, waar is der **kaart**-ver-kohp?*	Pardon, waar is de kaartverkoop?

Where can I buy a ticket?

*waar kahn ik ern **kaart**-yer koh-pern?*	Waar kan ik een kaartje kopen?

I want to go to ...

ik vil naar ... khaan	Ik wil naar ... gaan.

Do I need to book?

*moot ik ray-zehr-**vear**-ern?*	Moet ik reserveren?

You need to book.

*ü/yer moot ray-zehr-**vear**-ern*	U/je moet reserveren.

I would like to book a seat to ...

*ik vil khraakh ern plaats ray-zehr-**vear**-ern naar ...*	Ik wil graag een plaats reserveren naar ...

I would like ...

ik vil khraakh ...	Ik wil graag ...

a one-way ticket	*ern **ehng**-ker-ler reys*	een enkele reis
a return ticket	*ern rer-**toor***	een retour
two tickets	*tway **kaar**-tyers*	twee kaartjes
tickets for all of us	***kaar**-tyers vor ee-der-ayn*	kaartjes voor iedereen
a student's fare	*ern stü-**dehn**-tern-tah-**reef***	een studententarief
a child's/ pensioner's fare	*ern **kin**-der/sehs-tikh **plers** kor-ting*	een kinder/60+ korting
1st class	*ear-ster **klahs***	eerste klas
2nd class	*tway-der **klahs***	tweede klas

It is full.
heht is vol   Het is vol.
Is it completely full?
*is heht hay-ler-**maal** vol?*   Is het helemaal vol?
Can I get a stand-by ticket?
kahn ik ern stand-by ticket   Kan ik een stand-by ticket
***krey**-khern?*   krijgen?

Air

CHECKING IN LUGGAGE PICKUP	INCHECKEN BAGAGE

Is there a flight to …?
is air ern vlerkht naar … ?   Is er een vlucht naar …?
When is the next flight to …?
*wah-**near** is der vol-khern-der vlerkht naar … ?* | Wanneer is de volgende vlucht naar …?

How long does the flight take?
hoo-lahng dürt der vlerkht?   Hoelang duurt de vlucht?

What is the flight number?
waht is heht vlerkht-ner-mer?   Wat is het vluchtnummer?

You must check in at ...
ü moot in-tyehk-ern bey ...   U moet inchecken bij ...

airport tax	**lerkht-haa-vern-ber-lahst-ing**	luchthavenbelasting
boarding pass	**in-stahp-kaart**	instapkaart
customs	**doo-aa-ner**	douane

Bus

BUS/TRAM STOP	BUSHALTE/TRAMHALTE

Where is the bus/tram stop?
waar is der bers-hahl-ter?   Waar is de bushalte?

Which bus goes to ...?
wehl-ker bers khaat naar ...?   Welke bus gaat naar?

Does this bus go to ...?
khaat day-zer bers naar ...?   Gaat deze bus naar ...?

How often do buses pass by?
hoo vaak komt der bers?   Hoe vaak komt de bus?

Could you let me know when we get to ...?
kernt ü/kern yer mer laa-tern way-tern wah-near wer in ... aan-ko-mern?   Kunt U/kun je me laten weten wanneer we in ... aankomen?

DUTCH

I want to get off!
*ik vil **ert**-stahp-pern!*   Ik wil uitstappen!

What time is the ... bus?
hoo laat is der ... bers?   Hoe laat is de ... bus?

next	***vol**-khern-der*	volgende
first	***ear**-ster*	eerste
last	***laat**-ster*	laatste

Train

DINING CAR	RESTAURATIEWAGEN
EXPRESS	SNELTREIN
PLATFORM NO	PERRON/SPOOR NO
SLEEPING CAR	SLAAPWAGON

Is this the right platform for ...?
*is dir heht **yer**-ster pehr-**ron***   Is dit het juiste perron
vor ...?   voor ...?

The train leaves from
platform ...
*der treyn ver-**trehkt** vahn*   De trein vertrekt van per-
*pehr-**ron** ...*   ron ...

dining car	***ayt**-waa-khon*	eetwagon
express	***snehl**-treyn*	sneltrein
local	***stop**-treyn*	stoptrein
sleeping car	***slaap**-waa-khon*	slaapwagon

Passengers must ...
*pahs-sah-**zheers***   Passagiers moeten ...
moo-tern ...

change trains	*oh-ver-stahp-pern*	overstappen
go to platform	*naar pehr-ron*	naar perron
number ...	*ner-mer ...*	nummer ...

Metro

DUTCH

| METRO/UNDERGROUND
CHANGE (for coins) | METRO
WISSELGELD/
WISSELAUTOMAAT |
| THIS WAY TO
WAY OUT | RICHTING
UITGANG |

Which line takes me to ...?
wehl-ker leyn brehngt mer naar ...?

Welke lijn brengt me naar ...?

What is the next station?
waht is het vol-khern-der staht-shon?

Wat is het volgende station?

Taxi

Can you take me to ...?
kernt ü mey naar ... brehng-ern?

Kunt U mij naar ... brengen?

Please take me to ...
brehng mey ahls-tü-bleeft naar ...

Breng mij alstublieft naar ...

How much does it cost to go to ...?
hoo-vayl kost heht naar ...?

Hoeveel kost het naar ...?

DUTCH

Instructions

Here is fine, thank you.
heer is khood, dahnk ü

Hier is goed, dank U.

The next corner, please.
der vol-khern-der hook, ahls-tü-bleeft

De volgende hoek, alstublieft.

Continue!
rey dor!

Rij door!

The next street to the left/right.
der vol-khern-der straat links/rehkhts

De volgende straat links/rechts.

Stop here!
stop heer!

Stop hier!

Please slow down.
reyt ahls-tü-bleeft lahng-zaam-er

Rijd alstublieft langzamer.

Please wait here.
wahkht heer ahls-tü-bleeft

Wacht hier alstublieft.

Some Useful Phrases

The train is delayed/cancelled.
der treyn is ver-traakht/ ahf-kher-lahst

De trein is vertraagd/ afgelast.

How long will it be delayed?
hoo-lahng is heht ver-traakht?

Hoelang is het vertraagd?

There is a delay of ... hours.
ehr is ern ver-traakh-ing vahn ... ür

Er is een vertraging van ... uur.

Can I reserve a place?
kahn ik ern plaats
ray-zer-vear-ern?

Kan ik een plaats
reserveren?

How long does the trip take?
hoo-lahng dürt de tokht?

Hoelang duurt de tocht?

Is it a direct route?
is heht ern rehkht-strayk-
ser ver-bin-ding?

Is het een rechtstreekse
verbinding?

Is this seat taken?
is day-zer plaats ber-zeht?

Is deze plaats bezet?

I want to get off at …
ik vil ert-stahp-pern bey …

Ik wil uitstappen bij …

Excuse me.
pahr-don

Pardon.

Where can I hire a bicycle?
waar kahn ik ern feets
hü-rern?

Waar kan ik een fiets huren?

Car

DETOUR	OMLEIDING
FREEWAY	AUTOWEG/AUTOSNEL-WEG
GARAGE	GARAGE
GIVE WAY	GEEF VOORRANG
MECHANIC	MONTEUR
NO ENTRY	VERBODEN IN TE RIJDEN
NO PARKING	VERBODEN TE PARKEREN
NORMAL	NORMAAL

DUTCH

ONE WAY	EENRICHTING
REPAIRS	REPARATIES
SELF SERVICE	ZELFBEDIENING
STOP	STOP
SUPER	SUPER
UNLEADED	(EURO-)LOODVRIJ

Where can I hire a car?
  waar kahn ik ern oh-toh hü-rern?

Waar kan ik een auto huren?

daily/weekly
  pehr dahkh/wayk

per dag/week

Does that include insurance/mileage?
  zit daar ver-zay-ker-ing/ zit-tern daar kee-loh-may-ters bey in-ber-khray-pern?

Zit daar verzekering/ zitten daar kilometers bij inbegrepen?

Where's the next petrol station?
  waar is heht vol-khern-der behn-zee-ner-staht-shon?

Waar is het volgende benzinestation?

Please fill the tank.
  vol, khraakh

Vol, graag.

I want ... litres of petrol. (gas)
  ik vil ... lee-ter behn-zee-ner

Ik wil ... liter benzine.

Please check the oil and water.
  kon-tro-lear ahls-tü-bleeft oh-lee ehn waa-ter

Controleer alstublieft olie en water.

How long can I park here?
hoo-lahng kahn ik heer pahr-kear-ern? Hoelang kan ik hier parkeren?

Does this road lead to …?
khaat day-zer wehkh naar …? Gaat deze weg naar …?

air (for tyres)	*lerkht (vor bahn-dern)*	lucht (voor banden)
battery	*ahk-kü*	accu
brakes	*rehm-mern*	remmen
clutch	*kop-per-ling*	koppeling
driver's licence	*rey-ber-weys*	rijbewijs
engine	*moh-tor*	motor
lights	*likh-tern*	lichten
oil	*oh-lee*	olie
puncture	*lehk-ker bahnt*	lekke band
radiator	*raa-dee-yaa-tor*	radiator
road map	*way-khern-kaart*	wegenkaart
tyres	*bahn-dern*	banden
windscreen	*vor-rert*	voorruit

Car Problems

I need a mechanic.
ik hehp ern mon-ter noh-dikh Ik heb een monteur nodig.

What make is it?
wehlk mehrk is heht? Welk merk is het?

The battery is flat.
der ahk-kü is laykh De accu is leeg.

The radiator is leaking.
der raa-dee-yaa-tor lehkt De radiator lekt.

DUTCH

I have a flat tyre.
   ik hehp ern lehk-ker bahnt   Ik heb een lekke band.
It's overheating.
   heht raakt oh-ver-ver-hit   Het raakt oververhit.
It's not working.
   heht wehrkt neet   Het werkt niet.

Accommodation

CAMPING GROUND	CAMPING
GUESTHOUSE	PENSION
YOUTH HOSTEL	JEUGDHERBERG

I am looking for …
   ik zook …   Ik zoek …
Where is …?
   waar is …?   Waar is …?
a cheap hotel   *ern khood-kohp*   een goedkoop
          hoh-tehl   hotel
a good hotel   *ern khood hoh-tehl*   een goed hotel
a nearby hotel   *ern hoh-tehl dikht-*   een hotel dichtbij
          bey

What is the address?
   waht is heht ah-drehs?   Wat is het adres?
Could you write the address,
please?
   kernt ü/kern yer het   Kunt U/kun je het adres
   ah-drehs op-skhrey-vern,   opschrijven, alstublieft/
   ahls-tü-bleeft/ahls-yer-   alsjeblieft?
   bleeft?

At the Hotel

Do you have any rooms
available?
   *hayft ü **kaa**-mers vrey?*   Heeft U kamers vrij?

I would like (a) ...
   ik wil khraakh (ern) ...   Ik wil graag (een) ...

single room	*ayn-pehr-**sohns**-kaa-mer*	eenpersoonskamer
double room	*tway-per-**sohns**-kaa-mer*	tweeper-soonskamer
room with a bathroom	***kaa**-mer meht **baat**-kaa-mer*	een kamer met badkamer
to share a dorm bed	*ern **kaa**-mer **day**-lern beht*	een kamer delen bed

I want a room with a ...
   *ik vil ern **kaa**-mer meht ...*   Ik wil een kamer met ...

bathroom	***baht**-kaa-mer*	badkamer
shower	*doosh*	douche
television	*tay-ler-**vee**-see*	televisie
window	*raam*	raam

I'm going to stay for ...
   ik bleyf ...   Ik blijf ...

one day	*ayn dahkh*	één dag
two days	*tway **daa**-khern*	twee dagen
one week	*ayn wayk*	één week

Do you have identification?
   *hayft ü lay-khee-tee-**maat**-see?*   Heeft U legitimatie?

DUTCH

Your membership card, please.
üoo lit-maat-skhahps-kaart, ahls-tü-bleeft
Uw lidmaatschapskaart, alstublieft.

Sorry, we're full.
so-ree, wer zeyn vol
Sorry, we zijn vol.

How long will you be staying?
hoo-lahng bleyft ü?
Hoelang blijft U?

How many nights?
*hoo-vayl **nahkh**-tern?*
Hoeveel nachten?

It's … per day/per person.
*heht is … pehr dahkh/pehr pehr-**sohn***
Het is … per dag/per persoon.

How much is it per night/per person?
*hoo-vayl is heht pehr nahkht/per per-**sohn**?*
Hoeveel is het per nacht/per persoon?

Can I see it?
kahn ik heht zeen?
Kan ik het zien?

Are there any others?
*zeyn ehr **ahn**-der-er?*
Zijn er andere?

Are there any cheaper rooms?
*zeyn ehr khoot-**koh**-per-er kaa-mers?*
Zijn er goedkopere kamers?

Can I see the bathroom?
*kahn ik de **baht**-kaa-mer zeen?*
Kan ik de badkamer zien?

Is there a reduction for students/children?
*is ehr ray-**derk**-see vor stü-**dehn**-tern/**kin**-der-ern?*
Is er reductie voor studenten/kinderen?

Does it include breakfast?
*zit ehr ont-beyt bey
in-ber-khray-pern?*

Zit er ontbijt bij inbegrepen?

It's fine, I'll take it.
heht is khood, ik naym heht

Het is goed, ik neem het.

I'm not sure how long I'm
staying.
*ik wayt neet zay-ker
hoo-lahng ik bleyf*

Ik weet niet zeker hoelang
ik blijf.

Is there a lift?
is ehr ern lift?

Is er een lift?

Where is the bathroom?
waar is der baht-kaa-mer?

Waar is de badkamer?

Is there hot water all day?
*is ehr der hay-ler dahkh
wahrm waa-ter?*

Is er de hele dag warm
water?

Do you have a safe where I
can leave my valuables?
*hayft ü ern klers waar ik
meyn waar-der-vol-ler
sper-lern kahn laa-tern?*

Heeft U een kluis waar ik
mijn waardevolle spullen
kan laten?

Is there somewhere to wash
clothes?
*is ehr ehr-kherns om
klear-ern ter wahs-sern?*

Is er ergens om kleren te
wassen?

Can I use the kitchen?
*kahn ik der ker-kern
kher-brer-kern?*

Kan ik de keuken
gebruiken?

Can I use the telephone?
*kahn ik der tay-ler-fohn
kher-brer-kern?*

Kan ik de telefoon
gebruiken?

Requests & Complaints

Please wake me up at …
wehk mer ahls-tü-bleeft om …
Wek me alstublieft om …

The room needs to be cleaned.
der kaa-mer moot wor-dern skhohn-kher-maakt
De kamer moet worden schoongemaakt.

Please change the sheets.
ver-skhohn ahls-tü-bleeft der laa-kerns
Verschoon alstublieft de lakens.

I can't open/close the window.
ik kahn heht raam neet oh-pern/dikht doon
Ik kan het raam niet open/dicht doen.

I've locked myself out of my room.
ik hehp mer-zehlf ber-tern-kher-sloh-tern
Ik heb mezelf buiten-gesloten.

The toilet won't flush.
der way-say/heht twah-leht trehkt neet dor
De WC/het toilet trekt niet door.

I don't like this room.
day-zer kaa-mer ber-vahlt mer neet
Deze kamer bevalt me niet.

It's too small.	*heht is ter kleyn*	Het is te klein.
It's noisy.	*heht is lah-wai-ikh*	Het is lawaaiig.
It's too dark.	*heht is ter don-ker*	Het is te donker.
It's expensive.	*heht is dür*	Het is duur.

DUTCH

Some Useful Phrases

I would like to pay the bill.

ik wil khraakh	Ik wil graag afrekenen.
ahf-ray-ker-nern	

I am/We are leaving now.

ik ver-trehk/wey ver-trehk-kern nü	Ik vertrek/wij vertrekken nu.

name	*naam*	naam
surname	*ahkh-ter-naam*	achternaam
room number	*kaa-mer-ner-mer*	kamernummer

Some Useful Words

address	*ah-dres*	adres
air-conditioned	*air-kon-di-shernt*	air-conditioned
balcony	*bahl-korn*	balcon
bathroom	*baht-kaa-mer*	badkamer
bed	*beht*	bed
bill	*ray-ker-ning*	rekening
blanket	*day-kern*	deken
candle	*kaars*	kaars
chair	*stool*	stoel
clean	*skhohn*	schoon
cupboard	*kahst*	kast
dark	*don-ker*	donker
dirty	*smir-erkh*	smerig
double bed	*tway-per-sohns **beht***	tweepersoons bed
electricity	*ay-lehk-tree-see-teyt*	electriciteit
excluded	*ehks-klü-zeef*	exclusief
fan	*vehn-tee-laa-tor*	ventilator
included	*in-klü-zeef*	inclusief

DUTCH

key	*sler-terl*	sleutel
lift (elevator)	*lift*	lift
light bulb	*khlooee-lahmp*	gloeilamp
lock (n)	*slot*	slot
mattress	*maa-trahs*	matras
mirror	*spee-kherl*	spiegel
padlock	*hahng-slot*	hangslot
pillow	*kers-sern*	kussen
quiet	*stil*	stil
room (in hotel)	*kaa-mer*	kamer
sheet	*laa-kern*	laken
shower	*doosh*	douche
soap	*zayp*	zeep
suitcase	*kof-fer*	koffer
swimming pool	*zwehm-baht*	zwembad
table	*taa-ferl*	tafel
toilet	*way-say/twah-leht*	WC/toilet
toilet paper	*way-say/twah-leht pah-peer*	WC/toilet papier
towel	*hahn-dook*	handdoek
water	*waa-ter*	water
cold water	*kowt waa-ter*	koud water
hot water	*wahrm waa-ter*	warm water
window	*raam*	raam

Around Town

I'm looking for ...

ik zoek ...		Ik zoek ...
the art gallery	*heht kernst-mü-say-erm*	het kunstmuseum
the church	*der kairk*	de kerk

the city centre	*heht sehn-trerm*	het centrum
the ... embassy	*der ... ahm-baa-saa-der*	de ... ambassade
my hotel	*meyn hoh-tehl*	mijn hotel
the museum	*heht mü-say-erm*	het museum
the police	*der poh-leet-see*	de politie
the post office	*heht post-kahn-tor*	het postkantoor
a public toilet	*ern oh-pern-baa-rer way-say/oh-pern-baar twah-leht*	een openbare WC/openbaar toilet
the telephone centre	*der tay-ler-fohn-sen-traa-ler*	de telefoon-centrale
the tourist information office	*der vay-vay-vay/heht too-ris-tern-bü-ro*	de VVV (in the Netherlands)/het toeristenbureau

DUTCH

What time does it open?
  hoo laat oh-pernt heht?   Hoe laat opent het?
What time does it close?
  hoo laat slert heht?   Hoe laat sluit het?

What ... is this?
  wehl-ker ... is dit?   Welke ... is dit?

street	*straat*	straat
suburb	*vor-staht*	voorstad

For directions, see the Getting Around section, page 42.

DUTCH

At the Bank

I want to exchange some
money/travellers' cheques.

ik vil waht khehlt/reys-shehks (travellers' cheques) wis-ser-lern

Ik wil wat geld/reischeques (travellers' cheques) wisselen.

What is the exchange rate?

waht is der wis-serl-koors?

Wat is de wisselkoers?

How many guilders/francs per dollar?

hoo-vayl kherl-dern/frahn-kern pair dol-lahr?

Hoeveel gulden/franken per dollar?

Can I have money transferred here from my bank?

kahn ik khehlt vahn meyn bahnk heer-naar-too laa-tern oh-ver-maa-kern?

Kan ik geld van mijn bank hiernaartoe laten over-maken?

How long will it take?

hoo-lahng doot heht ehr-oh-ver?

Hoelang doet het erover?

Has my money arrived yet?

is meyn khehlt ahl aan-kher-koh-mern?

Is mijn geld al aangekomen?

bankdraft	*oh-ver-maa-king*	overmaking
bank notes	*bahnk-bil-jeht-tern*	bankbiljetten
cashier	*kahs-seer*	kassier
coins	*mern-tern*	munten
credit card	*krer-deet-kaart*	kredietkaart
exchange	*wis-ser-lern*	wisselen
loose change	*wis-serl-khehlt*	wisselgeld
signature	*hahnt-tay-ker-ning*	handtekening

DUTCH

At the Post Office

I would like to send ...
ik wil khraakh ... ver-stü-rern. Ik wil graag ... versturen.

a letter	*ern breef*	een brief
a postcard	*ern breef-kaart*	een briefkaart
a parcel	*ern pah-keht*	een pakket
a telegram	*ern tay-ler-khrahm*	een telegram

I would like some stamps.
ik wil khraakh waht post-zay-kherls Ik wil graag wat postzegels.

How much is the postage?
hoo-vayl is heht por-to? Hoeveel is het porto?

How much does it cost to send this to ...?
hoo-vayl kost heht om dit naar ... ter stü-rern? Hoeveel kost het om dit naar ... te sturen?

an aerogram	*ern lerkht-post-vehl*	een luchtpostvel
airmail	*lerkht-post*	luchtpost
envelope	*ahn-ver-lop*	envelop
mail box	*bree-vern-bers*	brievenbus
parcel	*pah-keht*	pakket
registered mail	*aan-kher-tay-kernt*	aangetekend
surface mail	*zay-post*	zeepost

Telephone

I want to ring ...
ik vil ... beh-lern Ik wil ... bellen.

The number is ...
heht ner-mer is ... Het nummer is ...

DUTCH

I want to speak for three minutes.

ik vil dree mee-nü-tern spray-kern

Ik wil drie minuten spreken.

How much does a three-minute call cost?

hoo-vayl kost ern kher-sprehk vahn dree mee-nü-tern?

Hoeveel kost een gesprek van drie minuten?

How much does each extra minute cost?

hoo-vayl kost ee-der-er mee-nüt ehk-straa?

Hoeveel kost iedere minuut extra?

I would like to speak to Mr Perez.

ik vil khraakh mer-near Perez spray-kern

Ik wil graag meneer Perez spreken.

I want to make a reverse-charges phone call.

ik vil ern ber-taa-ling ont-vahng-er kher-sprehk

Ik wil een betaling ontvanger gesprek.

It's engaged.

heht is ber-zeht

Het is bezet.

I've been cut off.

ik behn ahf-kher-bro-kern

Ik ben afgebroken.

Sightseeing

Do you have a guidebook/
local map?

hayft ü ern reys-khits/kaart   Heeft U een reisgids/kaart
vahn heht kher-beet?   van het gebied?

What are the main attractions?

waht zeyn der vor-naam-   Wat zijn de voornaamste
ster ber-zeens-waar-dikh-   bezienswaardigheden?
hay-dern?

What is that?

waht is daht?   Wat is dat?

How old is it?

hoo owt is heht?   Hoe oud is het?

Can I take photographs?

kahn ik foh-tohs   Kan ik foto's nemen?
nay-mern?

What time does it open/close?

hoo laat oh-pernt/slert   Hoe laat opent/sluit het?
heht?

ancient	*(zear) owt*	(zeer) oud
archaeological	*ahr-khay-oh-loh-khees*	archeologisch
beach	*strahnt*	strand
building	*kher-bow*	gebouw
bulb(s)	*bol(-lern)*	bol(len)
castle	*kah-stayl, berkht*	kasteel, burcht
cathedral	*kah-tay-draal*	kathedraal
church	*kairk*	kerk
clog(s)	*klomp(-ern)*	klomp(en)
concert hall	*kon-sairt-kher-bow*	concertgebouw
flower(s)	*bloom(-ern)*	bloem(en)

DUTCH

library	*bee-blee-oh-**tayk***	bibliotheek
main square	*pleyn/khrohter* **mahrkt**	plein/grote markt
market	*mahrkt*	markt
monastery	*kloh-ster*	klooster
monument	*moh-nü-**mehnt***	monument
mosque	*mos-**kay***	moskee
old city	*ow-der staht*	oude stad
palace	*pah-**leys***	paleis
opera house	*oh-per-aa-kher-bow*	operagebouw
ruins	*rü-ee-ner*	ruïne
stadium	*staa-dee-on*	stadion
statues	***stahnt**-bayl-dern*	standbeelden
synagogue	*see-nah-**khoh**-kher*	synagoge
temple	*tehm-perl*	tempel
tulip(s)	*terlp(-ern)*	tulp(en)
university	*ü-nee-vair-see-**teyt***	universiteit
windmill	***moh**-lern*	molen

Entertainment

What's there to do in the evenings?

*waht vahlt air **saa**-vonts ter doon?*

Wat valt er 's-avonds te doen?

Are there any discos?

*zeyn ehr **dis**-kohs?*

Zijn er disco's?

Are there places where you can hear local folk music?

*zeyn ehr **plaat**-sern waar jer **volks**-mü-zeek vahn der **strayk** kernt **hor**-ern?*

Zijn er plaatsen waar je volksmuziek van de streek kunt horen?

How much does it cost to get in?

hoo-vayl kost ahn-tray? Hoeveel kost entree?

cinema	*bee-os-kohp*	bioscoop
concert	*kon-sairt*	concert
discotheque	*dis-koh-tayk*	discotheek
theatre	*tay-aa-ter*	theater

In the Country
Weather

What's the weather like?

hoo is heht wear? Hoe is het weer?

The weather is ... today.

heht wear is vahn-daakh ... Het weer is vandaag ...

cloudy	*ber-wolkt*	bewolkt
cold	*kowt*	koud
foggy	*mis-terkh*	mistig
hot	*hayt*	heet
raining	*ray-kher-nern*	regenen
snowing	*snay-wern*	sneeuwen
sunny	*zon-nerkh*	zonnig
windy	*win-der-erkh*	winderig

Camping

Am I allowed to camp here?

mahkh ik heer kahm-pear-ern? Mag ik hier kamperen?

DUTCH

Is there a campsite nearby?
*is air ern **kehm**-ping*   Is er een camping dichtbij?
dikht-bey?

backpack	***rerkh**-zahk*	rugzak
can opener	***blik**-oh-per-ner*	blikopener
compass	*kom-**pahs***	kompas
firewood	***brahnt**-howt*	brandhout
gas cartridge	***khahs**-paa-trohn*	gaspatroon
hammock	***hahng**-maht*	hangmat
mattress	*maa-**trahs***	matras
penknife	***zahk**-mehs*	zakmes
rope	*tow*	touw
tent	*tehnt*	tent
tent pegs	***haa**-ring-ern*	haringen
torch (flashlight)	***zahk**-lahmp*	zaklamp
sleeping bag	***slaap**-zahk*	slaapzak
stove	***brahn**-der*	brander
water bottle	***vehlt**-flehs*	veldfles

Food

Dutch cuisine served in restaurants is not much to write home about, but a typical three-course 'tourist menu' (thick soup, meat with potatoes and vegetables, dessert) ensures you'll at least be well fed. Vegetarians are well catered for, and you'll find Indonesian and Chinese restaurants (usually combined) even in the smallest town.

Flemish cuisine is always gratifying, offering French finesse in big servings. For a cheap, filling snack on the run, go for *frites* (French fries) with mayonnaise – Belgians are justifiably proud of their frites. A typical meal in a restaurant consists of a hearty soup followed by the main dish. A potential highlight is *mos-selen*, mussels cooked in white wine, accompanied by frites and several goblets of *trappist* beer.

breakfast	*ont-beyt*	ontbijt
lunch	*mid-dahg-ay-tern/ lerntsh*	middageten/lunch
dinner	*aa-vont-ay-tern/ dee-nay*	avondeten/diner

Table for ..., please.
taa-ferl vor ..., ahls-tü-bleeft

Tafel voor ..., alstublieft.

Can I see the menu, please?
kahn ik heht mer-nü zeen, ahls-tü-bleeft?

Kan ik het menu zien, alstublieft?

I'd like the set lunch, please.
ik vil khraakh heht too-ris-tern-mer-nü, ahls-tü-bleeft

Ik wil graag het toeristen-menu, alstublieft.

What does it include?
waht is air-bey in-ber-khray-pern?

Wat is erbij inbegrepen?

Is service included?
is ber-dee-ning in-ber-khray-pern?

Is bediening inbegrepen?

Not too spicy please.
neet ter hayt/skhehrp/ pit-terkh ahls-tü-bleeft

Niet te heet/scherp/pittig alstublieft.

ashtray	*ahs-bahk*	asbak
the bill	*der ray-ker-ning*	de rekening

DUTCH

a cup	*ern kop*	een kop
a drink	*ern **drahnk**-yer*	een drankje
a fork	*ern vork*	een vork
a glass	*ern khlahs*	een glas
a knife	*ern mehs*	een mes
a plate	*ern bort*	een bord
a spoon	*ern lay-perl*	een lepel
teaspoon	*tay-lay-perl*	theelepel
toothpick	*tahn-dern-stoh-ker*	tandenstoker

Vegetarian Meals

I am a vegetarian.
   *ik behn vay-kher-**taa**-ree-yer*   Ik ben vegetariër.
I don't eat meat.
   ik ayt khayn vlays   Ik eet geen vlees.
I don't eat chicken, fish, or ham.
   ik ayt khayn kip, vis, off hahm   Ik eet geen kip, vis, of ham.

Breakfast & Lunch   Ontbijt & Middageten
Depending on the region, the main meal of the day is eaten either in the evening or at midday.

beschuit	Dutch crisp bread, eaten with cheese, *hagelslag* or *gestampte muisjes*.
griesmeelpap	Semolina porridge.
hagelslag	Fine, vermicelli-like strands of chocolate or coloured aniseed sugar, a hit with kids.
havermoutpap	Oatmeal porridge.
koek, ontbijtkoek	Dutch honey cake.
leverworst	Liver sausage.

muisjes	Sugar-coated aniseed. *Gestampte muisjes* are ground muisjes.
roggebrood	Pumpernickel, rye bread, black bread, usually eaten with cheese.
rookvlees	Smoked beef, thinly sliced.
theeworst	Literally 'tea-sausage': spiced and smoked, light-pink liver-sausage.
uitsmijter	Sliced bread with cold meat (usually ham or thinly sliced roast beef), covered with fried eggs and garnish (pickles, etc).

bacon	*spek*
bread (brown, white, wholemeal)	*brood (bruin, wit, volkoren)*
croissants	*halve maantjes*
egg(s)	*ei(eren)*
boiled egg	*gekookt ei*
fried eggs	*gebakken eieren*
fried eggs, sunny side up	*spiegeleieren*
hard-boiled	*hardgekookt*
scrambled eggs	*roerei*
soft-boiled	*zachtgekookt*
honey	*honing*
sausage	*worst*

Dairy Products   **Zuivelproducten**

buttermilk	*karnemelk*
buttermilk residue – a favourite home dessert	*hangop*
cheese	*kaas*
cheese spread	*smeerkaas*

DUTCH

cream	*room*
custard	*vla*
matured, ripe	*belegen*
milk	*melk*
new	*jong*
newly matured	*jong belegen*

Entrées	**Voorgerechten**
pastry (meat or fish)	*pastei*
soup	*soep*
oxtail	*ossestaart*
turtle	*schildpad*
vegetable	*groente*

Meat	**Vlees**
biefstuk tartaar	Raw minced beef with egg and spices.
blinde vink	Beef or veal wrapped in bacon, fried.
osseworst	Ox sausage, spiced and smoked.
pekelvlees	Salted meat.
rookworst	Smoked sausage (cooked, juicy).
slavink	Minced beef wrapped in bacon, fried.
sudderlap	Simmered meat (beef or pork).

bacon	*spek*
fillet of beef	*runderhaas*
fillet of beef, tenderloin	*ossehaas*
fillet of veal	*kalfsschijf*
goat	*geit*
lamb	*lam*
minced meat	*gehakt*
pork	*varken*
pork chop	*karbonade*

steak	*biefstuk*
sweetbread	*zwezerik*
veal collop, escalope	*kalfsoester*

Seafood / Visgerechten

groene haring	Fresh, raw herring, untreated apart from being cleaned and kept on ice. Don't dismiss it until you've tried it.
haring	Herring, usually eaten raw with chopped onions at fish stalls.
lekkerbekje	Fried fish fillet.
meerval	Freshwater catfish.
nieuwe haring	'New' herring, fresh and mild-flavoured, in theory the first herring of the season, a favourite at fish stalls.
rolmops	Pickled herring wrapped around gherkin and/or onion.
zeewolf	Saltwater catfish.
zoute haring	Salted herring, kipper.

cod	*kabeljauw*
eel	*paling/aal*
fish	*vis*
freshwater-	*zoetwater-*
haddock	*schelvis*
hake, stockfish	*stokvis*
lobster	*kreeft*
mussels	*mosselen*
octopus, squid	*inktvis*
pike	*snoek*
plaice	*schol*

salmon	*zalm*
shrimps, prawns	*garnalen*
trout	*forel*
tuna	*tonijn*
whiting	*wijting*

Poultry & Game — Gevogelte

chicken	*kip*
duck	*eend*
goose	*gans*
hare	*haas, haze-*
haunch of venison	*reebout*
pheasant	*fazant*
quail	*kwartel*
rabbit	*konijn*
turkey	*kalkoen*
wild pig/boar	*zwijn*

Vegetables — Groente

beans	*bonen, boontjes*
bean sprouts	*taugé*
beetroot	*bieten*
broad beans	*tuinbonen*
Brussels sprouts	*spruitjes*
butter-beans	*sperziebonen*
cabbage	*kool*
carrot	*peen*
carrots (small)	*wortel(tje)s*
cauliflower	*bloemkool*
chicory	*brussels lof*

corn on the cob	*maiskolf*
cucumber	*komkommer*
curly kale	*boerenkool*
endive	*andijvie*
French fries	*patates, patates frites*
garden-cress	*sterrekers*
green beans	*slabonen*
leek	*prei*
lentils	*linzen*
lettuce	*sla*
marrow peas (often served with bacon)	*kapucijners*
mushroom (big)	*paddestoel*
mushrooms (small & cultured)	*champignons*
onion	*ui* (Flemish: *ajuin*)
peas	*erwten*
potato(es)	*aardappel(en)*
new potatoes (small)	*jonge/nieuwe aardappelen*
mashed potatoes	*aardappelpuree*
podded peas, sugar peas	*peultjes*
pumpkin, squash	*pompoen*
purslane	*postelein*
red cabbage	*rode kool*
split peas	*spliterwten*
Swedish turnip	*koolraap*
turnip-tops	*raapstelen*

One-Pan Dishes   Éénpansgerechten

hachee   Hash.

hete bliksem   Apples, potatoes and onions, stewed and served hot.

DUTCH

DUTCH

hutspot met klapstuk	Carrots, potatoes and onions, mashed together and served with boiled thin flank (often pork).
jachtschotel	Casserole consisting of layers of sliced potatoes, meat (often bacon), onions and apples, baked and served with red cabbage or apple sauce.
stamppot	Curly kale or endives, and potatoes, mashed together and served with boiled smoked sausage.
zuurkool met spek	Sauerkraut with chunks of bacon.

Snacks   Hapjes, Versnaperingen

bamibal	Egg roll with Chinese-noodle filling.
bitterballen	Small, round meat croquettes, usually served with mustard.
croque monsieur	See *tosti*.
frika(n)del	A roast sausage of minced meat.
frites met/zonder	French fries with/without mayonnaise.
kroket	Croquette with meat/fish/shrimp filling (*'vlees/vis/garnalen-kroket'*). Usually meat (beef) if filling not specified.
loempia	Egg roll.
nasibal	Egg roll with fried-rice filling.
russisch ei	Hard-boiled egg filled with mayonnaise and capers.
sausijzebroodje	Sausage roll.
tosti	Bread, usually with ham and cheese, grilled. (Flemish: *croque monsieur*)

Indonesian Food   Indonesisch Eten

The ubiquitous Indonesian cuisine is a tasty legacy of Dutch colonial history. White rice (boiled or steamed) is the mandatory foundation of most dishes. Don't use chopsticks, or a knife and fork: those in the know eat their Indonesian food with a spoon, perhaps with the aid of a fork, from deep plates.

bami goreng	Fried thick noodles with onions, pork, shrimp and spices, often topped with a fried egg.
bami rames	Boiled thick noodles with various 'side dishes' on the same plate, not mixed in, often topped with a fried egg.
emping	Flattened melinjo nuts, deep-fried and salted, a slightly bitter accompaniment to meals.
gado-gado	Steamed vegetables (crispy) and hard-boiled eggs, served with peanut sauce.
ketjap	Soy sauce, either sweet, *manis*, or salty, *asin*. Usually sweet if not specified.
kroepoek	Shrimp crackers.
nasi goreng	Same as *bami goreng,* but with rice; sometimes shredded omelette instead of fried egg.
nasi rames	Same as *bami rames,* but with rice; in effect a one-plate *rijsttafel*.
rempejek	Fried, spiced wafers, usually with peanuts.
rendang	Meat (beef or mutton) curry – dry, very spicy.
rijsttafel	'Rice table', an Indonesian colonial dish consisting of white rice with heaps of side dishes. A great splurge.
sambal	Chilli paste. Varieties include *oelek* (red, very spicy) and *badjak* (dark, onion-based, mild).

DUTCH

saté, sateh	Indonesian kebab, marinaded in *ketjap*-based sauce.
sayor (sayur) lodeh	Vegetable soup in coconut-based broth, to be poured over white rice.
spekkoek	Multi-layered spice cake

banana	*pisang*
beef	*daging*
chicken	*ajam*
dried shrimp paste	*trasi*
fish	*ikan*
goat (mutton)	*kambing*
pork	*babi*
shrimp, prawn	*udang*
vegetable pickle	*atjar*
vegetables	*sayor (sayur)*

Condiments, Spices & Garnish	**Kruiden, Specerijen & Garnering**
aniseed	*anijs*
capers	*kapper(tje)s*
chervil	*kervel*
chives	*bieslook*
cinnamon	*kaneel*
cloves	*kruidnagels*
fennel	*venkel*
garlic	*knoflook*
gherkin	*augurk*
ginger	*gember*
gravy	*jus*
laurel, bay	*laurier*
mace	*foelie*

mawseed, poppyseed	*maanzaad*
nutmeg	*nootmuskaat*
olive oil	*olijfolie*
parsley	*peterselie, pieterselie*
salt	*zout*
small, pickled onions	*zilveruitjes*
sugar	*suiker*
vinegar	*azijn*

Methods of Cooking

baked, fried	*gebakken*
boiled, cooked	*gekookt*
broiled, fried, roasted	*gebraden*
crispy	*krokant*
deep-fried	*gefrituurd*
done (steak, etc)	*gaar*
rare (steak, etc)	*even aangebakken*
roasted	*geroosterd*
salty	*zout*
smoked	*gerookt*
sour	*zuur*
spicy	*scherp/heet/pittig*
steamed	*gestoomd*
stewed	*gestoofd*
sweet	*zoet*
(very) well done (steak, etc)	*goed gaar*

Fruit — Fruit, Vruchten, Ooft

apple	*appel*
apricots	*abrikozen*
banana	*banaan*

DUTCH

berries (blue, bil, black)	*bessen (blauw, bos, braam)*
cherries	*kersen*
dried currants	*krenten*
grapes (white, black)	*druiven (witte, zwarte)*
lemon	*citroen*
mulberries	*moerbeien*
orange	*sinaasappel*
peach	*perzik*
pear	*peer*
pineapple	*ananas*
plum, prune	*pruim*
raisins, sultanas	*rozijnen*
raspberries	*frambozen*
strawberries	*aardbeien*

Dessert, Biscuits & Sweets Dessert/Nagerecht/ Naspijs, Koekjes & Snoep

aardbeien met slagroom	Strawberries with whipped cream.
appelbeignet	Apple fritter.
appelmoes	Apple sauce (chunky, if done properly).
bokkepoot	Literally 'billy-goat leg': a compound biscuit with filling and almond slivers, both ends dipped in chocolate.
boterletter, boterstaaf	Pastry with soft marzipan filling.
drop	Liquorice, often salty (the Dutch national 'sweet', hundreds of varieties and shapes).
flensjes	Thin pancakes, crepes.
pannekoeken	Pancakes.
roomijs	Ice cream (cream-based, as opposed to water-based sherbet, or *'waterijs'*).

DUTCH

moorkop	Large cream-puff with chocolate icing.
oliebol	Dough fritter with currants, served with caster sugar. Popular New Year's treat.
poffertjes	A mound of tiny round pancakes, served with caster sugar.
speculaas	Brown biscuit, spiced (cinnamon, nutmeg, cloves), often with almond slivers.
stroopwafel	Two thin wafers glued together with treacle.
tompoes, tompouce	Thick custard between two layers of flaky pastry, topped with icing.
vlaai, Limburgse vlaai	Tangy fruit pie on bread-dough base.
wentelteefjes	Stale bread, soaked in egg, milk and cinnamon, fried and served with sugar.

Drinks – Nonalcoholic

chocolate milk	*Chocomel*
coffee	*koffie*
juice	*sap*
orange juice	*jus, jus d'orange*
freshly squeezed	*vers geperst*
tea	*thee*
with milk/lemon	*met melk/citroen*
water with ice	*water met ijs*

Drinks – Alcoholic

Beerenburg	A herbal 'genever' from Friesland.
genever, jenever	Dutch gin, based on juniper berries, drunk neat and chilled from small glasses, like schnapps. *Jonge* ('young') is smooth and relatively easy to drink, *oude* ('old') has a

DUTCH

	strong juniper flavour and can be an acquired taste.
lambic	Popular Belgian beer, spontaneously fermented. Many varieties: *gueuze* is sour(ish), *kriek* and *framboise* are sweet (cherry and raspberry flavoured, respectively).
sneeuwwitje	Literally 'Snow White': 50/50 lemonade and beer (shandy).
trappist	Dark and often very strong Belgian beer, drunk from goblets. Originally brewed by Trappist monks. Countless brands and varieties, graded by alcohol content (*dubbel, tripel*).

beer	*bier*
lager	*pils*
brandy	*vieux*
wine	*wijn*
dry	*droog*
house wine	*huiswijn*
bubbly, sparkling	*mousserend*
red	*rood*
white	*wit*
sweet	*zoet*

Shopping

How much is it ...?
   hoo-vayl kost heht ...?   Hoeveel kost het ...?

bookshop	*book-wing-kerl*	boekwinkel
camera shop	*foh-toh-wing-kerl*	fotowinkel

clothing store	*klay-ding-zaak*	kledingzaak
delicatessen	*day-lee-kaa-tehs-ser*	delicatesse
general store,	*wing-kerl vor*	winkel voor
shop	*ahl-ler-ley waa-rern*	allerlei waren
laundry	*wahs-ser-eht-ter*	wasserette
market	*mahrkt*	markt
newsagency	*teyt-skhrif-tern-wing-kerl*	tÿdschrijftenwinkel
stationer's	*kahn-tor-book-hahn-derl*	kantoorboekhandel
pharmacy	*droh-khist*	drogist
shoeshop	*skhoo-nern-wing-kerl*	schoenenwinkel
souvenir shop	*soo-ver-neer-wing-kerl*	souvenirwinkel
supermarket	*sü-per-mahrkt*	supermarkt
vegetable shop	*khroon-ter-wing-kerl*	groentewinkel
grocery shop	*krer-der-neer*	kruidenier

DUTCH

I would like to buy …
   ik zow khraakh … vil-lern koh-pern
   Ik zou graag … willen kopen.
Do you have others?
   hayft ü ahn-der-er?
   Heeft U andere?
I don't like it.
   heht ber-vahlt mey neet
   Het bevalt mij niet.
Can I look at it?
   kahn ik heht ber-key-kern?
   Kan ik het bekijken?
I'm just looking.
   ik keyk ahl-layn
   Ik kijk alleen.

DUTCH

Can you write down the price?
kernt ü der preys op-skhrey-vern?
Kunt U de prijs opschrijven?

Do you accept credit cards?
ahk-sehp-teart ü krer-deet-kaar-tern/kreh-dit kahrts?
Accepteert U kredietkaarten/
credit cards?

Could you lower the price?
kernt ü om-laakh meht der preys?
Kunt U omlaag met de prijs?

I don't have much money.
ik hehp neet vayl khehld
Ik heb niet veel geld.

Can I help you?
kahn ik ü/yer hehl-pern?
Kan ik U/je helpen?

Will that be all?
is daht ahl-lers?
Is dat alles?

Would you like it wrapped?
zahl ik heht vor ü in-pahk-kern?
Zal ik het voor U inpakken?

Sorry, this is our only one.
so-ree, dit is der ay-ni-kher (dee wer hehb-bern)
Sorry, dit is de enige (die we hebben).

How much/many do you want?
hoo-vayl wilt ü?
Hoeveel wilt U?

Souvenirs

clogs	*klomp-ern*	klompen
earrings	*or-behl-lern*	oorbellen
handicraft	**hahnt**-wehrk	handwerk
necklace	**hahls**-snoor/**hahls**-keht-ting	halssnoer/halsket-ting (cord/links)

pottery	*aar-der-wehrk*	aardewerk
ring	*ring*	ring
rug	*klayt*	kleed

Clothing

clothing	*klay-ding*	kleding
coat	*yahs*	jas
dress	*yerk*	jurk
jacket	*yahs-yer*	jasje
jumper (sweater)	*trer*	trui
shirt	*hehmt*	hemd
shoes	*skhoo-nern*	schoenen
skirt	*rok*	rok
trousers	*brook*	broek

It doesn't fit.
  heht pahst neet   Het past niet.

It is too …
  heht is ter …   Het is te …

big/small	*khroht/kleyn*	groot/klein
short/long	*kort/lahng*	kort/lang
tight/loose	*now/weyt*	nauw/wijd

Materials

cotton	*kah-toon*	katoen
handmade	*hahnt-wehrk*	handwerk
leather	*lear/lay-der*	leer/leder
of brass	*vahn mehs-sing*	van messing
of gold	*vahn khowt*	van goud
of silver	*vahn zil-ver*	van zilver
silk	*zey-der*	zijde

DUTCH

Toiletries

comb	*kahm*	kam
condoms	*kon-dohms*	condooms
deodorant	*day-oh-doh-rahnt*	deodorant
hairbrush	*bor-sterl*	borstel
moisturising cream	*hert-krehm*	huidcrème
razor (blade)	*skhear-mehs-yer*	scheermesje
razor (electric)	*skhear-ahp-pah-raat*	scheerapparaat
sanitary napkins	*maant-ver-bahnd*	maandverband
shampoo	*syahm-poh*	shampoo
shaving cream	*skhear-zayp*	scheerzeep
soap	*zayp*	zeep
sunblock cream	*zon-ner-brahnt-oh-lee*	zonnebrandolie
tampons	*tahm-pons*	tampons
tissues	*tis-yoos/pah-pee-rern zahk-dook-yers*	tissues/papieren zakdoekjes
toilet paper	*way-say-pah-peer/twah-leht-pah-peer*	WC-papier/toiletpapier
toothbrush	*tahn-dern-bor-sterl*	tandenborstel
toothpaste	*tahnt-pahs-taa*	tandpasta

Stationery & Publications

map	*kaart*	kaart
newspaper	*krahnt*	krant
newspaper in English	*ehng-erl-ser krahnt*	Engelse krant
novels in English	*ehng-erl-ser roh-mahns*	Engelse romans
paper	*pah-peer*	papier

| pen (ballpoint) | *bahl-pehn* | balpen |
| scissors | *skhaar* | schaar |

Photography

How much is it to process this film?
hoo-vayl kost heht om day-zer film ter ont-wik-ker-lern?
Hoeveel kost het om deze film te ontwikkelen?

When will it be ready?
wahn-near is heht klaar?
Wanner is het klaar?

I'd like a film for this camera.
ik vil khraag film vor day-zer kaa-mer-aa
Ik wil graag film voor deze kamera.

B&W (film)	*zvahrt-vit*	zwart-wit
camera	*kaa-mer-aa*	kamera
colour (film)	*kler(-ern-film)*	kleur(enfilm)
film	*film*	film
flash	*flits*	flits
lens	*lens*	lens
light meter	*likht-may-ter*	lichtmeter

Smoking

A packet of cigarettes, please.
ern pahk-yer see-khaar-eht-tern, ahls-tü-bleeft
Een pakje sigaretten, alstublieft.

Are these cigarettes strong/mild?
zeyn day-zer see-khaar-eht-tern zwaar/likht?
Zijn deze sigaretten zwaar/licht?

Do you have a light?
hayft ü/hehp yer ern   Heeft U/heb je een vuurtje?
vür-tyer?

cigarette papers	*vlooee*	vloei
cigarettes	*see-khaar-**eht**-tern*	sigaretten
filtered	*meht **fil**-ter*	met filter
lighter	***aan**-stay-ker*	aansteker
matches	*loo-see-**fehrs***	lucifers
menthol	***men**-tol*	menthol
pipe	*peyp*	pijp

Colours

black	*zvahrt*	zwart
blue	*blow*	blauw
brown	*brern*	bruin
green	*khroon*	groen
pink	*ro-ser*	rose
red	*roht*	rood
white	*vit*	wit
yellow	*khayl*	geel

Sizes & Comparisons

small	*kleyn*	klein
big	*khroht*	groot
heavy	*zvaar*	zwaar
light	*likht*	licht
more	*mear*	meer
less	***min**-der*	minder
too much/many	*ter-**vayl***	teveel
many	*vayl*	veel
enough	*kher-**nookh***	genoeg

| also | *ohk* | ook |
| a little bit | *ern **bayt**-yer* | een beetje |

Health

Where is …?		
waar is …?		Waar is …?
the doctor	*der **dok**-ter*	de dokter
the hospital	*het **zee**-kern-hers*	het ziekenhuis
the chemist	*der **droh**-khist*	de drogist
the dentist	*der **tahnt**-ahrts*	de tandarts

I am sick.
ik behn zeek　　　　　　　　　Ik ben ziek.

My friend is sick.
*meyn vreend/vreend-**in** is*　　Mijn vriend (m)/vriendin (f)
zeek　　　　　　　　　　　　is ziek.

Could I see a female doctor?
*kahn ik ern **vrow**-er-ler-ker*　Kan ik een vrouwelijke arts
ahrts zeen?　　　　　　　　　zien?

What's the matter?
waht is ehr aan der hahnt?　　Wat is er aan de hand?

Where does it hurt?
waar doot heht peyn?　　　　Waar doet het pijn?

It hurts here.
heht doot heer peyn　　　　　Het doet hier pijn.

My … hurts.
meyn … doot peyn　　　　　Mijn … doet pijn.

Parts of the Body

back	*rerkh*	rug
chest	*borst*	borst
ear	*or*	oor

DUTCH

eye	*ohkh*	oog
finger	*ving-er*	vinger
foot	*voot*	voet
head	*hohft*	hoofd
leg	*bayn*	been
mouth	*mont*	mond
skin	*hert*	huid
stomach	*maakh*	maag
teeth	*tahn-dern*	tanden
throat	*kayl*	keel

Ailments

I have …
   ik hehp …   Ik heb …

anaemia	*bloot-ahr-moo-der*	bloedarmoede
a blister	*ern blaar*	een blaar
a burn	*ern ver-brahn-ding*	een verbranding
a cold	*ern ver-kowd-heyt*	een verkoudheid
constipation	*ver-stop-ping*	verstopping
a sore throat	*ern zear-er kayl*	een zere keel
diarrhoea	*dee-ah-ray*	diarree
fever	*korts*	koorts
glandular fever	*zeek-ter vahn pfai-fer*	ziekte van Pfeiffer
a headache	*hohft-peyn*	hoofdpijn
indigestion	*in-dee-khehs-tee*	indigestie
an infection	*ern ont-stay-king*	een ontsteking
influenza	*khreep*	griep
lice	*ler-zern*	luizen
low/high blood pressure	*hoh-kher/laa-kher bloot-drerk*	hoge/lage bloed-druk
a sprain	*ern ver-ster-king*	een verstuiking

sunburn	*zon-ner-brahnt*	zonnebrand
a temperature	*korts*	koorts
a venereal disease	*ern ver-near-ee-ser zeek-ter*	een venerische ziekte

Some Useful Words & Phrases

I'm …
  ik behn … — Ik ben …

diabetic	*ser-ker-zeek*	suikerziek
epileptic	*ay-pee-lehp-tees*	epileptisch
asthmatic	*ahst-maa-tees*	astmatisch

I'm allergic to antibiotics/penicillin.
  ik behn ah-lehr-khees vor ahn-tee-bee-oh-tee-kaa/ pay-nee-see-lee-ner — Ik ben allergisch voor antibiotica/penicilline.

I'm pregnant.
  ik behn zwahng-er — Ik ben zwanger.

I'm on the pill.
  ik kher-brerk der pil — Ik gebruik de pil.

I haven't had my period for … months.
  ik behn ahl … maan-dern neet on-kher-stehlt kher-wayst — Ik ben al … maanden niet ongesteld geweest.

I have been vaccinated.
  ik behn in-kher-ehnt — Ik ben ingëent.

I feel better/worse.
  ik vool mer bay-ter/slehkh-ter — Ik voel me beter/slechter.

accident	*on-kher-lerk*	ongeluk
addiction	*ver-slaa-ving*	verslaving
antibiotics	*ahn-tee-bee-oh-tee-kaa*	antibiotica
antiseptic	*ahn-tee-sehp-tee-kerm*	antisepticum
bandage	*ver-bahnt*	verband
blood pressure	*bloot-drerk*	bloeddruk
blood test	*bloot-tehst*	bloedtest
contraceptive	*vor-ber-hoots-mid-derl*	voorbehoeds-middel
injection	*in-yek-see*	injectie
itch	*yerk*	jeuk
menstruation	*mehn-strü-aat-see*	menstruatie
nausea	*mis-ser-lerk-heyt*	misselijkheid

At the Chemist

I need medication for …
   ik hehp may-dee-sey-nern noh-derkh vor …
Ik heb medicijnen nodig voor …

I have a prescription.
   ik hehp ern rer-sehpt
Ik heb een recept.

At the Dentist

I have a toothache.
   ik hehp kees-peyn/tahnt-peyn
Ik heb kiespijn (molars)/ tandpijn (incisors).

I've lost a filling.
   ik behn ern ver-ling ver-lor-ern
Ik ben een vulling verloren.

I've broken a tooth.
ik hehp ern tahnt
kher-broh-kern

Ik heb een tand gebroken.

My gums hurt.
meyn tahnt-vlays doot peyn

Mijn tandvlees doet pijn.

I don't want it extracted.
ik vil neet daht heht
kher-trok-kern wort

Ik wil niet dat het getrokken wordt.

Please give me an anaesthetic.
khayf mer ahls-tü-bleeft ern
ver-doh-ving

Geef me alstublieft een verdoving.

Time & Dates

What time is it?
hoo laat is heht?

Hoe laat is het?

It is … (o'clock)
heht is … ür

Het is … uur.

in the morning	*smor-kherns*	's-morgens
in the afternoon	*smid-dahkhs*	's-middags
in the evening	*saa-vonts*	's-avonds

What date is it today?
wehl-ker daa-term is heht
vahn-daakh?

Welke datum is het vandaag?

Days of the Week

Monday	*maan-dahkh*	maandag
Tuesday	*dins-dahkh*	dinsdag
Wednesday	*voons-dahkh*	woensdag
Thursday	*don-der-dahkh*	donderdag

Friday	*vrey-dahkh*	vrijdag
Saturday	*zaa-ter-dahkh*	zaterdag
Sunday	*zon-dahkh*	zondag

Months

January	*jah-nü-aa-ree*	januari
February	*fay-brü-aa-ree*	februari
March	*maart*	maart
April	*ah-pril*	april
May	*mey*	mei
June	*yü-nee*	juni
July	*yü-lee*	juli
August	*ow-khers-ters*	augustus
September	*sehp-tehm-ber*	september
October	*ok-toh-ber*	oktober
November	*noh-vehm-ber*	november
December	*day-sehm-ber*	december

Seasons

summer	*zoh-mer*	zomer
autumn	*hehrfst, naa-yaar*	herfst, najaar
winter	*win-ter*	winter
spring	*lehn-ter, vor-yaar*	lente, voorjaar

Present

today	*vahn-daakh*	vandaag
this morning	*day-zer mor-khern*	deze morgen
tonight	*vahn-aa-vont*	vanavond
this week/year	*day-zer wayk/dit yaar*	deze week/dit jaar
now	*nü*	nu

DUTCH

Past

yesterday	*khis-ter-ern*	gisteren
day before yesterday	*ear-khis-ter-ern*	eergisteren
yesterday morning	*khis-ter-ern-mor-khern*	gisterenmorgen
last night	*khis-ter-ern-aa-vont*	gisterenavond
last week/year	*vor-i-kher wayk/vor-ikh yaar*	vorige week/vorig jaar

Future

tomorrow	*mor-khern*	morgen
day after tomorrow	*oh-ver-mor-khern*	overmorgen
tomorrow morning	*mor-khern-okh-ternt*	morgenochtend
tomorrow afternoon/evening	*mor-khern-mid-dahkh/mor-khern-aa-vont*	morgenmiddag/ morgenavond
next week	*vol-khern-der wayk*	volgende week
next year	*vol-khernd yaar*	volgend jaar

During the Day

afternoon	*mid-dahkh*	middag
dawn, very early morning	*daa-khe-raat, smor-kherns vrookh*	dageraad, 's-morgens vroeg
day	*dahkh*	dag
early	*vrookh*	vroeg
midnight	*mid-der-nahkht*	middernacht
morning	*okh-ternt*	ochtend
night	*nahkht*	nacht
noon	*twaalf ür smid-dahkhs*	12 uur 's-middags

| sundown | *zons-on-der-khahng* | zonsondergang |
| sunrise | *zons-op-khahng* | zonsopgang |

Numbers & Amounts

0	*nerl*	nul
1	*ayn*	één
2	*tway*	twee
3	*dree*	drie
4	*veer*	vier
5	*veyf*	vijf
6	*zehs*	zes
7	*zay-vern*	zeven
8	*ahkht*	acht
9	*nay-khern*	negen
10	*teen*	tien
11	*elf*	elf
12	*twaalf*	twaalf
13	*dehr-teen*	dertien
14	*vear-teen*	veertien
15	*veyf-teen*	vijftien
16	*zehs-teen*	zestien
17	*zay-vern-teen*	zeventien
18	*ahkh-teen*	achttien
19	*nay-khern-teen*	negentien
20	*tvin-terkh*	twintig
30	*dehr-terkh*	dertig
40	*vear-terkh*	veertig
50	*veyf-terkh*	vijftig
60	*zehs-terkh*	zestig
70	*zay-vern-terkh*	zeventig
80	*tahkh-terkh*	tachtig

90	**nay**-khern-terkh	negentig
100	**hon**-dert	honderd
1000	**der**-zernt	duizend
one million	ayn mil-**yoon**	één miljoen

1st	**ear**-ster	eerste – 1e
2nd	**tway**-der	tweede – 2e
3rd	**dehr**-der	derde – 3e

¼	ern **kwahrt**	een kwart
⅓	ern **dehr**-der	een derde
½	ern **hahlf**	een half
¾	**dree**-kwahrt	driekwart

Some Useful Words

a little (amount)	ern **bay**-tyer	een beetje
double	**der**-berl	dubbel
a dozen	ern doh-**zeyn**	een dozijn
Enough!	kher-**nookh**!	Genoeg!
few	**wey**-nikh-er	weinige
less	**min**-der	minder
many	**vay**-ler	vele
more	**mear**	meer
once	**ayns**/ayn-**maal**	eens/eenmaal
a pair	ern **paar**	een paar
percent	pro-**sehnt**	procent
some	**som**-mer-kher	sommige
too much	ter-**vayl**	teveel
twice	**tway**-maal	tweemaal

DUTCH

Abbreviations

Afd	Dept
ANWB	Dutch motoring federation
BTW	VAT (value-added tax)
bv, bijv	eg
BV	Pty, private company
EG	EC
enz	etc
fl or f	Dutch guilder
F or BF	Belgian franc
GOS	CIS (Commonwealth of Independent States)
M/Mevr	Mr/Mrs, Ms
NV	Ltd, Unlimited
ps/zoz	ps/pto
TCB	Belgian Motoring (automobile) Club
-str/-weg/-pl	St/Rd/Sq
v.Chr./n.Chr.	AD/BC
VN	UN
VS	USA
VVV	Dutch tourist information

French

French

Introduction

French, like Italian, Spanish, Romanian and Portuguese, is one of the Romance languages – those descended from Latin. It began to emerge as a distinct language in the 9th century AD. The earliest surviving text in French is that of the *Strasbourg Oaths* (842 AD), an agreement uniting two of Charlemagne's grandsons against the third in a quarrel over the division of the empire. It was not until the 11th century, however, that a vernacular literature really established itself in France, with the development of verse epics called *chansons de gestes*.

During the 13th and 14th centuries, the emergence of France as a centralised state favoured the spread of the dialect of the Parisian region (Francien), to the detriment of regional dialects and the Provençal language in the south.

The edict of Villers-Cotterets, issued by François I in 1539, made the use of French compulsory for official documents. During the French Rennaissance, in the 16th century, efforts were made to enrich and dignify the national tongue, to make it a worthy vehicle for serious literature. This involved coining words from Greek and Latin roots, and the adoption of etymological spellings, which later reformers have not been able to rationalise. During the 17th century there was a reaction to this trend. The poet Malherbe and the grammarian Vaugelas, a founding member of the French Academy, *Académie française*, were influential in a movement to 'purify' the language and codify its usage, establishing norms which have, to a large extent, remained in force.

The Academy, established in 1635, has preserved its purist stand, opposing, in recent years, the introduction of English words such as 'look' or 'background'. The widespread use of such 'franglais', though it may pose a threat to the integrity of the French language, does not make communication significantly easier for the Anglophone in France.

There are about 90 million Francophones throughout the world, of whom about 54 million live in France. French is one of the official languages in Belgium, Switzerland and Luxembourg, which have around four million, 1.2 million and 300,000 Francophones respectively. French is also spoken by about 150,000 inhabitants of the Val d'Aosta in north-western Italy, and it has a million speakers in Monaco. Major areas outside Europe where you'll find French spoken are Africa, Indochina, the Pacific, Canada (Quebec), and the USA (especially Maine and Louisiana).

French grammar is broadly similar to that of the other Romance languages. An important distinction is made in French between *tu* and *vous* (singular), which both correspond to 'you.' *Tu* is only used in addressing people you know well, children, and animals. When addressing an adult who is not a personal friend, *vous* should be used unless the person invites you to use *tu (Tu peux me tutoyer)*. In general, younger people insist less on this distinction, and they may use *tu* right from the beginning of an acquaintance.

All nouns in French are either masculine or feminine, or both, and adjectives reflect the gender. The feminine form of both nouns and adjectives is indicated by a silent 'e' added to the masculine form: student, *étudiant* (m)/*étudiante* (f). As in the example here, throughout this chapter the feminine word or variant follows the masculine. The gender of a noun is often indicated by a preceding article 'the/a/some': *le/un/du* (m), *la/une/de la* (f); or possessive adjective 'my/your/his/her': *mon/ton/son* (m), *ma/ta/sa* (f). The possessive adjectives agree in number and gender with the thing possessed: his/her mother, *sa mère*.

There are three ways of asking questions in French: you can invert the subject and the verb *(Avez-vous l'heure?)*; you can begin with *est-ce que* and keep the normal word order *(Est-ce que vous avez l'heure?)*; or you can rely on intonation to indicate that you are asking a question *(Vous avez l'heure?)*. The first way of asking questions is rather formal. The second two ways are more common in spoken French, and so will be used for most of the questions in this section.

Pronunciation

Stress in French is much weaker than in English – all it really does is lengthen the final syllable of the word – so it is important for the Anglophone to make an effort to pronounce each syllable with approximately equal stress.

French has a number of sounds which are notoriously difficult to produce. The main causes of trouble are:

1) The distinction between **ü** (as in *tu*) and **oo** (as in *tout*). For both sounds, the lips are rounded and projected forward, but for **ü**, the tongue is towards the front of the mouth, its tip against the lower front teeth, while for **oo** the tongue is towards the back of the mouth, its tip behind the gums of the lower front teeth.

2) The nasal vowels. During the production of nasal vowels the breath escapes partly through the nose and partly through the mouth. There are no nasal vowels in English; in French there

are three, indicated in the text as **õ**, **ẽ**, **ã**, as in *bon vin blanc*, 'good white wine'. These sounds occur where a syllable ends in a single **n** or **m**: the **n** or **m** in this case is not pronounced, but indicates the nasalisation of the preceding vowel.

ã   as for the 'ah' sound in 'father', but with a slightly smaller opening between the lips, and the breath escaping partly through the nose. The usual spellings are **an**, **am**, **en**, and **em**.

õ   as for the 'o' in 'pot', but with the lips closer and rounded, and the breath escaping partly through the nose. The usual spelling is **on**, **om**. It is important to distinguish this sound from **ã**.

ẽ   as for the 'eh' sound in 'bet', but with a slightly larger opening between the lips, and the breath escaping partly through the nose. The usual spellings are **in**, **im**, **yn**, **ym**, **ain**, **aim**, **ein**, **eim**, **en** preceded by **i** or **é**, **un** or **um**.

Remember that for **õ**, the jaws are closer together and the lips rounded. Practice distinguishing pairs of words such as *tonton*, **tõtõ**, 'uncle', and *tentant*, **tãtã**, 'tempting.'

3) l and r. The French **l** is always pronounced with the tip of the tongue touching the back of the upper incisors, and the surface of the tongue higher than for an English 'l'. Be especially careful to maintain this tongue position for **ls** at the ends of words, as in *il* or *elle*. The standard **r** of Parisian French is produced by moving the bulk of the tongue backwards to constrict the air flow in the pharynx, while the tip of the tongue rests behind the lower front teeth. It is quite similar to the noise made by some people before spitting, but with much less friction. For those who know Spanish, it also like the *jota*, except that it is 'softer' and voiced (involves vibration of the vocal cords).

In general, try not to diphthongise vowels – keep the tongue in the same position during their entire production, and project the lips forward and round them well to produce the rounded vowels **o**, **ü**, **er** and **oo**.

FRENCH

Greetings & Civilities
Top Useful Phrases

Hello.
bō-zhoor   Bonjour.

Goodbye.
oh rer-vwahr   Au revoir.

Yes./No.
wee/nō   Oui./Non.

Excuse me.
ehk-skü-zei mwah   Excusez-moi.

May I? Do you mind?
voo pehr-meh-tei? sah ner   Vous permettez? Ça ne vous
voo fei ryē?   fait rien?

Sorry. (excuse me, forgive me)
pahr-dō   Pardon.

Please.
seel voo plei   S'il vous plaît.

Thank you.
mehr-see   Merci.

Many thanks.
mehr-see boh-koo   Merci beaucoup.

That's fine. You're welcome.
trei byē. zher voo zā pree   Très bien. Je vous en prie.

Greetings

Good morning.
bō-zhoor — Bonjour.

Good afternoon.
bō-zhoor — Bonjour.

Good evening/night.
bō-swahr — Bonsoir.

How are you?
ko-mā tah-lei voo? — Comment-allez vous?

Well, thanks.
byē mehr-see! — Bien, merci!

Forms of Address

Madam/Mrs	*mah-dahm*	Madame
Sir/Mr	*mer-syer*	Monsieur
Miss	*mahd-mwah-zehl*	Mademoiselle
companion, friend	*ah-mee*	ami (m)/amie (f)

Small Talk

Meeting People

What is your name?
voo voo zah-plei ko-mā? — Vous vous appelez comment?

My name is …
zher mah-pehl … — Je m'appelle …

I'd like to introduce you to …
zhem-rei voo prei-zā-tei … — J'aimerais vous présenter …

I'm pleased to meet you.
ā-shā-tei — Enchanté/-ée.

FRENCH

FRENCH

Nationalities

Where are you from?
voo ver-ne doo?   Vous venez d'où?

I am ...
zher vyẽ ...   Je viens ...

from Australia	*do-strah-lee*	d'Australie
from Canada	*dü kah-nah-dah*	du Canada
from England	*dã-gler-tehr*	d'Angleterre
from France	*der frãs*	de France
from New Zealand	*der noo-vehl zei-lãd*	de Nouvelle Zélande
from Scotland	*dei-kos*	d'Écosse
from Switzerland	*der swees*	de Suisse
from the USA	*dei zei-tah zü-nee*	des États-Unis
from Wales	*dü pei-ee der gahl*	du Pays de Galles

Age

How old are you?
voo zah-vei kehl ahzh?   Vouz avez quel âge?
I am ... years old.
zhei ... ã   J'ai ... ans.

Occupations

What (work) do you do?
keh-sker voo feht dã lah vee?   Qu'est-ce que vous faites dans la vie?

I am (a/an) …
   zher swee …   Je suis …

artist	*ahr-teest*	artiste
business person	*om/fahm dah-fehr*	homme (m)/
		femme (f) d'affaires
doctor	*mehd-sē*	médecin
engineer	*ē-zhen-yerr*	ingénieur
farmer	*ah-gree-kül-terr*	agriculteur
journalist	*zhoor-nah-leest*	journaliste
lawyer	*ah-vo-kah*	avocat
mechanic	*mei-kah-nee-syē*	mécanicien (m)
	mei-kah-nee-syehn	mécanicienne (m)
nurse	*ē-feer-myei*	infirmier (m)
	ē-feer-myehr	infirmière (f)
office worker	*ā-plwah-yei der*	employé/-ée de
	bü-roh	bureau
scientist	*syā-tee-feek*	scientifique
student	*ei-tü-dyā*	étudiant (m)
	ei-tü-dyāt	étudiante (f)
teacher	*pro-feh-serr*	professeur
waiter	*sehr-verr*	serveur (m)
	sehr-verz	serveuse (f)
writer	*ei-kreev-ē*	écrivain

FRENCH

Religion

What is your religion?
   kehl ei votr rer-lee-zhyō?   Quelle est votre religion?
I am not religious.
   zher ner swee pah   Je ne suis pas croyant.
   krwah-yā

I am …
zher swee …
Je suis …

Buddhist	*boo-deest*	bouddhiste
Catholic	*kah-to-leek*	catholique
Christian	*krei-tyē/kreit-yehn*	chrétien (m)
		chrétienne (f)
Hindu	*ē-doo*	hindou (m)
		hindoue (f)
Jewish	*zhweef/zhweev*	juif (m)/juive (f)
Muslim	*mü-zül-mā*	musulman (m)
	mü-zül-mahn	musulmane (f)

Family

Are you married?
voo zeht mah-ryei?
Vous êtes marié/-ée?

I am single.
zher swee sei-lee-bah-tehr
Je suis célibataire.

I am married.
zher swee mah-ryei
Je suis marié/-ée.

How many children do you
have?
voo zah-vei kō-byē dā-fā?
Vous avez combien
d'enfants?

I don't have any children.
zher nei pah dā-fā
Je n'ai pas d'enfants.

I have a daughter/a son.
zhei ün feey/ē fees
J'ai une fille/un fils.

How many brothers/sisters do
you have?
*voo zah-vei kō-byē der
frehr/serr?*
Vous avez combien de
frères/soeurs?

Is your husband/wife here?
eh-sker votr mahree/fahm ei lah?

Est-ce que votre mari/femme est lá?

Do you have a boyfriend/girlfriend?
eh-sker voo zah-vei ē per-tee tah-mee/ün per-teet ah-mee?

Est-ce que vous avez un petit ami/une petite amie?

brother	*ler frehr*	le frère
children	*lei zāfā*	les enfants
daughter	*lah feey*	la fille
family	*lah fah-meey*	la famille
father	*ler pehr*	le père
grandfather	*ler grā-pehr*	le grand-père
grandmother	*lah grā-mehr*	la grand-mère
husband	*ler mah-ree*	le mari
mother	*lah mehr*	la mère
sister	*lah serr*	la soeur
son	*ler fees*	le fils
wife	*lah fahm*	la femme

Feelings

I (don't) like …
… (ner) mer plei (pah)

… (ne) me plaît (pas).

I am sorry. (condolence)
zher swee dei-zo-lei

Je suis désolé/-ée.

I am grateful.
zher voo swee rer-ko-neh-sā/rer-ko-neh-sāt

Je vous suis reconnaissant (m)/reconnaissante (f).

FRENCH

I am …
zhei …

cold/hot	*frwah/shoh*	froid/chaud
hungry/thirsty	*fĕ/swahf*	faim/soif
right	*rei-zō*	raison
sleepy	*so-meihy*	sommeil

J'ai …

I am …
zher swee …

Je suis …

angry	*fah-shei*	fâché/-ée
happy	*er-rer*	heureux (m)
	er-rerz	heureuse (f)
in a hurry	*preh-sei*	pressé/-ée
sad	*treest*	triste
tired	*fah-tee-gei*	fatigué/-ée
well	*byē*	bien

Language Difficulties

Do you speak English?
  voo pahr-lei ā-glei?
Vous parlez anglais?

Does anyone speak English?
  ehs-keel-yah kehl-kē kee
  pahrl ā-glei?
Est-ce qu'il y a à quelqu'un
qui parle anglais?

I speak a little …
  zher pahrl ē per der …
Je parle un peu de …

I don't speak …
  zher ner pahrl pah
Je ne parle pas …

I (don't) understand.
  zher (ner) kō-prā (pah)
Je (ne) comprends (pas).

Could you speak more slowly?
  eh-sker voo poo-ryei
  pahr-lei plü lā-tmā?
Est-ce que vous pourriez
parler plus lentement?

Could you repeat that?
*eh-sker voo poo-ryei
rei-pei-tei?*

Est-ce que vous pourriez
répéter?

How do you say ...?
ko-mā tehs-kō dee ... ?

Comment est-ce qu'on dit ...?

What does ... mean?
ker ver deer ...?

Que veut dire ...?

I speak ...
zher pahrl ...

Je parle ...

English	*ā-glei*	anglais
French	*frā-sei*	français
German	*ahl-mā*	allemand
Italian	*ee-tah-lyē*	italien

FRENCH

Some Useful Phrases

Sure.
byē sür

Bien sûr.

Just a minute.
ah-tā-dei ün mee-nüt

Attendez une minute.

It's important.
sei tē-por-tā

C'est important.

It's not important.
ser nei pah zē-por-tā

Ce n'est pas important.

It's (not) possible.
*sei po-seebl/ser nei pah
po-seebl*

C'est possible/Ce n'est pas
possible.

Good luck!
bon shās!

Bonne chance!

Wait!
ah-tā-dei!

Attendez!

Signs

BAGGAGE COUNTER	CONSIGNE
CHECK-IN COUNTER	ENREGISTREMENT
CUSTOMS	DOUANE
EMERGENCY EXIT	ISSUE DE SECOURS
ENTRANCE	ENTRÉE
EXIT	SORTIE
FREE ADMISSION	ENTRÉE GRATUITE
HOT/COLD	CHAUDE/FROIDE
INFORMATION	RENSEIGNEMENTS
NO ENTRY	ENTRÉE INTERDITE
NO SMOKING	DÉFENSE DE FUMER
OPEN/CLOSED	OUVERT/FERMÉ
PROHIBITED	INTERDIT
RESERVED	RÉSERVÉ
TELEPHONE	TÉLÉPHONE
TOILETS	TOILETTES

Emergencies

POLICE	POLICE
POLICE STATION	(COMMISSARIAT DE)

Help!
   oh ser-coor!   Au secours!
It's an emergency!
   sei tür-zhā!   C'est urgent!

There's been an accident!
eel-yah ü ē nak-see-dā!

Il y a eu un accident!

Call a doctor!
ah-plei ē meid-sē!

Appelez un médecin!

Call an ambulance!
ah-plei ün ā-bü-lās!

Appelez une ambulance!

I've been raped.
zhei ei-tei vyo-lei

J'ai été violée.

I've been robbed!
zhei ei-tei volei!

J'ai été volé/-ée!

Call the police!
ah-plei lah po-lees!

Appelez la police!

Where is the police station?
oo ei ler ko-mee-sahr-yah der po-lees?

Où est le commissariat de police?

Go away!
lei-sei mwah trā-keel!

Laissez-moi tranquille!

Thief!
oh vo-lerr!

Au voleur!

I am ill.
zher swee mah-lahd

Je suis malade.

My friend is ill.
mō nah-mee ei mah-lahd

Mon ami/-e est malade.

I am lost.
zher mer swee ei-gah-rei

Je me suis égaré/-ée.

Where are the toilets?
oo sō lei twah-leht?

Où sont les toilettes?

Could you help me please?
eh-sker voo poo-ryei mei-dei seel voo plei?

Est-ce que vous pourriez m'aider, s'il vous plaît?

Could I please use the
telephone?
   eh-sker zher poo-rei
   ū-tee-lee-zei ler tei-lei-fon?

Est-ce que je pourrais
utiliser le téléphone?

I'm sorry. I apologise.
   zher swee dei-zo-lei
   zher mehk-skūz

Je suis désolé/-ée.
Je m'excuse.

I didn't realise I was doing
anything wrong.
   zher nei sah-vei pah ker
   zhah-vei tor der ler fehr

Je ne savais pas que j'avais
tort de le faire.

I didn't do it.
   ser nei pah mwah kee lah fei

Ce n'est pas moi qui l'a fait.

I wish to contact my embassy/
consulate.
   zher ver kō-tahk-tei
   lā-bah-sahd/ler kō-sū-lah

Je veux contacter
l'Ambassade/le Consulat.

I speak English.
   zher pahrl ā-glei

Je parle anglais.

I have medical insurance.
   zhei der lah-sū-rās
   mah-lah-dee

J'ai de l'assurance maladie.

My possessions are insured.
   mei byē sō tah-sū-rei

Mes biens sont assurés.

... was stolen.
   ō mah vo-lei ...

On m'a volé ...

I've lost ...
   zhei pehrdū ...

J'ai perdu ...

my bags	*mei bah-gahzh*	mes bagages
my handbag	*mō sahk ah mē*	mon sac à main
my money	*mō nahr-zhā*	mon argent
my travellers' cheques	*mei shehk der vwah-yahzh*	mes cheques de voyage
my passport	*mō pahs-por*	mon passeport

Paperwork

name	*nō ei prei-nō*	nom et prénom
address	*ah-drehs*	adresse
date of birth	*daht der neh-sās*	date de naissance
place of birth	*lyer der neh-sās*	lieu de naissance
age	*ahzh*	âge
sex	*sehks*	sexe
nationality	*nah-syo-nah-lee-tei*	nationalité
religion	*kō-feh-syō*	confession
reason for travel	*rei-zō dü vwah-yahzh*	raison du voyage
profession	*mei-tyei*	métier
marital status	*see-twah-syō der fah-meey*	situation de famille
passport	*pahs-por*	passeport
passport number	*nü-mer-oh der pahs-por*	numéro de passeport
visa	*vee-zah*	visa
identification	*pyehs dee-dā-tee-tei*	pièce d'identité
birth certificate	*ehk-streh der neh-sās*	extrait de naissance
driver's licence	*pehr-mee der kō-dweer*	permis de conduire
car owner's title	*teetr der pro-pree-yei-tei dün vwah-tür*	titre de propriété d'une voiture
car registration	*kahrt greez*	carte grise

customs	*dwahn*	douane
immigration	*ee-mee-grah-syõ*	immigration
border	*frõ-tyehr*	frontière

Getting Around

ARRIVALS	ARRIVÉES
BUS STATION	GARE ROUTIÈRE
BUS STOP	ARRÊT D'AUTOBUS
DEPARTURES	DÉPARTS
SUBWAY	MÉTRO
TICKET OFFICE	GUICHET
TIMETABLE	HORAIRE
TRAIN STATION	GARE

What time does ... leave/
arrive?

   ... pahr/ahreev ah kehl err?   ... part/arrive à quelle
heure?

the (air)plane	*lah-vyõ*	l'avion
the boat	*ler bah-toh*	le bateau
the bus (city)	*l(o-to-)büs*	l'(auto)bus
the bus (intercity)	*l(o-to-)kahr*	l'(auto)car
the train	*ler trẽ*	le train
the tram	*ler trahm-wei*	le tramway

Directions

Where is ...?

   oo ei ...?   Où est ...?

How do I get to ...?
ko-mã fehr poor ah-lei ah ...?
Comment faire pour aller á ...?

Is it far from/near here?
sei lwẽ/pah lwẽ dee-see?
C'est loin/pas loin d'ici?

Can I walk there?
zher per ee ah-lei ah pyei?
Je peux y aller à pied?

Can you show me (on the map)?
eh-sker voo poo-vei mer ler mõ-trei (sür lah kahrt)?
Est-ce que vous pouvez me le montrer (sur la carte)?

Are there other means of getting there?
ehs-keel-yah ẽ nohtr mwah-yẽ dee ah-lei?
Est-ce qu'il y a un autre moyen d'y aller?

I want to go to ...
zher ver ah-lei ah ...
Je veux aller à ...

Go straight ahead.
kõ-teen-wei too drwah
Continuez tout droit.

It's two blocks down.
sei der rü plü lwah
C'est deux rues plus loin.

Turn left ...
toor-nei ah gohsh ...
Tournez à gauche ...

Turn right ...
toor-nei ah drwaht ...
Tournez à droite ...

at the next corner
oh pro-shẽ kwẽ
au prochain coin

at the traffic lights
oh fer
aux feux

behind	*deh-ryehr*	derrière
in front of	*der-vã*	devant
far	*lwẽ*	loin
near	*prosh*	proche
opposite	*ã fahs der*	en face de

Booking Tickets

Excuse me, where is the ticket office?
ehk-skü-zei mwah oo ei ler gee-shei?
Excusez-moi, où est le guichet?

Where can I buy a ticket?
oo ehs-ker zher per ahsh-tei ẽ bee-yei?
Où est-ce que je peux acheter un billet?

I want to go to …
zher ver ah-lei ah …
Je veux aller â …

Do I need to book?
ehs-keel foh rei-zehr-vei ün plahs/lei plahs?
Est-ce qu'il faut réserver une place/les places?

You need to book.
eel foh rei-zehr-vei ün plahs/lei plahs
Il faut réserver une place/les places.

I would like to book a seat to …
zher voo-drei re-zehr-vei ün plahs poor …
Je voudrais réserver une place pour …

It is full.
sei kõ-plei
C'est complet.

Is it completely full?
eel nyah vreh-mã pah der plahs?
Il n'y a vraiment pas de place?

Can I get a stand-by ticket?
ehs-ker zher per ahsh-tei ē bee-yei sā gah-rā-tee?

Est-ce que je peux acheter un billet sans garantie?

I would like …
zher voo-drei …

Je voudrais …

a one-way ticket	*ē bee-yei ah-lei sēpl*	un billet aller simple
a return ticket	*ē bee-yei ah-lei ei rertoor*	un billet aller et retour
two tickets	*der bee-yei*	deux billets
tickets for all of us	*dei bee-yei poor noo toos*	des billets pour nous tous
a student's fare	*ē bee-yei ah tah-reef rei-dwee (zher swee zei-tü-dyā/ zei-tü-dyāt)*	un billet à tarif réduit (je suis étudiant (m)/ étudiante (f))
a child's/ pensioner's fare	*ē bee-yei ah tah-reef rei-dwee (sei poor ē ā-fā/zher swee rer-treh-tei)*	un billet à tarif réduit (c'est pour un enfant/je suis retraité/-ée)
1st class	*prer-myehr klahs*	Première classe
2nd class	*ser-gōd/der-zyehm klahs*	Seconde/Deuxième classe

Air

CHECKING IN	ENREGISTREMENT
LUGGAGE PICKUP	LIVRAISON DE BAGAGES

Is there a flight to …?
ehs-keel-yah ē vol poor …?

Est-ce qu'il y a un vol pour …?

When is the next flight to …?
ah kehl err pahr ler pro-shē nah-vyō poor …?

A quelle heure part le prochain avion pour …?

How long does the flight take?
ler vol dür kō-byē der tā?

Le vol dure combien de temps?

What is the flight number?
kehl ei ler nü-mer-oh dü vol?

Quel est le numéro du vol?

You must check in at …
voo der-ve voo prei-sā-tei ah lā-rei-zhee-strermā ah …

Vous devez vous présenter à l'enregistrement à …

airport tax	*tahks dah-ei-ro-por*	taxes d'aéroport
boarding pass	*kahrt dā-bahr-ker-mā*	carte d'embarquement
customs	*dwahn*	douane

Bus

BUS/TRAM STOP	ARRÊT D'AUTOBUS/DE TRAMWAY

Where is the bus/tram stop?
oo ei lah-rei do-to-büs/der trahm-wei?

Où est l'arrêt d'autobus/de tramway?

Which bus goes to …?
kehl büs vah ah …?

Quel bus va à …?

Does this bus go to …?
ehs-ker ser büs vah ah …?

Est-ce que ce bus va à …?

How often do buses pass by?
lei büs pahs ah kehl frei-kās?

Les bus passent à quelle fréquence?

What time is the … bus?
ler büs … pahs ah kehl err?

Le bus … passe à quelle heure?

next	*pro-shē*	prochain (m)
	pro-shehn	prochaine (f)
first	*prer-myei*	premier (m)
	prer-myehr	première (f)
last	*dehr-nyei*	dernier (m)
	dehr-nyehr	dernière (f)

Could you let me know when we get to …?
ehs-ker voo poo-vei mer ler deer kā noo zah-ree-vō ah …?

Est-ce que vous pouvez me le dire quand nous arrivons à …?

I want to get off!
zher ver dehs-ādr!

Je veux descendre!

FRENCH

Train

DINING CAR	WAGON-RESTAURANT
EXPRESS	RAPIDE
PLATFORM	QUAI
SLEEPING CAR	WAGON-LIT

Is this the right platform
for …?
   sei byē ler kei poor …?   C'est bien le quai pour …?

Passengers must …
   lei vwah-yah-zherr   Les voyageurs doivent …
   dwahv …

| change trains | *shā-zhei der trē* | changer de train |
| change platforms | *shā-zhei der kei* | changer de quai |

The train leaves from
platform …
   ler trē pahr dü kei …   Le train part du quai …

dining car	*vah-gō rehs-toh-rā*	wagon-restaurant
express	*rah-peed*	rapide
local	*lo-kahl*	local
sleeping car	*vah-gō lee*	wagon-lit

Metro

METRO/UNDERGROUND	MÉTRO
CHANGE (for coins)	DISTRIBUTEUR DE MONNAIE
THIS WAY TO	CORRESPONDANCE
WAY OUT	SORTIE

Which line takes me to …?
   kehl leeny/rahm vah ah …?   Quelle ligne/rame va à …?

What is the next station?
*kehl ei lah pro-shehn
stah-syõ?*

Quelle est la prochaine
station?

Taxi

Can you take me to …?
*ehs-ker voo poo-vei mer
kõ-dweer ah …?*

Est-ce que vous pouvez me
conduire à …?

Please take me to …
*kõ-dwee-ze mwah ah …,
seel voo plei*

Conduisez-moi à …, s'il
vous plaît.

How much does it cost to go
to …?
*kehl ei ler pree der lah
koors zhüs-kah …?*

Quel est le prix de la course
jusqu'à …?

Instructions

Here is fine, thank you.
ee-see sah vah, mehr-see

Ici ça va, merci.

The next corner, please.
*oh pro-shẽ kwẽ der rü,
seel voo plei*

Au prochain coin de rue,
s'il vous plaît.

Continue!
kõ-tee-nwe!

Continuez!

The next street to the left/right.
*lah pro-shehn rü ah gohsh/
drwaht*

La prochaine rue à gauche/
droite.

Stop here!
ah-reh-tei voo ee-see!

Arrêtez-vous ici!

Please slow down.
*roo-lei plü lãt-mã, seel voo
plei*

Roulez plus lentement, s'il
vous plaît.

FRENCH

Please wait here.
ah-tā-de ee-see seel voo plei   Attendez ici, s'il vous plaît.

Some Useful Phrases

The train is delayed/cancelled.
ler trē ah dü rer-tahr/ah   Le train a du retard/a été
ei-tei ah-nü-lei   annulé.

How long will it be delayed?
eel yo-rah kō-byē der tā der   Il y aura combien de temps
rer-tahr?   de retard?

There is a delay of … hours.
eel yo-rah ē rer-tahr der …   Il y aura un retard de …
err   heures.

Can I reserve a place?
ehs-ker zher per rei-zehr-   Est-ce que je peux réserver
vei ün plahs?   une place?

How long does the trip take?
ler trah-zhei dü-rer-rah   Le trajet durera combien de
kō-byē der tā?   temps?

Is it a direct route?
sei tē trē dee-rehkt?   C'est un train direct?

Is that seat taken?
ehs-ker seht plahs ei   Est-ce que cette place est
to-kü-pei?   occupée?

I want to get off at …
zher ver dehs-ādr ah …   Je veux descendre à …

Excuse me.
ehk-skü-ze mwah   Excusez-moi.

Where can I hire a bicycle?
oo ehs-ker zher per lwei   Où est-ce que je peux louer
ē vei-loh?   un vélo?

FRENCH

Car

DETOUR	DÉVIATION
FREEWAY	AUTOROUTE
GARAGE	GARAGE/STATION SERVICE
GIVE WAY	CÉDEZ LA PRIORITÉ
MECHANIC	MÉCANICIEN
NO ENTRY	ENTRÉE INTERDITE
NO PARKING	STATIONNEMENT INTERDIT
NORMAL	NORMALE
ONE WAY	SENS UNIQUE
REPAIRS	RÉPARATIONS
SELF SERVICE	LIBRE-SERVICE
STOP	STOP
SUPER	SUPER
UNLEADED	SANS PLOMB

Where can I rent a car?
oo ehs-ker zher per lwei ün vwah-tür?
Où est-ce que je peux louer une voiture?

How much is it daily/weekly?
kehl ei ler tah-reet pahr zhoor/pahr ser-mehn?
Quel est le tarif par jour/par semaine?

Does that include insurance/mileage?
ehs-ker lah-sü-rās/ler kee-lo-mei-trahzh ei kõ-pree?
Est-ce que l'assurance/le kilométrage est compris?

Where's the next petrol station?
oo ei lah pro-shehn stah-syō sehr-vees?

Où est la prochaine station service?

Please fill the tank.
ler plē seel voo plei

Le plein, s'il vous plaît.

I want … litres of petrol (gas).
do-ne mwah … leetr dehs-ās seel voo plei

Donnez-moi … litres d'essence, s'il vous plaît.

Please check the oil and water.
kō-tro-lei lweel ei loh seel voo plei

Controllez l'huile et l'eau, s'il vous plaît.

How long can I park here?
poor kō-byē der tā ehs-ker zher peux stah-syō-nei ee-see?

Pour combien de temps est-ce que je peux stationner ici?

Does this road lead to?
ehs-ker seht root mehn ah …?

Est-ce que cette route mène à …?

air (for tyres)	*ler kō-prehs-err (poor gō-flei le pner)*	le compresseur (pour gonfler les pneus)
battery	*lah bah-tree*	la batterie
brakes	*le frē*	les freins
clutch	*lā-bre-yahzh*	l'embrayage
driver's licence	*ler pehr-mee der kō-dweer*	le permis de conduire
engine	*ler mo-terr*	le moteur
lights	*le fahr*	les phares
oil	*lweel*	l'huile

puncture	*lah krer-ve-zō*	la crevaison
radiator	*ler rah-dyah-ter*	le radiateur
road map	*lah kahrt roo-tyehr*	la carte routière
tyres	*le pner*	les pneus
windscreen	*ler pahr breez*	le pare-brise

Car Problems

I need a mechanic.
zhei ber-zwē dē mei-kah-nee-syē

J'ai besoin d'un mécanicien.

What make is it?
kehl ei lah mahrk?

Quelle est la marque?

The battery is flat.
lah bah-tree ei tah plah

La batterie est à plat.

The radiator is leaking.
ler rah-dyah-terr fwee

Le radiateur fuit.

I have a flat tyre.
ler pner sei dei-gō-flei

Le pneu s'est dégonflé.

It's overheating.
ler mo-terr shohf

Le moteur chauffe.

It's not working.
eel/ehl ner mahrsh pah

Il (m)/elle (f) ne marche pas.

Accommodation

CAMPING GROUND	CAMPING
GUEST HOUSE	PENSION DE FAMILLE
HOTEL	HÔTEL
MOTEL	MOTEL
YOUTH HOSTEL	AUBERGE DE JEUNESSE

FRENCH

I am looking for ...
zher shehrsh ...   Je cherche ...

Where is ...?
oo es-keel-yah ... ?   Où est-ce qu'il y a ...?

a cheap hotel	*ē-noh-tehl bō mahr-shei*	un hôtel bon marché
a good hotel	*ē-bō-noh-tehl*	un bon hôtel
a nearby hotel	*ē-noh-tehl pah lwē dee-see*	un hôtel pas loin d'ici
a clean hotel	*ē-noh-tehl propr*	un hôtel propre

What is the address?
kehl ei lah-drehs?   Quelle est l'adresse?

Could you write the address, please?
ehs-ker voo poo-vei ei-kreer lah-drehs seel voo plei?   Est-ce vous pouvez écrire l'adresse, s'il vous plaît?

At the Hotel

Do you have any rooms available?
ehs-ker voo zah-vei de shābr leebr?   Est-ce que vous avez des chambres libres?

I would like ...
zher voo-drei ...   Je voudrais ...

a single room	*ün shābr ah ē lee*	une chambre à un lit
a double room	*ün shābr doobl*	une chambre double

a room with a bathroom	*ün shābr ah-vehk ün sahl der bē*	une chambre avec une salle de bain
to share a dorm	*koo-shei dā zē dor-twahr*	coucher dans un dortoir
a bed	*ē lee*	un lit

I want a room with …
zher ver ün shābr ah-vehk …

Je veux une chambre avec …

a bathroom	*ün sahl der bē*	une salle de bain
a shower	*ün doosh*	une douche
a television	*ün tei-lei-vee-zyō*	une télévision
a window	*ün fer-nehtr*	une fenêtre

I'm going to stay for …
zher rehs-ter-rei …

Je resterai …

one day	*ē zhoor*	un jour
two days	*der zhoor*	deux jours
one week	*ün ser-mehn*	une semaine

Do you have identification?
ehs-ker voo zha-vei ün pyehs dee-dā-tee-tei?

Est-ce que vous avez une pièce d'identité?

Your membership card, please.
votr kahrt dah-dei-rā seel voo plei

Votre carte d'adhérent, s'il vous plaît.

Sorry, we're full.
dei-zo-lei me sei kō-plei

Désolé, mais c'est complet.

How long will you be staying?
voo rehs-ter-re kō-byē der tā?

Vous resterez combien de temps?

How many nights?
kō-byē der nwee?

Combien de nuits?

It's ... per day/per person.
ler pree ei ... pahr zhoor/
pahr pehr-son

Le prix est ... par jour/par
personne.

How much is it per night/per
person?
kehl ei ler pree pahr
nwee/pahr pehr-son?

Quel est le prix par nuit/par
personne?

Can I see it?
zher per lah vwahr?

Je peux la voir?

Are there any others?
eel yā-nah dohtr?

Il y en a d'autres?

Are there any cheaper rooms?
voo nah-vei ryē der
shābr mei-yerr mahr-shei?

Vous n'avez rien de
chambres meilleur marché?

Can I see the bathroom?
zher per vwahr lah sahl der
bē?

Je peux voir la salle de bain?

Is there a reduction for
students/children?
ehs-ker voo zah-vei ē
tah-reef rei-dwee poor lei
zei-tü-dyā/le zā-fā?

Est-ce que vous avez un
tarif réduit pour les
étudiants/les enfants?

Does it include breakfast?
ehs-ker ler per-tee
dei-zher-nei ei kō-pree?

Est-ce que le petit déjeuner
est compris?

It's fine, I'll take it.
sei byē zher lah prā

C'est bien, je la prends.

I'm not sure how long I'm staying.
zher ner sei pah ehg-zahk-ter-mã kõ-byẽ der tã zher rehs-ter-rei

Je ne sais pas exactement combien de temps je resterai.

Is there a lift (elevator)?
ehs-keel-yah ẽ nah-sã-serr?

Est-ce qu'il y a un ascenseur?

Where is the bathroom?
oo ei lah sahl der bẽ?

Où est la salle de bain?

Is there hot water all day?
ehs-keel-yah der loh shohd pã-dã toot lah zhoor-nei?

Est-ce qu'il y a de l'eau chaude pendant toute la journée?

Do you have a safe where I can leave my valuables?
ehs-ker voo zah-vei ẽ kofr for poor dei-poh-zei mei zob-zhei der vah-lerr?

Est-ce que vous avez un coffre-fort pour déposer mes objets de valeur?

Is there somewhere to wash clothes?
ehs-keel-yah ẽ ã-drwah oo õ per fehr lah lehs-eev?

Est-ce qu'il y a un endroit où on peut faire la lessive?

Can I use the kitchen?
ehs-ker zher per mer sehr-veer der lah kwee-zeen?

Est-ce que je peux me servir de la cuisine?

Can I use the telephone?
ehs-ker zher per ü-tee-lee-zei ler tei-lei-fon?

Est-ce que je peux utiliser le téléphone?

Requests & Complaints

Please wake me up at ...
  rei-vei-yei mwah ah ..., seel voo plei
Réveillez-moi à ..., s'il vous plaît.

The room needs to be cleaned.
  eel foh neh-twah-yei lah shãbr
Il faut nettoyer la chambre.

Please change the sheets.
  shã-zhei lei drah, seel voo plei
Changez les draps, s'il vous plaît.

I can't open/close the window.
  lah fer-nehtr ei blo-kei
La fenêtre est bloquée.

I've locked myself out of my room.
  zher mer swee ã-fehr-mei der-or
Je me suis enfermé/-ée dehors.

The toilet won't flush.
  lah shahs doh ner mahrsh pah
La chasse d'eau ne marche pas.

I don't like this room.
  seht shãbr ner mer plei pah
Cette chambre ne me plaît pas.

It's too small.
  ehl ei troh per-teet
Elle est trop petite.

It's noisy.
  ehl ei brü-yãt
Elle est bruyante.

It's too dark.
  ehl ei troh sõbr
Elle est trop sombre.

It's expensive.
  sei shehr
C'est cher.

Some Useful Phrases

I am/We are leaving now.
zher pahr/noo pahr-tō mē-tnã — Je pars/Nous partons maintenant.

I would like to pay the bill.
zher voo-dre rei-glei (lah not) — Je voudrais régler (la note).

name	*prei-nō*	prénom
surname	*nō*	nom
room number	*nü-mei-roh der shãbr*	numéro de chambre

Some Useful Words

address	*lah-drehs*	l'adresse
air-conditioned	*klee-mah-tee-zei*	climatisé
balcony	*ler bahl-kō*	le balcon
bathroom	*lah sahl der bẽ*	la salle de bain
bed	*ler lee*	le lit
bill	*lah not*	la note
blanket	*lah koo-vehr-tür*	la couverture
candle	*lah boo-zhee*	la bougie
chair	*lah shehz*	la chaise
clean	*propr*	propre
cupboard	*ler plah-kahr*	le placard
dark	*sōbr*	sombre
dirty	*sahl*	sale
double bed	*ler lee doobl*	le lit double
electricity	*lei-lehk-tree-see-tei*	l'électricité
excluded	*pah kō-pree*	pas compris

FRENCH

fan	*ler vã-tee-lah-terr*	le ventilateur
included	*kõ-pree*	compris
key	*lah klei*	la clé
lift (elevator)	*lah-sã-serr*	l'ascenseur
light bulb	*lã-pool*	l'ampoule
lock (n)	*lah seh-rür*	la serrure
mattress	*ler maht-lah*	le matelas
mirror	*ler meer-wahr*	le miroir
padlock	*ler kahd-nah*	le cadenas
pillow	*lo-rei-yei*	l'oreiller
quiet	*ler kahlm*	le calme
room (in hotel)	*lah shãbr*	la chambre
sheet	*ler drah*	le drap
shower	*lah doosh*	la douche
soap	*ler sah-võ*	le savon
suitcase	*lah vah-leez*	la valise
swimming pool	*lah pee-seen*	la piscine
table	*lah tahbl*	la table
toilet	*lah kü-veht*	la cuvette
toilet paper	*ler pah-pyei*	le papier
	ee-zhyei-neek	hygiénique
towel	*ün sehr-vyeht der bẽ*	une serviette de bain
water	*loh*	l'eau
cold water	*loh frwahd*	l'eau froide
hot water	*loh shohd*	l'eau chaude
window	*lah fer-nehtr*	la fenêtre

Around Town

I'm looking for …
zher shehrsh …   Je cherche …

the art gallery	*ler mü-zei dahr*	le musée d'art
a bank	*ün bāk*	une banque
the church	*lei-gleez*	l'église
the city centre	*ler sātr veel*	le centre-ville
the … embassy	*lā-bah-sahd der …*	l'ambassade de …
my hotel	*mõ noh-tehl*	mon hôtel
the market	*ler mahr-shei*	le marché
the museum	*ler mü-zei*	le musée
the police	*lah po-lees*	la police
the post office	*ler bü-roh der post*	le bureau de poste
a public toilet	*dei twah-leht*	des toilettes
the telephone centre	*lei kah-been tei-lei-fo-neek*	les cabines téléphoniques
the tourist information office	*lo-fees der too-reesm/ ler sē-dee-kah dee-nee-syah-teev*	l'office de tourisme/le syndicat d'initiative

FRENCH

What time does it open?
*kehl ei lerr der
loo-vehr-tür?*   Quelle est l'heure de
                                    l'ouverture?

What time does it close?
*kehl ei lerr der
fehr-mer-tür?*   Quelle est l'heure de
                                    fermeture?

What street/suburb is this?
sei kehl rü/kehl kahr-tye?   C'est quelle rue/quel quartier?

For directions, see the Getting Around section, pages 114-115.

FRENCH

At the Bank

I want to exchange some
money/traveller's cheques.
> *zher ver shã-zhei der*
> *lahr-zhã/dei shehk der*
> *vwah-yahzh*

Je veux changer de l'argent/
des chèques de voyage.

What is the exchange rate?
> *kehl ei ler koor dü shãzh?*

Quel est le cours du change?

How many francs per dollar?
> *kõ-byẽ der frã ler dolahr?*

Combien de francs le dollar?

Can I have money transferred
here from my bank?
> *ehs-ker zher per fehr ee-see*
> *ẽ veer-mã der mõ kõt ã bãk?*

Est-ce que je peux faire ici
un virement de mon compte
en banque?

How long will it take to
arrive?
> *kõ-byẽ der tã ehs-keel*
> *foh-drah ah-tãdr?*

Combien de temps est-ce
qu'il faudra attendre?

Has my money arrived yet?
> *ehs-ker mõ nahr-zhã ei*
> *tah-ree-vei?*

Est-ce que mon argent est
arrivé?

bank draft	*ün treht bã-kehr*	une traite bancaire
bank notes	*dei bee-yei der bãk*	des billets de banque
cashier	*ler kehs-yei*	le caissier (m)
	lah kehs-yehr	la caissière (f)
coins	*der lah mone/dei pyehs*	de la monnaie/des pièces
credit card	*ün kahrt der krei-dee*	une carte de crédit

exchange	*ler shāzh*	le change
loose change	*der lah per-teet mone*	de la petite monnaie
signature	*lah seen-yah-tür*	la signature

At the Post Office

I would like to send ...
zher voo-drei ā-vwah-yei ... Je voudrais envoyer ...

a letter	*ün lehtr*	une lettre
a postcard	*ün kahrt pos-tahl*	une carte postale
a parcel	*ē ko-lee*	un colis
a telegram	*ē tei-lei-grahm*	un télégramme

I would like some stamps.
zher voo-drei dei tēbr Je voudrais des timbres.

How much does it cost to send this to ...?
ah kō-byē ehs-keel foh ah-frā-sheer sei-see poor ...? À combien est-ce qu'il faut affranchir ceci pour ...?

an aerogram	*ē-nah-ei-ro-grahm*	un aérogramme
air mail	*pahr ah-vyō*	par avion
envelope	*ün āv-lop*	une enveloppe
mail box	*ün bwaht oh lehtr*	une boîte aux lettres
parcel	*ē ko-lee*	un colis
registered mail	*ā rer-ko-mā-dei*	en recommandé
surface mail	*pahr vwah der tehr/ pahr vwah mah-ree-teem*	par voie de terre/ par voie maritime

FRENCH

FRENCH

Telephone

I want to ring ...
zher voo-drei ah-plei ...
Je voudrais appeler ...

The number is ...
ler nü-mei-roh ei ...
Le numéro est ...

I want to speak for three
minutes.
zher ver pahr-lei poor
trwah mee-nüt
Je veux parler pour trois
minutes.

How much does a three-
minute call cost?
kehl ei ler pree dün
ko-mü-nee-kah-syö der
trwah mee-nüt?
Quel est le prix d'une
communication de trois
minutes?

How much does each extra
minute cost?
kehl ei ler pree der shahk
mee-nüt sü-plei-mã-tehr?
Quel est le prix de chaque
minute supplémentaire?

I would like to speak to Mr
Perez.
zher voo-drei pahr-lei
ah-vehk mer-syer peh-rehs
Je voudrais parler avec
Monsieur Perez.

I want to make a reverse-
charges phone call.
zher ver tei-lei-fo-nei ã
pei-sei-vei
Je veux téléphoner en PCV.

It's engaged.
la leeny ei to-kü-pei
La ligne est occupée.

I've been cut off.
noo zah-võ ei-tei koo-pei
Nous avons été coupés.

Sightseeing

Do you have a guidebook/
local map?
*ehs-ker voo zah-ve ē geed
too-ree-steek/ün kahrt der
lah rei-zhyō?*

Est-ce que vous avez un
guide touristique/une carte
de la région?

What are the main attractions?
*kehl sō le zā-drwah le plü
zē-tei-rehs-ā?*

Quels sont les endroits les
plus intéressants?

What is that?
kehs-ker sei (ker sah)?

Qu'est-ce que c'est (que ça)?

How old is it?
eel/ehl ah kehl ahzh?

Il (m)/Elle (f) a quel âge?

Can I take photographs?
*ehs-ker zher per prādr
dei fo-toh?*

Est-ce que je peux prendre
des photos?

What time does it open/close?
*kehl ei lerr doo-vehr-tür/
der fehr-mer-tür?*

Quelle est l'heure
d'ouverture/de fermeture?

ancient	*ā-teek*	antique
archaeological	*ahr-kei-o-lo-zheek*	archéologique
beach	*lah plahzh*	la plage
building	*ler bah-tee-mā*	le batiment
castle	*ler shah-toh*	le château
cathedral	*lah kah-tei-drahl*	la cathédrale
church	*lei-gleez*	l'église
concert hall	*lah sahl der kō-sehr*	la salle de concert
library	*lah bee-blyo-tehk*	la bibliothèque
main square	*lah plahs sā-trahl*	la place centrale
market	*ler mahr-shei*	le marché

FRENCH

monastery	*ler mo-nah-stehr*	le monastère
monument	*ler mo-nü-mā*	le monument
mosque	*lah mos-kei*	la mosquée
old city	*lah vyehy veel*	la vieille ville
palace	*lei pah-lei*	le palais
opera house	*(ler tei-ahtr der)*	(le théâtre de)
	lo-pei-rah	l'opéra
ruins	*lei rü-ween*	les ruines
stadium	*ler stahd*	le stade
statues	*lei stah-tü*	les statues
synagogue	*lah see-nah-gog*	la synagogue
temple	*ler tāpl*	le temple
university	*lü-nee-vehr-see-tei*	l'université

Entertainment

What's there to do in the evenings?
> *kehs-kō per fehr ler swahr?* Qu'est-ce qu'on peut faire le soir?

Are there any discos?
> *ehs-keel-yah dei dees-ko-tehk?* Est-ce qu'il y a des discothèques?

Are there places where you can hear local folk music?
> *ehs-keel-yah dei zē-drwah oo ō per ei-koo-tei der lah mü-seek folk-lo-reek lo-kahl?* Est-ce qu'il y a des endroits où on peut écouter de la musique folklorique locale?

How much does it cost to get in?
> *kehl ei ler pree der lā-trei?* Quel est le prix de l'entrée?

cinema	*ler see-nei-mah*	le cinéma
concert	*ler kŏ-sehr*	le concert
discotheque	*lah dees-ko-tehk*	la discothèque
theatre	*ler tei-ahtr*	le théâtre

In the Country
Weather

What's the weather like?
kehl tā feh-teel?   Quel temps fait-il?

The weather is ... today.
eel fei ... oh-zhoor-dwee   Il fait ... aujourd'hui.

Will it be ... tomorrow?
ehs-keel fer-ra ... der-mē?   Est-ce qu'il fera ... demain?

It is ...
eel fei ...   Il fait ...

cold	*frwah*	froid
foggy	*dü broo-yahr*	du brouillard
hot	*shoh*	chaud
sunny	*boh*	beau
windy	*dü vā*	du vent

It's cloudy.	*ler tā ei koo-vehr*	Le temps est couvert.
It's frosty.	*eel zhehl*	Il gèle.
It's raining.	*eel pler*	Il pleut.
It's snowing.	*eel nehzh*	Il neige.

FRENCH

Camping

Am I allowed to camp here?
   ehs-ker zher per kã-pei
   ee-see?
                       Est-ce que je peux camper
                       ici?

Is there a campsite nearby?
   ehs-keel-yah ē kã-peeng
   preh dee-see
                       Est-ce qu'il y a un camping
                       près d'ici?

backpack	*ler sah-kah-doh*	le sac-à-dos
can opener	*loovr bwaht*	l'ouvre-boîtes
compass	*lah boo-sol*	la boussole
crampons	*lei krã-põ*	les crampons
firewood	*ler bwah ah brü-lei*	le bois à brûler
gas cartridge	*lah kahr-toosh ah gahz*	la cartouche à gaz
hammock	*ler ah-mahk*	le hamac
ice axe	*ler pyo-lei*	le piolet
mattress	*ler maht-lah*	le matelas
penknife	*ler kah-neef*	le canif
rope	*lah kord*	la corde
tent	*lah tãt*	la tente
tent pegs	*lei pee-kei der tãt*	les piquets de tente
torch (flashlight)	*lah lãp der posh*	la lampe de poche
sleeping bag	*ler sahk der koo-shahzh*	le sac de couchage
stove	*ler rei-shoh*	le réchaud
water bottle	*lah goord*	la gourde

Food

breakfast	*ler per-tee dei-zher-nei*	le petit déjeuner
lunch	*ler dei-zher-nei*	le déjeuner
dinner	*ler dee-nei*	le dîner

Table for ..., please.
ün tahbl poor ... pehr-son, seel voo plei

Une table pour ... personnes, s'il vous plaît.

Can I see the menu please?
ehs-ker zher per vwahr lah kahrt?

Est-ce que je peux voir la carte?

I would like the set lunch, please.
zher prä ler mer-nü

Je prends le menu.

What does it include?
kehs-ker sah kõ-prä?

Qu'est-ce que ça comprend?

Is service included in the bill?
ehs-ker ler sehr-vees ei kõ-pree?

Est-ce que le service est compris?

Not too spicy please.
pah troh ei-pee-sei seel-voo plei

Pas trop épicé s'il vous plaît.

an ashtray	*ē sä-drye*	un cendrier
the bill	*lah-dee-syõ*	l'addition
a cup	*ün tahs*	une tasse
dessert	*ler de-sehr*	le dessert
a drink	*ün bwah-sõ*	une boisson
a fork	*ün foor-sheht*	une fourchette
fresh	*freh/frehsh*	frais (m)/fraîche (f)

a glass	ē vehr	un verre
a knife	ē koo-toh	un couteau
a plate	ē plah	un plat
spicy	ei-pee-sei	épicé
a spoon	ün kwee-yehr	une cuillère
stale	pah freh/frehsh	pas frais (m)/ fraîche (f)
sweet	sü-krei	sucré/-ée
teaspoon	ün per-teet kwee-yehr	une petite cuillère
toothpick	ē kür dā	un cure-dent

Vegetarian Meals

I am a vegetarian.

zher swee vei-zhei-tahr-yē/ vei-zhei-tahr-yehn

Je suis végétarien (m)/ végétarienne (f).

I don't eat meat.

zher ner māzh pah der vyād

Je ne mange pas de viande.

I don't eat chicken, or fish, or ham.

zher ner māzh pah der poo-lei, der pwah-sō, oo der zhā-bō

Je ne mange pas de poulet, de poisson, ou de jambon.

Breakfast

breakfast cereal	*de la céréale*
a croissant	*un croissant*
a hard-boiled egg	*un oeuf dur*
bread, butter, jam	*du pain, du beurre, de la confiture*

Petit Dejeuner

Snacks   Casse-croûtes

un cornet de frites
A paper cone of chips.
une crêpe au sucre/au citron/au miel/à la confiture
Thin pancake with sugar/with lemon/with honey/with jam.
un croque-madame
Grilled cheese-and-ham sandwich with a fried egg.
un croque-monsieur
Grilled cheese-and-ham sandwich.
marrons chauds
Roast chestnuts.
un sandwich fromage/jambon
A cheese/ham sandwich.

In the Delicatessen	Á la Charcuterie
bean salad	*des haricots en salade*
a carton of …	*une barquette …*
cheese	*du fromage*
gherkins	*des cornichons*
ham	*du jambon*
mayonnaise	*de la mayonnaise*
a portion of …	*une part de …*
liver/rabbit/farmhouse pâté	*du pâté de foie/de lapin/de campagne*
potted meat (pork or goose)	*des rillettes*
Russian salad	*de la salade russe*
a slice	*une tranche*

FRENCH

Starters	**Hors d'Œuvres/ Entrées**
anchovies	*anchois*
artichoke hearts	*coeurs d'artichaut*
clear soup	*consommé*
hard-boiled egg with mayonnaise	*oeuf mayonnaise*
hearts of palm	*coeurs de palmier*
Marseillais fish soup	*bouillabaisse*
mussels with shallots in white-wine sauce	*moules marinières*
oysters	*huîtres*
raw vegetables with dressings	*crudités*
scallops	*coquilles Saint-Jacques*
shellfish soup	*bisque*
snails	*escargots*
thick soup, usually vegetable	*potage*

Meat & Poultry	**Viandes et Volailles**
chicken	*poulet*
duck	*canard*
mutton	*mouton*
rabbit	*lapin*
ribsteak	*entrecôte*
sausage made of intestines	*andouille*
sirloin roast	*contrefilet*
sirloin steak	*faux filet*
spicy red sausage	*merguez*
thick slices of fillet	*tournedos*
tripe	*tripes*
turkey	*dinde, dindon, dindonneau*
veal	*veau*

FRENCH

Seafood — Fruits de Mer

Seafood	Fruits de Mer
bream	*brème*
clams	*palourdes*
eels	*anguilles*
fresh cod	*cabillaud*
herring	*hareng*
John Dory	*Saint-Pierre*
king prawns	*gambas*
lobster	*homard*
mackerel	*maquereau*
octopus	*poulpe*
prawns	*crevettes roses*
salmon	*saumon*
salt cod	*morue*
sea bream	*daurade*
shrimps	*crevettes grises*
squid	*calmar*
spiny lobster	*langouste*
trout	*truite*
tuna	*thon*

Vegetables — Légumes

Vegetables	Légumes
asparagus	*asperges*
avocado	*avocat*
broad beans	*fèves*
cabbage	*chou*
cauliflower	*choufleur*
chickpeas	*pois chiches*
corn	*maïs*
cucumber	*concombre*
dwarf kidney beans	*flageolets*
french or string beans	*haricots verts*

FRENCH

FRENCH

garlic	*ail*
gherkin	*cornichon*
leek	*poireau*
lettuce	*laitue*
mushrooms	*champignons*
onion	*oignon*
peas	*petits pois*
potato	*pomme de terre*
pumpkin	*citrouille*
radish	*radis*
rice	*riz*
spinach	*épinards*
sweet pepper or capsicum	*poivron*
truffles	*truffes*

Typical Dishes   Plat Typiques

boeuf bourgignon
    Beef stew with burgundy, onions and mushrooms.

cassoulet
    Casserole of beans and meat (often goose).

choucroute
    Pickled cabbage with sausages, bacon and salami.

coq au vin
    Chicken cooked with wine, onions and mushrooms.

poulet roti
    Roast chicken.

ratatouille
    Eggplant, zucchini, tomato and garlic dish.

steak au poivre
    Steak with pepper sauce.

steak frites
　　Steak with chips.
steak tartare
　　Raw chopped beef, raw onion and egg yolk.

Sample Menu: One

An average menu from Toulouse: *Une entrée, une viande, une boisson* – an entrée, a meat dish, and a drink.

Entrées

confit de canard
　　Conserve of duck.
terrine de poisson
　　Fish pâté.
salade multicolore au basilic
　　Salad with peppers, tomatoes, radishes, cucumber, egg, corn and basil.
salade au bleu
　　Salad with blue cheese and walnuts.
salade crudité
　　Raw vegetable salad.

Meat Dishes

andouillette sauce au poivre
　　Tripe sausage with pepper sauce.
brochette de coeurs
　　Heart kebab.
entrecôte grillée, sauce au bleu ou au poivre
　　Grilled rib steak with blue cheese or pepper sauce.
cotriade
　　Fillet of fish with seafood and a saffron sauce.

brochette de volailles au citron
Poultry kebab with lemon.
tagliatelles Bolognaise ou au bleu
Tagliatelli with bolognese or blue cheese sauce.
¼ *de vin compris*
A quarter of a litre of wine included.

Sample Menu: Two
A typical budget Parisian menu:

un kir
Blackcurrant juice and white wine.
hors d'oeuvres à volonté
A choice of entrées.

plat au choix
A choice of the following main courses:
   pavé grillé
   A thick steak, grilled.
      côte d'agneau
      Lamb cutlet.
   truite aux amandes
   Trout with almonds.
   brochettes mixtes
   Kebabs.

fromage ou dessert
Cheese or dessert.
vin compris
(Table) wine included.

Sample Menu: Three
A more expensive Parisian menu:

Entrées

concombre à la crème – ciboulette
  Cucumber with cream and chives.
salade de tomates – basilic, huile vierge
  Tomato salad with basil and virgin olive oil.
suchi de poisson cru – sur lit de soja croquant
  Raw fish sushi on a bed of crunchy soya bean sprouts.
fromage blanc battu aux fines herbes
  Cream cheese blended with sweet herbs.
méli-mélo de légumes vapeur
  Mixed steamed vegetables.
boudin antillais – feuille de chêne, pommes tièdes en robe
  West-Indian sausage with lettuce and hot potatoes in their
  jackets.

Main Courses

filets de rascasse grillés aux tagliatelles safranées
  Grilled fillets of scorpion fish with tagliatelli seasoned with
  saffron.
emincé de haddock fumé, pommes mousselines
  Slivers of smoked haddock with mashed potatoes.
moelleux de porc au curry, riz sauvage
  Tender pork curry with wild rice.
demi cannette rotie, pommes château
  Half a roast duckling with quartered potatoes sautéed in
  butter.
emincé de poulet mariné, aux grains de coriandre en salade
  Slivers of marinated chicken with coriander seeds and salad.

Fruit & Nuts

almonds	*amandes*
apple	*pomme*
cherries	*cerises*
chestnuts	*marrons*
grapefruit	*pamplemousse*
grapes	*raisins*
greegages (kind of plum)	*mirabelles*
hazlenuts	*noisettes*
peach	*pêche*
peanuts	*cacahouètes*
pear	*poire*
plum	*prune*
raspberries	*framboises*
strawberries	*fraises*
walnuts	*noix*
watermelon	*pastèque*

Desserts

charlotte
   Custard and fruit in lining of almond fingers.
clafoutis
   Fruit tart, usually with berries.
fromage blanc
   Cream cheese.
glace
   Ice cream.
île flottante, crème vanille
   Soft meringues floating on custard with vanilla cream.
mousse au chocolat, crème anglaise
   Chocolate mousse with custard.

parfait
  Frozen mousse.
poires Belle Hélène
  Pears and ice-cream in a chocolate sauce.
sorbet aux choix
  A choice of sorbets.
tarte aux pommes fines
  Apple tart.

Drinks – Nonalcoholic

a short black coffee	*un café*
a large/small milk coffee	*un grand/petit crème*
a grapefruit juice	*un jus de pamplemousee*
an orange juice	*un jus d'orange*
a cup of tea	*un thé*
lemon/white tea	*thé au citron/au lait*

Drinks – Alcoholic

Pre-dinner Drinks	**Apéritifs**
blackcurrant juice and white wine	*kir*
blackcurrant juice and champagne	*kir royale*
aniseed liqueur, served with water	*pastis*
beer mixed with a sweet liqueur	*picon bière*
cognac and grape juice	*pineau*
fermented gentian	*suze*

FRENCH

Wines	**Vins**
dry	*sec*
mature and sparkling	*méthode champenoise*
red	*rouge*
sparkling	*mousseux*
sweet	*demi-sec*
table wine	*vin de table/vin ordinaire*
very dry	*brut*
very sweet	*doux*
white	*blanc*

Shopping

How much is it?
sei kō-byē?   C'est combien ?

bookshop	*ün lee-breh-ree*	une librairie
camera shop	*ün boo-teek der fo-to-grahf*	une boutique de photographe
clothing store	*ē mah-gah-zē der kō-fehk-syō*	un magasin de confection
delicatessen	*ün shahr-kü-tree*	une charcuterie
general store, shop	*ē mah-gah-zē dah-lee-mā-tah-syō zhei-nei-rahl*	un magasin d'alimentation générale
laundry	*ün blā-shees-ree*	une blanchisserie
market	*ē mahr-shei*	un marché
newsagency/ stationers	*ün pah-pei-tree*	une papeterie
pharmacy	*ün fahr-mah-see*	une pharmacie
shoeshop	*ē mah-gah-zē der shoh-sür*	un magasin de chaussures

souvenir shop	ē mah-gah-zē der soov-neer	un magasin de souvenirs
supermarket	ē sü-pehr-mahr-shei	un supermarché
vegetable shop	ē mahr-shã der lei-güm	un marchand de légumes

I would like to buy …
  zher voo-drei …
Je voudrais …

Do you have others?
  ehs-ker voo zã nah-vei dohtr?
Est-ce que vous en avez d'autres?

I don't like it.
  ser-lah ner mer plei pah
Cela ne ma plaît pas.

Can I look at it?
  ehs-ker zher per ler/lah vwahr?
Est-ce que je peux le/la voir?

I'm just looking.
  zher ner fei ker rer-gahr-dei
Je ne fais que regarder.

Can you write down the price?
  ehs-ker voo poo-vei ei-kreer ler pree?
Est-ce que vous pouvez écrire le prix?

Do you accept credit cards?
  ehs-ker zher per peh-yei ah-vehk mah kahrt der krei-dee?
Est-ce je peux payer avec ma carte de crédit?

Could you lower the price?
  voo ner poo-vei pah bei-sei ler pree?
Vous ne pouvez pas baisser le prix?

I don't have much money.
  zher nei pah boh-koo dahr-zhã
Je n'ai pas beaucoup d'argent.

Can I help you?	
zher per voo zei-dei?	Je peux vous aider?
Will that be all?	
ohtr shohz?	Autre chose?
Would you like it wrapped?	
zher voo lãv-lop?	Je vous l'enveloppe?
Sorry, this is the only one.	
dei-zo-lei eel-nyah ker	Désolé/-ée, il n'y a que
ser-lwee see/sehl see	celui-ci (m)/celle-ci (f).
How much/many do you want?	
voo dei-zee-rei kō-byē?	Vous désirez combien?

Souvenirs

earrings	*dei bookl do-rehy*	des boucles d'oreilles
handicraft	*dei zob-zhei ahr-teez-ah-noh*	des objets artisanaux
jewellery	*der lah bee-zhoo-tree*	de la bijouterie
lace	*der lah dã-tehl*	de la dentelle
miniature statue	*ün stah-tweht*	une statuette
necklace	*ē ko-lyei*	un collier
poster	*ē pos-tehr*	un poster
pottery	*dei po-tree*	des poteries
ring	*ün bahg*	une bague
rug	*ē per-tee tah-pee/ün kahr-peht*	un petit tapis/une carpette

Clothing / Vêtements

coat	*ē mã-toh*	un manteau
dress	*ün rob*	une robe
jacket	*ün vehst*	une veste
jumper (sweater)	*ē pü-lo-verr*	un pullover
shirt	*ün sher-meez*	une chemise
shoes	*de shoh-sür*	des chaussures
skirt	*ün zhüp*	une jupe
trousers	*ē pā-tah-lō*	un pantalon

It doesn't fit.
ser nei pah lah bon tahy   Ce n'est pas la bonne taille.

It is too …
sei troh …   C'est trop …

big	*grã*	grand
small	*per-tee*	petit
long	*lō*	long
short	*koor*	court
tight	*ei-trwah*	étroit
loose	*lahrzh*	large

Materials

cotton	*ã ko-tõ*	en coton
handmade	*fei ah lah mē*	fait à la main
leather	*ã kweer*	en cuir
of brass	*ã kweevr*	en cuivre
of gold	*ã nor*	en or
of silver	*ã nahr-zhã*	en argent
silk	*ã swah*	en soie
wool	*ã lehn*	en laine

Toiletries

comb	*ē pehny*	un peigne
condoms	*dei prei-zehr-vah-teef*	des préservatifs
deodorant	*ē dei-o-do-rā*	un déodorant
hairbrush	*ün bros ah sher-ver*	une brosse à cheveux
moisturising cream	*der lah krehm ee-drah-tāt*	de la crème hydratante
razor	*ē rahz-wahr*	un rasoir
sanitary napkins	*dei sehr-vyeht ee-zhyei-neek*	des serviettes hygiéniques
shampoo	*dü shāp-wē*	du shampooing
shaving cream	*der lah moos ah rah-zei*	de la mousse à raser
soap	*dü sah-vō*	du savon
sunblock cream	*der la krehm oht pro-tehk-syō*	de la crème haute protection
tampons	*dei tāpō ee-zhyei-neek*	des tampons hygiéniques
tissues	*dei moo-shwahr ā pah-pyei*	des mouchoirs en papier
toilet paper	*dü pah-pyei ee-zhyei-neek*	du papier hygiénique
toothbrush	*ün bros ah dā*	une brosse à dents
toothpaste	*dü dā-tee-frees*	du dentifrice

Stationery & Publications

map	*ün kahrt*	une carte
newspaper	*ē zhoor-nahl*	un journal
newspaper in English	*ē zhoor-nahl ā nā-glei*	un journal en anglais

novels in English	*dei ro-mã ã nã-glei*	des romans en anglais
paper	*dü pah-pyei*	du papier
pen (ballpoint)	*ē stee-loh (beey)*	un stylo (bille)
scissors	*dei see-zoh*	des ciseaux

Photography

How much is it to process this film?
kõ-byē koo-trah ler deiv-lop-mã der ser feelm?
Combien coûtera le développement de ce film?

When will it be ready?
kã teh-sker ser-lah ser-rah preh?
Quand est-ce que cela sera prêt?

I'd like a film for this camera.
zher voo-drei ē feelm poor seht ah-pah-rehy der fo-toh
Je voudrais un film pour cet appareil de photo.

B&W (film)	*nwahr ei blã*	noir et blanc
camera	*ē nah-pah-rehy der fo-toh*	un appareil de photo
colour (film)	*koo-lerr*	couleurs
film	*ē feelm*	un film
flash	*ē flahsh*	un flash
lens	*ē nob-zhehk-teef*	un objectif
light meter	*ē pohz-mehtr*	un posemètre

Smoking

A packet of cigarettes, please.
ē pah-ket der see-gah-reht seel voo plei
Un paquet de cigarettes, s'il vous plaît.

Are these cigarettes
strong/mild?
   ehs-ker sei see-gah-reht   Est-ce que ces cigarettes
   sō fort/lei-zhehr?   sont fortes/légères?
Do you have a light?
   voo zah-ve dü fer?   Vous avez du feu?

cigarette papers	*dei pah-pyei ah see-gah-reht*	des papiers à cigarettes
cigarettes	*dei see-gah-reht*	des cigarettes
filtered	*a-vehk feeltr*	avec filtre
lighter	*ē bree-kei*	un briquet
matches	*dei zah-lü-meht*	des allumettes
menthol	*mā-to-lei*	mentholées
pipe	*ün peep*	une pipe
tobacco (pipe)	*dü tah-bah (poor lah peep)*	du tabac (pour la pipe)

Colours

black	*nwahr*	noir/-e
blue	*bler*	bleu/-e
brown	*brē/brün*	brun (m)/brune (f)
green	*vehr/vehrt*	vert (m)/verte (f)
pink	*rohz*	rose
red	*roozh*	rouge
white	*blā*	blanc (m)
	blāsh	blanche (f)
yellow	*zhohn*	jaune

Sizes & Comparisons

small	*per-tee/per-teet*	petit/-e
big	*grā/grād*	grand/-e

heavy	*loor/loord*	lourd/-e
light	*lei-zhei/lei-zhehr*	léger (m)/légère (f)
more	*plü*	plus
less	*mwē*	moins
too much/many	*troh*	trop
many	*boh-koo*	beaucoup
enough	*ah-se*	assez
also	*oh-see*	aussi
a little bit	*ē per*	un peu

FRENCH

Health

Where is …?
  oo ei …?   Où est …?

the doctor	*ler meid-sē*	le médecin
the hospital	*lo-pee-tahl*	l'hôpital
the chemist	*ler fahr-mah-syē*	le pharmacien
the dentist	*ler dā-teest*	le dentiste

I am sick
  zher swee mah-lahd   Je suis malade.
My friend is sick.
  mõ nah-mee ei mah-lahd   Mon ami/-e est malade.
Could I see a female doctor?
  ehs-ker zher per vwahr ün   Est-ce que je peux voir une
  meid-sē fahm?   médecin femme?
What's the matter?
  kehs-kee ner vah pah?   Qu'est-ce qui ne va pas?
Where does it hurt?
  oo ehs-ker voo zah-vei   Où est-ce que vous avez
  mahl?   mal?

It hurts here.
 zhei ün doo-lerr ee-see   J'ai une douleur ici.

My ... hurts.
 mõ/mah ... mer fei mahl   Mon (m)/ma (f) ... me fait
 mal.

Parts of the Body

ankle	*sher-veey*	cheville
arm	*brah*	bras
back	*doh*	dos
chest	*pwah-treen*	poitrine
ear	*o-rehy*	oreille
eye	*er-y*	oeil
finger	*dwah*	doigt
foot	*pyei*	pied
hand	*mē*	main
head	*teht*	tête
heart	*kerr*	coeur
leg	*zhãb*	jambe
mouth	*boosh*	bouche
nose	*nei*	nez
ribs	*kot*	côtes
skin	*poh*	peau
spine	*ei-sheen*	échine
stomach	*ehs-to-mah*	estomac
teeth	*dã*	dents
throat	*gorzh*	gorge

Ailments

I have ...
 zhei ...   J'ai ...
an allergy   *ün ah-lehr-zhee*   une allergie

a blister	*ün ã-pool*	une ampoule
a burn	*ün brü-lür*	une brûlure
a cough	*ün too*	une toux
diarrhoea	*lah dyah-rei*	la diarrhée
fever	*der lah fyehvr*	de la fièvre
glandular fever	*la mo-no-nü-klei-ohz ẽ-fehk-syerz*	la mononucléose infectieuse
a headache	*mahl ah lah teht*	mal à la tête
hepatitis	*lei-pah-teet*	l'hépatite
indigestion	*ün ẽ-dee-zhehs-tyõ*	une indigestion
an infection	*ün ẽ-fehk-syõ*	une infection
influenza	*lah greep*	la grippe
lice	*dei poo*	des poux
a pain	*ün doo-lerr*	une douleur
sore throat	*mahl ah lah gorzh*	mal à la gorge
a stomachache	*mahl oh vãtr*	mal au ventre
a venereal disease	*ün mah-lah-dee vei-nei-ryehn*	une maladie vénérienne
worms	*dei vehr*	des vers

FRENCH

I have a cold.
zher swee ã-rü-mei
Je suis enrhumé/-ée.

I have constipation.
zher swee kõ-stee-pei
Je suis constipé/-ée.

I have low/high blood pressure.
zher fei der lee-pehr-tã-syõ/ lee-poh-tã-syõ
Je fais de l'hypertension/ l'hypotension.

I have a sprain.
zher mer swee do-nei ün ã-tors
Je me suis donné une entorse.

I have sunburn.
zhei pree ĕ koo der so-lehy   J'ai pris un coup de soleil.

Some Useful Words & Phrases

I'm ...
  zher swee ...   Je suis ...

diabetic	*dyah-bei-teek*	diabétique
epileptic	*ei-pee-lehp-teek*	épileptique
asthmatic	*ah-smah-teek*	ashtmatique
anaemic	*ah-nei-meek*	anémique

I'm allergic to antibiotics/
penicillin
  zher swee ah-lehr-zheek oh   Je suis allergique aux anti-
  zā-tee-byo-teek/ah lah   biotiques/à la pénicilline
  pei-nee-see-leen
I'm pregnant.
  zher swee ā-sēt   Je suis enceinte.
I'm on the pill.
  zher prā lah pee-lül   Je prends la pilule.
I haven't had my period for
... months.
  zher nei pah ü mei rehgl   Je n'ai pas eu mes règles
  der-pwee ... mwah   depuis ... mois.
I have been vaccinated.
  zher mer swee fei   Je me suis fait vacciné/-ée.
  vahk-see-nei
I have my own syringe.
  zhei mah propr serrēg   J'ai ma propre seringue.
I feel better/worse.
  zher mer sā myer/plü mahl   Je me sens mieux/plus mal.

FRENCH

accident	*ē nahk-see-dā*	un accident
addiction	*lah dei-pā-dās/lah tok-see-ko-mah-nee*	la dépendance/la toxicomanie
antibiotics	*dei zā-tee-byo-teek*	des antibiotiques
antiseptic	*der lā-tee-sehp-teek*	de l'antiseptique
aspirin	*der lah-spee-reen*	de l'aspirine
bandage	*ē pās-mā*	un pansement
bite	*ün mor-sür*	une morsure
blood pressure	*lah tā-syō (ahr-te-ryehl)*	la tension (artérielle)
blood test	*ü-nah-nah-leez der sā*	une analyse de sang
contraceptive	*ē kō-trah-sehp-teef*	un contraceptif
injection	*ün nē-zhehk-syō/ün pee-kür*	une injection/une piqûre
injury	*ün blehs-ür*	une blessure
menstruation	*lei rehgl*	les règles
nausea	*lah noh-zei*	la nausée
oxygen	*lok-see-zhehn*	l'oxygène
vitamins	*dei vee-tah-meen*	des vitamines

FRENCH

At the Chemist

I need medication for ...
  zhei ber-zwē dē mei-dee-kah-mā poor ... J'ai besoin d'un médicament pour ...
I have a prescription.
  zhei ün or-do-nās J'ai une ordonnance.

At the Dentist

I have a toothache.
  zhei mahl oh dā J'ai mal aux dents.

I've lost a filling.
zhei pehr-dü ẽ plō-bahzh J'ai perdu un plombage.
I've broken a tooth.
zher mer swee kah-sei ün dã Je me suis cassé une dent.
My gums hurt.
me zhã-seev mer fõ mahl Mes gencives me font mal.
I don't want it extracted.
zher ner ver pah ker voo Je ne veux pas que vous
lah-rah-shye l'arrachiez.
Please give me an anaesthetic.
ah-vehk ah-nehs-tei-zee seel Avec anesthésie, s'il vous
voo plei plaît.

Time & Dates

Note that the French normally use the 24-hour clock.

What time is it?
kehl err ei teel? Quelle heure est-il?

It is …
eel ei … err Il est … heures.
in the morning *dü mah-tẽ* du matin
in the afternoon *der lah-preh mee-dee* de l'après midi
in the evening *dü swahr* du soir

What date is it today?
noo som kehl zhoor Nous sommes quel jour
oh-zhoor-dwee? aujourd'hui?

FRENCH

Days of the Week

Monday	*lē-dee*	lundi
Tuesday	*mahr-dee*	mardi
Wednesday	*mehr-krer-dee*	mercredi
Thursday	*zher-dee*	jeudi
Friday	*vā-drer-dee*	vendredi
Saturday	*sahm-dee*	samedi
Sunday	*dee-māsh*	dimanche

Months

January	*zhā-vye*	janvier
February	*feiv-rye*	février
March	*mahrs*	mars
April	*ah-vreel*	avril
May	*meh*	mai
June	*zhwē*	juin
July	*zhwee-yeh*	juillet
August	*oo(t)*	août
September	*sehp-tābr*	septembre
October	*ok-tobr*	octobre
November	*no-vābr*	novembre
December	*dei-sābr*	décembre

Seasons

summer	*lei-tei*	l'été
autumn	*lo-ton*	l'automne
winter	*lee-vehr*	l'hiver
spring	*ler prē-tā*	le printemps

Present

today	*oh-zhoor-dwee*	aujourd'hui
this morning	*ser mah-tē*	ce matin

tonight	*ser swahr*	ce soir
this week/year	*seht ser-mehn/ah-nei*	cette semaine/année
now	*mēt-nā*	maintenant

Past

yesterday	*yehr*	hier
day before yesterday	*ah-vã tyehr*	avant-hier
yesterday morning	*yehr mah-tē*	hier matin
last night	*yehr swahr*	hier soir
last week/year	*lah-nei/lah ser-mehn dehr-nyehr*	l'année/la semaine dernière

Future

tomorrow	*der-mē*	demain
day after tomorrow	*ah-preh der-mē*	après-demain
tomorrow morning	*der-mē mah-tē*	demain matin
tomorrow afternoon/evening	*der-mē ah-preh mee-dee/swahr*	demain après midi/soir
next week	*lah ser-mehn proshehn*	la semaine prochaine
next year	*lah-nei pro-shehn*	l'année prochaine

During the Day

afternoon	*lah-preh mee-dee*	l'après-midi
dawn, very early morning	*lohb*	l'aube
day	*ler zhoor*	le jour
early	*toh*	tôt
midnight	*meen-wee*	minuit
morning	*ler mah-tē*	le matin

night	*lah nwee*	la nuit
noon	*mee-dee*	midi
sundown	*ler koo-shei dü*	le coucher du
	so-lehy	soleil
sunrise	*ler ler-vei dü so-lehy*	le lever du soleil

Numbers & Amounts

0	*zeiroh*	zéro
1	*ē*	un
2	*der*	deux
3	*trwah*	trois
4	*kahtr*	quatre
5	*sēk*	cinq
6	*sees*	six
7	*seht*	sept
8	*weet*	huit
9	*nerf*	neuf
10	*dees*	dix
11	*ōz*	onze
12	*dooz*	douze
13	*trehz*	treize
14	*kah-torz*	quatorze
15	*kēz*	quinze
16	*sehz*	seize
17	*dee-seht*	dix-sept
18	*dee-zweet*	dix-huit
19	*deez-nerf*	dix-neuf
20	*vē*	vingt
21	*vē tei ē*	vingt et un
22	*vē der*	vingt-deux
30	*trāt*	trente

FRENCH

40	*kah-rāt*	quarante
50	*sē-kāt*	cinquante
60	*swah-sāt*	soixante
70	*swah-sāt dees*	soixante-dix
80	*kahtr vē*	quatre-vingts
90	*kahtr vē dees*	quatre-vingt-dix
100	*sā*	cent
1000	*meel*	mille
one million	*ē mee-lyō*	un million

1st	*prer-myei*	premier (m) (1er)
	prer-myehr	première (f) (1ère)
2nd	*ser-gō/ser-gōd*	second/-e (2e)
	der-zyehm	deuxième
3rd	*trwah-zyehm*	troisième (3e)

¼	*ē kahr*	un quart
⅓	*ē tyehr*	un tiers
½	*ē der-mee*	un demi
¾	*trwah kahr*	trois quarts

Some Useful Words

a little (amount)	*ē per*	un peu
double	*doobl*	double
a dozen	*ün doo-zehn*	une douzaine
Enough!	*ah-se!*	Assez!
few	*per der/kehl-ker*	peu de/quelques
less	*mwē*	moins
many	*boh-koo der*	beaucoup de
more	*plü*	plus
once	*ün fwah*	une fois

a pair	*ün pehr*	une paire
percent	*poor sã*	pour cent
some	*dü/der lah/de*	du/de la/des
too much	*troh*	trop
twice	*der fwah*	deux fois

Abbreviations

ap. J.-C./av. J.-C.	AD/BC
BCBG	'Sloane Ranger', from a 'good' family
la CE	EC
la CGT	association of French trade unions
HLM	public housing flats
M/Mme/Mlle	Mr/Mrs/Ms
l'ONU	UN
le PC	the Communist Party
le PS	the Socialist Party
PTT	on post boxes and post offices
RER	system of trains serving the outer suburbs of Paris
le RPR	right-wing political party
Rte/Av	Rd/Av
le SIDA	AIDS
TTC	all inclusive
l'UDF	right-wing political party

FRENCH

German

German

Introduction

It might be a surprise to know that German is, in fact, a close relative of English. English, German and Dutch are all known as West Germanic languages. It means that you know lots of German words already – *Arm*, *Finger*, *Gold* – and you'll be able to figure out many others – *Mutter* (mother), *trinken* (drink), *gut* (good). A primary reason why English and German have grown apart is that the Normans, on invading England in 1066, brought with them a large number of non-Germanic words. It's meant that English has lots of synonyms, with the more basic word being Germanic, and the more literary or specialised one coming from French; for instance, 'start' and 'green' as opposed to 'commence' and 'verdant'.

German grammar is often described as difficult – it is often cited that there are many different ways to say 'the', and that words have 'lots of endings'. However, most of these concepts that seem so alien actually have remnants in English. German also has the advantage of being comparatively easy to pronounce. It is beyond the scope of this book to outline how to put your own sentences together from scratch, but there are many examples of model sentences where you can choose the key word you want: for instance 'It is too … (big/small/short/long)'.

German is spoken throughout Germany and Austria, and in most of Switzerland. It is also extremely useful in Eastern Europe, especially with older people. Although you may hear different dialects, there is a strong tradition of a prescribed official language, used in this book, which will always be understood. In some tourist centres English is so widely spoken that you may not have a chance to use German, even if you want to! However, as soon as you try to meet ordinary people or move out of the big cities, especially in what was East Germany, the situation is totally different. Your efforts to speak the local language will be very much appreciated and will make your trip much more enjoyable and fulfilling. *Gute Reise!*

Pronunciation

German is a relatively 'phonetic' language; that is, its spelling isn't as weird as English! You can almost always tell how a word is pronounced by the way it's spelt. Some letters can be pronounced several ways, but you can normally tell which way to use from the context.

Unlike English or French, German does not have silent letters: you pronounce the **k** at the start of the word *Knie*, 'knee', the **p** at the start of *Psychologie,* 'psychology', and the **e** at the end of *ich habe*, 'I have'.

One distinctive feature of German is that all nouns are written with a capital letter. The language has a fairly complicated grammar involving gender, whereby words are given masculine, feminine or neuter forms. In this chapter, the feminine form is given first, the masculine second.

Vowels

As in English, vowels can be pronounced long (like the 'o' in 'pope') or short (like the 'o' in 'pop'). As a rule, German vowels are long before one consonant and short before two consonants: the **o** is long in the word *Dom*, 'cathedral', but short in the word *doch*, 'after all'.

GERMAN

Letter/s	Pronunciation Guide	Sounds
a	ah	short, as the 'u' sound in 'cut'
	aa	long, as in 'father'
au	ow	as in 'vow'
ä	a	short, as in 'act'
	air	long, as in 'hair'
äu	oy	as in 'boy'
	eh	short, as the 'e' in 'bet'
e	eh	short, as in 'bet'
	ay	long, as in 'day'
ei	ai	as the 'ai' in 'aisle'
	oy	as in 'boy'
eu	oy	as in 'boy'
i	ee	long, as in 'see'
i	i	short, as in 'in'
ie	ee	as in 'see'
o	oh	long, as in 'note'
	o	short, as in 'pot'
ö	er	as the 'er' in 'fern'
u	u	as the 'u' in 'pull'
ü	ü	like the 'u' in 'pull' but with stretched lips

Consonants

Most German consonants sound similar to their English counterparts. One important difference is that **b**, **d** and **g** sound like 'p', 't' and 'k', respectively, at the end of a word.

Letter/s	Pronunciation Guide	Sounds
b	*b/p*	normally the English 'b', but 'p' at end of a word
ch	*kh*	the *ch* in Scottish *loch*
d	*d/t*	normally as the English 'd', but 't' at end of a word
g	*gh/k/ch*	normally as the hard English 'g', but 'k' at the end of a word, and *ch*, as in the Scottish *loch*, at the end of a word and after **i**
j	*y*	as the 'y' in 'yet'
qu	*kv*	'k' plus 'v'
r	*r*	as the English 'r', but rolled at the back of the mouth
s	*s/z*	normally as the 's' in 'sun'; when followed by a vowel, as the 'z' in 'zoo'
sch	*sh*	as the 'sh' in 'ship'
sp, st	*shp/sht*	at the start of a word, 's' sounds like the 'sh' in 'ship'
tion	*tsiohn*	the **t** sounds like the 'ts' in 'hits'
ß	*s*	as in 'sun' (in some books, written as **ss**)
v	*f*	as the 'f' in 'fan'
w	*v*	as the 'v' in 'van'
z	*ts*	as the 'ts' in 'hits'

GERMAN

Stress

Stressed syllables are highlighted in bold in the pronunciation guide. However, stress in German is very straightforward; the overwhelming majority of German words are stressed on the first syllable. Some prefixes are not stressed (such as *besetzt* is stressed on the **setzt**); and certain foreign words, especially from French, are stressed on the last syllable (*Organisation*, *Appetit*).

Greetings & Civilities
Top Useful Phrases

Hello. (Good day)
ghu-tehn taak — Guten Tag.

Goodbye.
owf vee-dehr-zayn — Auf Wiedersehen.

Yes./No.
yaa/nain — Ja./Nein.

Excuse me.
ehnt-shul-di-ghung — Entschuldigung.

May I? Do you mind?
dahrf ikh?/makht ehs ee-nehn eht-vahs ows? — Darf ich? Macht es Ihnen etwas aus?

Sorry. (excuse me, forgive me)
ehnt-shul-di-ghung — Entschuldigung.

Please.
bi-teh — Bitte.

Thank you.
dahng-keh — Danke.

Many thanks.
fee-lehn dahngk — Vielen Dank.

That's fine. You're welcome.
bi-teh zayr — Bitte sehr.

Greetings

Good morning.
ghu-tehn mor-ghehn — Guten Morgen.

Good afternoon.
   ghu-tehn taak

Guten Tag.

Good evening/night.
   ghu-tehn aa-behnt/
   ghu-teh nahkht

Guten Abend./Gute Nacht.

How are you?
   vee ghayt ehs ee-nehn?

Wie geht es Ihnen?

Well, thanks.
   dahng-keh, ghut

Danke, gut.

Forms of Address

Madam/Mrs	*ghnair-di-gheh*	Gnädige Frau/
	frow/frow	Frau
Sir/Mr	*main hehr/hehr*	Mein Herr/Herr
Miss	*froy-lain*	Fräulein
companion,	*froyn-din*	Freundin (f)
friend	*froynt*	Freund (m)

As yet there is no equivalent of Ms, *Frau* is regarded as a respectful address for older women whether they are married or not.

Small Talk
Meeting People

What is your name?
   *vee **hai**-sehn zee?*

Wie heißen Sie?

My name is …
   *ikh **hai**-seh …*

Ich heiße …

I'd like to introduce you to …
   kahn ikh ee-nehn …
   for-shteh-lehn?

Kann ich Ihnen …
vorstellen?

GERMAN

I'm pleased to meet you.
   ahn-gheh-naym   Angenehm.

Nationalities
Where are you from?
   *voh-**hayr** ko-mehn zee?*   Woher kommen Sie?

I am from …
   *ikh **ko-meh** ows* …   Ich komme aus …

Australia	*ow-**straa**-li-yehn*	Australien
Canada	*kah-nah-dah*	Kanada
England	*ehng-lahnt*	England
Germany	*doych-lahnt*	Deutschland
Ireland	*ir-lahnt*	Irland
New Zealand	*noy-zay-lahnt*	Neuseeland
Scotland	*shot-lahnt*	Schottland
Switzerland	*dayr shvaits*	der Schweiz
the USA	*dayn fay-**rai**-nikh-*	den Vereinigten
	*tehn **shtaa**-tehn*	Staaten
Wales	*wailz*	Wales

Age
How old are you?
   vee ahlt zint zee?   Wie alt sind Sie?
I am … years old.
   *ikh bin … **yaa**-reh ahlt*   Ich bin … Jahre alt.

Occupations
What (work) do you do?
   *ahls vahs **ahr**-bai-tehn zee?*   Als was arbeiten Sie?
I am a/an …
   ikh bin …   Ich bin …

artist	*künst*-lehr-in	Künstlerin (f)
	künst-lehr	Künstler (m)
business person	gheh-**shafts**-frow	Geschäftsfrau (f)
	gheh-**shafts**-mahn	Geschäftsmann (m)
doctor	*arts*-tin/ahrtst	Ärztin (f)/Arzt (m)
engineer	in-zheh-ni-*yer*-in	Ingenieurin (f)
	in-zhe-ni-*yer*	Ingenieur (m)
factory worker	fah-**breek**-ahr-bai-tehr-in/fah-**breek**-ahr-bai-tehr	Fabrikarbeiterin (f) Fabrikarbeiter (m)
farmer	*boy*-yehr-in	Bäuerin (f)
	bow-ehr	Bauer (m)
journalist	zhur-nah-**list**-in	Journalistin (f)
	zhur-nah-**list**	Journalist (m)
lawyer	**rehkhts**-ahn-vahlt-in	Rechtsanwältin (f)
	rekhts-ahn-vahlt	Rechtsanwalt (m)
mechanic	meh-**khah**-ni-kehr-in	Mechanikerin (f)
	meh-**khah**-ni-kehr	Mechaniker (m)
nurse	**krahng**-kehn-shveh-stehr	Kranken-schwester (f)
	krahng-kehn-pflay-ghehr	Kranken-pfleger (m)
office worker	bü-**roh**-ahn-gheh-shtehl-teh	Büroangestellte (f)
	bü-**roh**-ahn-gheh-shtehl-tehr	Büroange-stellter (m)
scientist	*vi*-sehn-shahft-lehr-in	Wissenschaft-lerin (f)
	vi-sehn-shahft-lehr	Wissenschaftler (m)
student	shtu-**dehnt**-in	Studentin (f)
	shtu-**dehnt**	Student (m)

teacher	*lay-rehr-in*	Lehrerin (f)
	lay-rehr	Lehrer (m)
waiter	*kehl-nehr-in*	Kellnerin (f)
	kehl-nehr	Kellner (m)
writer	*shrift-shtehl-ehr-in*	Schriftstellerin (f)
	shrift-shtehl-ehr	Schriftsteller (m)

Religion

What is your religion?
vahs ist i-reh reh-li-ghi-ohn? — Was ist Ihre Religion?

I am not religious.
ikh bin nikht reh-li-gi-ers — Ich bin nicht religiös.

I am …
ikh bin … — Ich bin …

Buddhist	*bu-dist-in*	Buddhistin (f)
	bu-dist	Buddhist (m)
Catholic	*kah-to-leek-in*	Katholikin (f)
	kah-to-leek	Katholik (m)
Christian	*khrist-in*	Christin (f)
	khrist	Christ (m)
Hindu	*hin-du*	Hindu
Jewish	*yü-din*	Jüdin (f)
	yü-deh	Jude (m)
Muslim	*mos-lehm*	Moslem

Family

Are you married?
zint zee fehr-hai-rah-teht? — Sind Sie verheiratet?

I am single.
ikh bin un-fehr-hai-rah-teht — Ich bin unverheiratet.

I am married.
*ikh bin fehr-**hai**-rah-teht*
Ich bin verheiratet.

How many children do you have?
*vee-**fee**-leh **kin**-dehr haa-behn zee?*
Wieviele Kinder haben Sie?

I don't have any children.
ikh haa-beh kai-neh kin-dehr
Ich habe keine Kinder.

I have a daughter/a son.
ikh haa-beh ai-neh tokh-tehr/ai-nehn zohn
Ich habe eine Tochter/einen Sohn.

Do you have any brothers or sisters?
*haa-behn zee nokh gheh-**shvi**-stehr?*
Haben Sie noch Geschwister?

Is your husband/wife here?
ist ihr mahn/ih-reh frow heer?
Ist Ihr Mann/Ihre Frau hier?

Do you have a boyfriend/girlfriend?
haa-behn zee ai-nehn froynt/ai-neh froynd-in?
Haben Sie einen Freund/eine Freundin?

brother	*bru-dehr*	Bruder
children	*kin-dehr*	Kinder
daughter	*tokh-tehr*	Tochter
family	*fah-**mi**-li-eh*	Familie
father	*faa-tehr*	Vater
grandfather	*ghrohs-vaa-tehr*	Großvater
grandmother	*ghrohs-mu-tehr*	Großmutter

husband	*mahn*	Mann
mother	*mu-tehr*	Mutter
sister	**shveh**-*stehr*	Schwester
son	*zohn*	Sohn
wife	*frow*	Frau

Feelings

I (don't) like …
 … *gheh-**falt** mir (nikht)*   … gefällt mir (nicht).

I am angry.	*ikh bin **ber**-zeh*	Ich bin böse.
I am cold.	*mir ist kahlt*	Mir ist kalt.
I am grateful.	*ikh bin **dahngk**-bahr*	Ich bin dankbar.
I am happy.	*ikh bin **ghlük**-likh*	Ich bin glücklich.
I am hot.	*mir ist hais*	Mir ist heiß.
I am hungry.	*ikh **haa**-beh **hung**-ehr*	Ich habe Hunger.
I am in a hurry.	*ikh **haa**-beh ehs ai-likh*	Ich habe es eilig.
I am right.	*ikh **haa**-beh rehkht*	Ich habe recht.
I am sad.	*ikh bin **trow**-rikh*	Ich bin traurig.
I am sleepy.	*ikh bin **mü**-deh*	Ich bin müde.
I am sorry.	*ehs tut mir lait*	Es tut mir leid.
I am thirsty.	*ikh **haa**-beh durst*	Ich habe Durst.
I am tired.	*ikh bin **mü**-deh*	Ich bin müde.
I am (un)well.	*ikh **fü**-leh mikn (nikht) vohl*	Ich fühle mich (nicht) wohl.
I am worried.	*ikh **mah**-kheh mir **zor**-ghehn*	Ich mache mir Sorgen.

Language Difficulties

Do you speak English?
*shpreh-khehn zee **ehng-lish**?*

Sprechen Sie Englisch?

Does anyone here speak English?
shprikht heer yay-mahnt ehng-lish?

Spricht hier jemand Englisch?

I speak a little …
ikh shpreh-kheh ain bis-khehn …

Ich spreche ein bißchen …

I don't speak …
ikh shpreh-kheh kain …

Ich spreche kein …

I (don't) understand.
ikh fehr-shtay-eh (nikht)

Ich verstehe (nicht).

Could you speak more slowly please?
kern-tehn zee bi-teh lahng-zahm-ehr shpreh-khehn?

Könnten Sie bitte langsamer sprechen?

Sorry? (I didn't hear.)
bi-teh?

Bitte?

Could you repeat that?
kern-tehn zee dahs vee-dehr-hoh-lehn?

Könnten Sie das wiederholen?

How do you say …?
vahs haist … owf doych?

Was heißt … auf deutsch?

What does … mean?
vahs beh-doy-teht …?

Was bedeutet …?

I speak …
ikh shpreh-kheh …

Ich spreche …

English   ***ehng-lish***

Englisch

GERMAN

French	*frahn-tser-zish*	Französisch
German	*doych*	Deutsch
Italian	*i-tah-li-ay-nish*	Italienisch
Japanese	*yah-paa-nish*	Japanisch

Some Useful Phrases

Sure.
klahr! — Klar!

Just a minute.
ain moh-mehnt! — Ein Moment!

It's (not) important.
ehs ist (nikht) vikh-tikh — Es ist (nicht) wichtig.

It's (not) possible.
*ehs ist (nikht) **mergh**-likh* — Es ist (nicht) möglich.

Wait!
vahr-tehn zee maal! — Warten Sie mal!

Good luck!
feel ghlük! — Viel Glück!

Signs

LEFT LUGGAGE	GEPÄCKAUFBE-WAHRUNG
CHECK-IN COUNTER	ABFERTIGUNG
CUSTOMS	ZOLL
EMERGENCY EXIT	NOTAUSGANG
ENTRANCE	EINGANG
EXIT	AUSGANG
FREE ADMISSION	EINTRITT FREI
HOT/COLD	HEISS/KALT
INFORMATION	AUSKUNFT

GERMAN

NO ENTRY	KEIN ZUTRITT
NO SMOKING	RAUCHEN VERBOTEN
OPEN/CLOSED	OFFEN/GESCHLOSSEN
PROHIBITED	VERBOTEN
RESERVED	RESERVIERT
TELEPHONE	TELEFON
TOILETS	TOILETTEN (WC)

Emergencies

POLICE	POLIZEI
POLICE STATION	POLIZEIWACHE

Help!
hil-feh!
Hilfe!

It's an emergency!
ehs ist ain noht-fahl!
Es ist ein Notfall!

There's been an accident!
ehs haht ai-nehn un-fahl gheh-ghay-behn!
Es hat einen Unfall gegeben!

Call a doctor!
hoh-lehn zee ai-nehn ahrtst!
Holen Sie einen Arzt!

Call an ambulance!
ru-fehn zee ai-nehn krahng-kehn-vaa-ghehn!
Rufen Sie einen Krankenwagen!

I've been raped.
ikh bin fehr-vahl-tikht vor-dehn
Ich bin verwaltigt worden.

I've been robbed!
*ikh bin beh-**shtoh**-lehn* Ich bin bestohlen worden!
***vor**-dehn!*

Call the police!
*ru-fehn zee dee po-li-**tsai**!* Rufen Sie die Polizei!

Where is the police station?
*voh ist dee poh-li-**tsai**-vah-* Wo ist die Polizeiwache?
kheh?

Go away!
***ghay**-ehn zee vehk!* Gehen Sie weg!

I'll call the police!
*ikh **ru**-feh ai-nehn* Ich rufe einen Polizisten!
*po-li-**tsist**-ehn!*

Thief!
deep! Dieb!

I am ill.
ikh bin krahngk Ich bin krank.

My friend is ill.
***mai**-neh **froynd**-in (f)/* Meine Freundin (f)/Mein
froynt (m) ist krahngk Freund (m) ist krank.

I am lost.
*ikh **haa**-beh mikh fehr-**irt*** Ich habe mich verirrt.

Where are the toilets?
*voh ist dee toh-ah-**leh**-teh?* Wo ist die Toilette?

Could you help me please?
ker-nehn zee mir bi-teh Könnten Sie mir bitte
***hehl**-fehn?* helfen?

Could I please use the
telephone?
kern-teh ikh bi-teh dahs Könnte ich bitte das Telefon
*teh-leh-**fohn** beh-**nu**-tsehn?* benutzen?

I'm sorry. I apologise.
   ehs tut mir lait
   *ehnt-**shul**-di-ghehn zee*
   bi-teh

Es tut mir leid.
Entschuldigen Sie bitte.

I didn't realise I was doing anything wrong.
   *ikh vahr mir nikht beh-**vust**,*
   *eht-vahs **un**-rehkht-ehs*
   *gheh-**tahn** tsu **haa**-behn*

Ich war mir nicht bewußt,
etwas Unrechtes getan zu
haben.

I didn't do it.
   *dahs **haa**-beh ikh nikht*
   *gheh-**tahn***

Das habe ich nicht getan.

I wish to contact my embassy/consulate.
   *ikh **merkh**-teh mikh mit*
   ***mai**-nehr boht-**shahft**/*
   ***mai**-nehm kon-zu-**laat** in*
   *fehr-**bin**-dung **zeht**-tsehn*

Ich möchte mich mit meiner
Botschaft/meinem Konsulat
in Verbindung setzen.

I speak English.
   *ikh **shpreh**-kheh*
   ***ehng**-lish*

Ich spreche Englisch.

I have medical insurance.
   *ikh bin in **ai**-nehr*
   ***krahng**-kehn-kah-seh*

Ich bin in einer
Krankenkasse.

My possessions are insured.
   ***mai**-neh **zah**-khehn zint*
   *fehr-**zi**-khehrt*

Meine Sachen sind
versichert.

GERMAN

I've lost …
*ikh **haa**-beh … vehr-**loh**-rehn* Ich habe … verloren.

my bags	*mai-neh rai-zeh-tah-shehn*	meine Reisetaschen
my handbag	*mai-neh hahnt-tah-sheh*	meine Handtasche
my money	*main ghehlt*	mein Geld
my travellers' cheques	*mai-neh rai-zeh-shehks*	meine Reiseschecks
my passport	*main(-ehn) pahs*	mein(en) Paß (Use -en in Ich habe meinen Paß verloren)

Paperwork

name	*naa-meh*	Name
address	*ah-dreh-seh*	Adresse
date of birth	*gheh-burts-daa-tum*	Geburtsdatum
place of birth	*gheh-burts-ort*	Geburtsort
age	*ahl-tehr*	Alter
sex	*gheh-shlehkht*	Geschlecht
nationality	*nah-tsi-o-nah-li-tayt*	Nationalität
religion	*reh-li-ghi-ohn*	Religion
profession	*beh-ruf*	Beruf
marital status	*fah-mi-li-ehn-shtahnt*	Familienstand
passport	*(rai-zeh-)pahs*	(Reise)paß
passport number	*pahs-nu-mehr*	Paßnummer
visa	*vi-zum*	Visum
identification	*ows-vais-pah-pee-reh*	Ausweispapiere

birth certificate	*gheh-**burts**-ur-kun-deh*	Geburtsurkunde
driver's licence	*fü-rehr-shain*	Führerschein
car owner's title/registration	*(krahft-)**faar**-tsoyk-breef*	(Kraft)fahrzeug-brief
customs	*tsol*	Zoll
immigration	*ain-vahn-dehr-ung*	Einwanderung
border	*ghrehn-tseh*	Grenze

Getting Around

ARRIVALS	ANKUNFT
BUS STOP	BUSHALTESTELLE
DEPARTURES	ABFAHRT
STATION	STATION
SUBWAY	U-BAHN (U)
TICKET OFFICE	FAHRKARTENSCHALTER
TIMETABLE	FAHRPLAN
TRAIN STATION	BAHNHOF (Bhf/Bf)

What time does ... leave?		
vahn fairt ... ahp?	Wann fährt ... ab?	
What time does ... arrive?		
vahn komt ... ahn?	Wann kommt ... an?	
the (air)plane	*dahs **fluk**-tsoyk*	das Flugzeug
the boat	*dahs bowt*	das Boot
the bus (city)	*dayr bus*	der Bus
the bus (intercity)	*dayr (ü-behr-lahnt-) bus*	der (Überland)bus

| the train | *dayr tsuk* | der Zug |
| the tram | *dee shtrah-sehn-baan* | die Straßenbahn |

Directions

Where is …?
voh ist …?
Wo ist …?

How do I get to …?
vee ko-meh ikh nahkh …?
Wie komme ich nach …?

Is it far from/near here?
ist ehs vait/in dayr na-yeh?
Ist es weit/in der Nähe?

Can I walk there?
kahn ikh tsu fus ghay-ehn?
Kann ich zu Fuß gehen?

Can you show me (on the map)?
ker-nehn zee mir (owf dayr kahr-teh) tsai-ghehn?
Können Sie mir (auf der Karte) zeigen?

Are there other means of getting there?
ghipt ehs ahn-deh-reh mer-ghlikh-kai-tehn, dort-hin tsu faa-rehn?
Gibt es andere Möglichkeiten, dorthin zu fahren?

I'm looking for …
ikh zu-kheh …
Ich suche …

Go straight ahead.
ghay-ehn zee gheh-raa-deh-ows
Gehen Sie geradeaus.

It's two streets down.
ehs ist tsvai shtrah-sehn vai-tehr
Es ist zwei Straßen weiter.

Turn left …
bee-ghehn zee … lingks ahp
Biegen Sie … links ab.

Turn right …
> **bee-ghehn zee … rehkhts ahp**

Biegen Sie … rechts ab.

at the next corner
> **bai dayr nakh-stehn eh-keh**

bei der nächsten Ecke

at the traffic lights
> **bai dayr ahm-pehl**

bei der Ampel

behind	**hin-tehr**	hinter
in front of	*for*	vor
far	*vait*	weit
near	**naa-eh**	nahe
opposite	**ghay-ghehn-ü-behr**	gegenüber

Booking Tickets

Excuse me, where is the ticket office?
> **ehnt-shul-di-ghung, voh ist dayr faar-kahr-tehn-shahl-tehr?**

Entschuldigung, wo ist der Fahrkartenschalter?

Where can I buy a ticket?
> **voh kahn ikh ai-neh faar-kahr-teh kow-fehn?**

Wo kann ich eine Fahrkarte kaufen?

I want to go to …
> **ikh merkh-teh nahkh … fah-rehn.**

Ich möchte nach … fahren.

Do I need to book?
> **mus mahn ai-nehn plahts reh-zehr-vee-rehn lah-sehn?**

Muß man einen Platz reservieren lassen?

GERMAN

You need to book.

*mahn mus **ai**-nehn plahts
reh-zehr-**vee-rehn lah**-sehn*

Man muß einen Platz
reservieren lassen.

I'd like to book a seat to ...

*ikh **merkh**-teh **ai**-nehn
plahts nahkh ... reh-zehr-
vee-rehn **lah**-sehn*

Ich möchte einen Platz nach
... reservieren lassen.

I would like ...

*ikh **merkh**-teh ...*		Ich möchte ...
a one-way ticket	*ai-neh ain-tsehl-kahr-teh*	eine Einzelkarte
a return ticket	*ai-neh **rük**-fahr-kahr-teh*	eine Rückfahrkarte
two tickets	*tsvai fahr-kahr-tehn*	zwei Fahrkarten
tickets for all of us	*fahr-kahr-tehn für uns **ah**-leh*	Fahrkarten für uns alle
student's concession	*mit fahr-prais-ehr-**mas**-i-ghung für shtu-**dehn**-tehn*	mit Fahrpreiser-mäßigung für Studenten
with child/ pensioner concession	*mit fahr-prais-ehr-**mas**-i-ghung für kindehr/**rehnt**-nehr*	mit Fahrpreiser-mäßigung für Kinder/Rentner
1st class	*ehr-steh klah-seh*	erste Klasse
2nd class	*tsvai-teh klah-seh*	zweite Klasse

It is full.

ehr ist ows-gheh-bukht

Er ist ausgebucht.

Is it completely full?

ist ehr ghahnts ows-gheh-bukht?

Ist er ganz ausgebucht?

Can I get a stand-by ticket?
*kahn ikh ain **stand**-bai ti-keht **kow**-fehn?*

Kann ich ein Standby-Ticket kaufen?

Air

CHECKING IN	ABFERTIGUNG
LUGGAGE PICKUP	GEPÄCKAUSGABE
REGISTRATION	GEPÄCKAUFGABE

Is there a flight to …?
ghipt ehs ai-nehn fluk nahkh …?

Gibt es einen Flug nach …?

When is the next flight to …?
*vahn ist dayr **nakh**-steh fluk nahkh …?*

Wann ist der nächste Flug nach …?

How long does the flight take?
*vee **lahng**-eh dow-ehrt dayr fluk?*

Wie lange dauert der Flug?

What is the flight number?
*vehl-kher **flug**-nu-mehr ist ehs?*

Welcher Flugnummer ist es?

You must check in at …
*zee **mü**-sehn um … ain-cheh-kehn*

Sie müssen um … einchecken.

airport tax	*fluk-hah-fehn-gheh-bür*	Flughafengebühr
boarding pass	*bort-kahr-teh*	Bordkarte
customs	*tsol*	Zoll

GERMAN

Bus

BUS/TRAM STOP	BUSHALTESTELLE/ STRAßENBAHNHALTE- STELLE

Where is the bus/tram stop?
voh ist dee bus-hahl-teh-shteh-leh/shtrah-sehn-bahn-hahl-teh-shteh-leh?

Wo ist die Bushaltestelle/ Straßenbahnhaltestelle?

Which bus goes to …?
vehl-khehr bus fairt nahkh …?

Welcher Bus fährt nach …?

Does this bus go to …?
fairt dee-zayr bus nahkh …?

Fährt dieser Bus nach …?

How often do buses pass by?
vee oft faa-rehn bu-seh for-bai?

Wie oft fahren Busse vorbei?

Could you let me know when we get to …?
kern-tehn zee mir bi-teh zaa-ghehn, vehn vir in … ahn-ko-mehn?

Könnten Sie mir bitte sagen, wenn wir in … ankommen?

I want to get off!
ikh merkh-teh ows-shtai-ghehn!

Ich möchte aussteigen!

What time is the … bus?
vahn fairt dayr … bus?

Wann fährt der … Bus?

next	**nakh**-steh bus	nächste
first	**ehr**-steh	erste
last	**lehts**-teh	letzte

Train

DINING CAR	SPEISEWAGEN
EXPRESS	SCHNELLZUG
PLATFORM NO	BAHNSTEIG
SLEEPING CAR	SCHLAFWAGEN

Passengers must ...
   pah-sah-zhee-reh   Passagiere müssen ...
   mü-sehn ...

change trains	*um-shtai-ghehn*	umsteigen
change platforms	*owf ai-nehn ahn-*	auf einen anderen
	deh-rehn baan-	Bahnsteig gehen
	shtaik ghay-ehn	

Is this the right platform
for ...?
   fairt dayr tsuk nahkh ... owf   Fährt der Zug nach ... auf
   dee-zehm baan-shtaik ahp?   diesem Bahnsteig ab?

The train leaves from
platform ...
   dayr tsuk fairt owf   Der Zug fährt auf Bahsteig
   baan-shtaik ... ahp   ... ab.

dining car	*shpai-zeh-vaa-ghehn*	Speisewagen
express	*shnehl-tsuk*	Schnellzug
local	*naa-vehr-kehrs-tsuk*	Nahverkehrszug
sleeping car	*shlaaf-vah-ghehn*	Schlafwagen

Metro

METRO/UNDERGROUND	U-BAHN
CHANGE (for coins)	WECHSELGELD
THIS WAY TO	AUSGANG ZU
WAY OUT	AUSGANG

Which line takes me to …?
   *vel-kheh **li**-ni-yeh fairt
   nahkh …?*
     Welche Linie fährt nach …?
What is the next station?
   *vee haist dayr **nakh**-steh
   baan-hof?*
     Wie heißt der nächste
     Bahnhof?

Taxi

Can you take me to …?
   *****kern**-ehn zee mir tsu …
   bring-ehn?*
     Können Sie mich zu …
     bringen?
Please take me to …
   *****bring**-ehn zee mikh **bi**-teh
   tsu …*
     Bringen Sie mich bitte zu …
How much is it to go to …?
   *vahs **ko**-steht ehs bis …?*
     Was kostet es bis …?

Instructions

Here is fine, thank you.
   *****hahl**-tehn zee **bi**-teh heer*
     Halten Sie bitte hier.
The next corner, please.
   *ahn dayr **nakh**-stehn
   eh-keh, **bi**-teh*
     An der nächsten Ecke, bitte.

Continue!
  vai-tehr!

Weiter!

The next street to the left/right.
  bee-ghehn zee ahn dayr
  nakh-stehn eh-keh lingks/
  rehkhts ahp

Biegen Sie an der nächsten Ecke links/rechts ab.

Stop here!
  haal-tehn zee bi-teh heer!

Halten Sie hier!

Please slow down.
  faa-rehn zee bi-teh
  lahng-sahm-ehr

Fahren Sie bitte langsamer.

Please wait here.
  bi-teh vahr-tehn zee heer

Bitte warten Sie hier.

Some Useful Phrases

The train is delayed/cancelled.
  dayr tsuk haht fehr-shpair-
  tung/falt ows

Der Zug hat Verspätung/ fällt aus.

How long will it be delayed?
  vee-feel fehr-shpair-tung
  virt ehr haa-behn?

Wieviel Verspätung wird er haben?

There is a delay of ... hours.
  ehr haht ... shtun-dehn
  fehr-shpair-tung

Er hat ... Stunden Verspätung.

Can I reserve a place?
  kahn ikh ai-nehn plahts
  reh-zehr-vee-rehn lah-sehn?

Kann ich einen Platz reservieren lassen?

How long does the trip take?
  vee lahng-eh dow-ehrt dee
  rai-zeh?

Wie lange dauert die Reise?

Is it a direct route?
*ist ehs **ai**-neh di-**rehk**-teh*
*fehr-**bin**-dung?*

Ist es eine direkte
Verbindung?

Is that seat taken?
*ist **dee**-zayr plahts*
*beh-**zehtst**?*

Ist dieser Platz besetzt?

I want to get off at …
*ikh **merkh**-teh in …*
*ows-**shtai**-ghehn*

Ich möchte in … aussteigen.

Excuse me.
*ehnt-**shul**-di-ghung*

Entschuldigung.

Where can I hire a bicycle?
*voh kahn ikh ain **faar**-raht*
mee-tehn?

Wo kann ich ein Fahrrad
mieten?

Car

DETOUR	UMLEITUNG
FREEWAY	AUTOBAHN
GARAGE	TANKSTELLE
GIVE WAY	VORFAHRT GEWÄHREN
MECHANIC	MECHANIKER
NO ENTRY	KEIN EINGANG
NO PARKING	PARKEN VERBOTEN
ONE WAY	EINBAHNSTRAßE
REPAIRS	REPARATUREN
SELF SERVICE	SELBSTBEDIENUNG
STOP	HALT
SUPER	SUPER
UNLEADED	BLEIFREI

Where can I hire a car?
voh kahn ikh ain ow-toh mee-tehn?

Wo kann ich ein Auto mieten?

How much is it daily/weekly?
vee-feel ko-steht ehs proh taak/proh voh-kheh?

Wieviel kostet es pro Tag/pro Woche?

Does that include insurance/mileage?
ist dee fehr-zi-khehr-ung/dahs ki-lo-may-tehr-ghehlt in-beh-ghri-fehn?

Ist die Versicherung/das Kilometergeld inbegriffen?

Where's the next petrol station?
voh ist dee nakh-steh tahngk-shteh-leh?

Wo ist die nächste Tankstelle?

Please fill the tank.
fol-tahng-kehn, bi-teh

Volltanken, bitte.

I want … litres of petrol (gas).
ghay-behn zee mir … li-tehr behn-tsin

Geben Sie mir … Liter Benzin.

Please check the oil and water.
bi-teh zay-ehn zee nahkh erl unt vah-sehr

Bitte sehen Sie nach Öl und Wasser.

How long can I park here?
vee lahg-eh kahn ikh heer pahr-kehn?

Wie lange kann ich hier parken?

Does this road lead to?
fürt dee-zeh shtrah-seh nahkh …?

Führt diese Straße nach …?

air (for tyres)	*luft*	Luft
battery	*bah-teh-ree*	Batterie

brakes	*brehm-zehn*	Bremsen
clutch	*kup-lung*	Kupplung
driver's licence	*fü-rehr-shain*	Führerschein
engine	*moh-tor*	Motor
lights	*shain-vehr-fehr*	Scheinwerfer
oil	*erl*	Öl
puncture	*rai-fehn-pah-neh*	Reifenpanne
radiator	*kü-lehr*	Kühler
road map	*shtraa-sehn-kahr-teh*	Straßenkarte
tyres	*rai-fehn*	Reifen
windscreen	*vint-shuts-shai-beh*	Windschutzscheibe

Car Problems

I need a mechanic.

ikh brow-kheh ai-nehn meh-khah-ni-kehr — Ich brauche einen Mechaniker.

What make is it?

vehl-kheh mar-keh ist ehs? — Welche Marke ist es?

The battery is flat.

dee bah-teh-ree ist layr — Die Batterie ist leer.

The radiator is leaking.

dayr kü-lehr ist un-dikht — Der Kühler ist undicht.

I have a flat tyre.

ikh hah-beh ai-neh pah-neh — Ich habe eine Panne.

It's overheating.

ehs loyft hais — Es läuft heiß.

It's not working.

ehs fungk-tsi-o-neert nikht — Es funktioniert nicht.

Accommodation

CAMPING GROUND	CAMPINGPLATZ
GUESTHOUSE	PENSION or GASTHAUS
HOTEL	HOTEL
MOTEL	MOTEL
YOUTH HOSTEL	JUGENDHERBERGE

I am looking for …
  ikh zu-kheh …   Ich suche …
Where is …?
  voh ist …?   Wo ist …?

a cheap hotel	*ain bi-li-ghehs hoh-tehl*	ein billiges Hotel
a good hotel	*ain ghu-tehs hoh-tehl*	ein gutes Hotel
a nearby hotel	*ain hoh-tehl in dayr na-yeh*	ein Hotel in der Nähe
a clean hotel	*ain zow-beh-rehs hoh-tehl*	ein sauberes Hotel

What is the address?
  vahs ist dee ah-dreh-seh?   Was ist die Adresse?
Could you write the address, please?
  kern-tehn zee bi-teh dee ah-dreh-seh owf-shrai-behn?   Könnten Sie bitte die Adresse aufschreiben?

GERMAN

GERMAN

At the Hotel

Do you have any rooms available?

	*haa-behn zee nokh **frai**-yeh **tsi**-mehr?*	Haben Sie noch freie Zimmer?

I would like …
*ikh **merkh**-teh …* — Ich möchte …

a single room	*ain **ain**-tsehl-tsi-mehr*	ein Einzelzimmer
a double room	*ain **do**-pehl-tsi-mehr*	ein Doppelzimmer
a room with a bathroom	*ain **tsi**-mehr mit baat*	ein Zimmer mit Bad
to share a dorm	*ai-nehn **shlaaf**-zaal tai-lehn*	einen Schlafsaal teilen
a bed	*ain beht*	ein Bett

I want a room with a …
*ikh **merkh**-teh ain **tsi**-mehr mit …* — Ich möchte ein Zimmer mit …

bathroom	*baat*	Bad
shower	*du-sheh*	Dusche
television	*fehrn-say-ehn*	Fernsehen
view	*ows-zikht*	Aussicht

I'm going to stay for …
*ikh **blai**-beh …* — Ich bleibe …

one day	*ai-neh nahkht*	eine Nacht
two days	*tsvai **nakh**-teh*	zwei Nächte
one week	*ai-neh vo-kheh*	eine Woche

Do you have identification?
*ker-nehn zee zikh
ows-vai-zehn?*

Könaen Sie sich ausweisen?

Your membership card, please.
mit-ghleets-ows-vais, bi-teh

Mitgliedsausweis, bitte.

Sorry, we're full.
*ehnt-shul-di-ghung, vir
haa-behn kai-neh tsi-mehr
frai*

Entschuldigung, wir haben
keine Zimmer frei.

How long will you be staying?
vee lahng-eh blai-behn zee?

Wie lange bleiben Sie?

How many nights?
vee-fee-leh nakh-teh?

Wieviele Nächte?

It's … per day/per person.
*ehs kos-teht … proh
nahkht/proh pehr-zohn*

Es kostet … pro Nacht/pro
Person.

How much is it per night/per
person?
*vee-feel kos-teht ehs proh
nahkht/proh pehr-zohn?*

Wieviel kostet es pro
Nacht/pro Person?

Can I see it?
kahn ikh ehs zay-ehn?

Kann ich es sehen?

Are there any others?
*haa-behn zee nokh
ahn-deh-reh?*

Haben Sie noch andere?

Is there anything cheaper?
*ghipt ehs eht-vahs
bi-li-ghehr-ehs?*

Gibt es etwas Billigeres?

Can I see the bathroom?
kahn ikh dahs baat zay-ehn?

Kann ich das Bad sehen?

GERMAN

Is there a reduction for
students/children?
*ghipt ehs ehr-**ma**-si-ghung
für shtu-**dehn**-tehn/**kin**-
dehr?*

Gibt es Ermäßigung für
Studenten/Kinder?

Does it include breakfast?
*ist frü-shtük in-beh-ghri-
fehn?*

Ist Frühstück inbegriffen?

It's fine, I'll take it.
*ehs ist ghut, ikh **nay**-meh
ehs*

Es ist gut, ich nehme es.

I'm not sure how long I'm
staying.
*ikh vais nikht, vee **lahng**-eh
ikh **blai**-beh*

Ich weiß nicht, wie lange
ich bleibe.

Is there a lift?
*ghipt ehs ai-**nehn** lift?*

Gibt es einen Lift?

Where is the bathroom?
voh ist dahs baat?

Wo ist das Bad?

Is there hot water all day?
*ghipt ehs dayn **ghahn**-tsehn
taak **vahrm**-ehs vah-**sehr**?*

Gibt es den ganzen Tag
warmes Wasser?

Do you have a safe where I
can leave my valuables?
*haa-behn zee ai-**nehn** sayf,
in daym ikh **mai**-neh vehrt-
zah-khehn **lah**-sehn kahn?*

Haben Sie einen Safe, in
dem ich meine Wertsachen
lassen kann?

Is there somewhere to wash
clothes?
*kahn mahn ir-**ghehnt**-voh
va-sheh vah-**shehn**?*

Kann man irgendwo
Wäsche waschen?

Can I use the kitchen?
kahn ikh dee kü-kheh beh-nu-tsehn?

Kann ich die Küche benutzen?

Can I use the telephone?
kahn ikh dahs teh-leh-fohn beh-nu-tsehn?

Kann ich das Telefon benutzen?

Requests & Complaints

Please wake me up at ...
bi-teh veh-kehn zee mikh um ...

Bitte wecken Sie mich um ...

The room needs to be cleaned.
main tsi-mehr ist nikht geh-mahkht

Mein Zimmer ist nicht gemacht.

Please change the sheets.
vekh-zehln zee bi-teh dee beht-va-sheh

Wechseln Sie bitte die Bettwäsche.

I can't open/close the window.
ikh kahn dahs fehn-stehr nikht owf-mah-khehn/tsu-mah-khehn

Ich kann das Fenster nicht aufmachen/zumachen.

I've locked myself out of my room.
ikh haa-beh mikh ows mai-nehm tsi-mehr ows-geh-shpehrt

Ich habe mich aus meinem Zimmer ausgesperrt.

The toilet won't flush.
dee shpü-lung in dayr to-ah-leh-teh fungk-tsi-o-neert nikht

Die Spülung in der Toilette funktioniert nicht.

I don't like this room.
*dahs **tsi**-mehr gheh-**falt** mir nikht* — Das Zimmer gefällt mir nicht.

It's too ...
ehs ist tsu ... — Es ist zu ...

small	*klain*	klein
noisy	*lowt*	laut
dark	***dung**-kehl*	dunkel
expensive	*toy-ehr*	teuer

Some Useful Phrases

I am/We are leaving now.
*ikh **rai**-zeh/vir **rai**-zehn yehtst* — Ich reise/Wir reisen jetzt.

I would like to pay the bill.
*kahn ikh **bi**-teh dee **rehkh**-nung **haa**-behn?* — Kann ich bitte die Rechnung haben?

name	***naa**-meh*	Name
surname	***nahkh**-naa-meh*	Nachname
room number	***tsi**-mehr-nu-mehr*	Zimmernummer

Some Useful Words

address	*ah-**dreh**-seh*	Adresse
air-conditioned	*mit **kli**-mah-ahn-laa-gheh*	mit Klimaanlage
balcony	*bahl-**kon***	Balkon
bath	*baat*	Bad
bed	*beht*	Bett
bill	***rehkh**-nung*	Rechnung

blanket	*vol-deh-keh*	Wolldecke
candle	**kehr**-*tseh*	Kerze
chair	*shtul*	Stuhl
clean	*zow-behr*	sauber
cupboard	*shrahngk*	Schrank
dark	**dung**-*kehl*	dunkel
dirty	**shmut**-*tsikh*	schmutzig
double bed	*do-pehl-beht*	Doppelbett
electricity	*eh-lehk-trits-i-***tairt**	Elektrizität
excluding ...	*ow-sehr/ows-gheh-no-mehn* ...	außer/ausgenommen ...
fan	*vehn-ti-***laa**-*tor*	Ventilator
... included	... *in-beh-ghri-fehn*	... inbegriffen
key	*shlü-sehl*	Schlüssel
lift (elevator)	*lift*	Lift
light bulb	*glü-bir-neh*	Glühbirne
lock (n)	*shlos*	Schloß
mattress	*mah-***trah**-*tseh*	Matratze
mirror	*shpee-ghehl*	Spiegel
padlock	*for-hang-eh-shlos*	Vorhängeschloß
pillow	*ki-sehn*	Kissen
quiet	*ru-ikh*	ruhig
room (in hotel)	*tsi-mehr*	Zimmer
sheet	*beht-laa-kehn*	Bettlaken
shower	*du-sheh*	Dusche
soap	*zai-feh*	Seife
suitcase	*ko-fehr*	Koffer
swimming pool	*shvim-baat*	Schwimmbad
table	*tish*	Tisch
toilet	*to-ah-***leh**-*teh*	Toilette

GERMAN

toilet paper	*to-ah-leh-tehn-pah-peer*	Toilettenpapier
towel	***hahnt-tukh***	Handtuch
water	*vah-sehr*	Wasser
cold water	*kahl-tehs vah-sehr*	kaltes Wasser
hot water	*vahrm-ehs vah-sehr*	warmes Wasser
window	*fehn-stehr*	Fenster

Around Town

I'm looking for ...
  ikh zu-kheh ...   Ich suche ...

the art gallery	*dee **kunst**-ghah-leh-ree*	die Kunstgallerie
a bank	***ai**-neh bahngk*	eine Bank
the church	*dee **kir**-kheh*	die Kirche
the city centre	*dee **i**-nehn-shtaht*	die Innenstadt
the ... embassy	*dee ... **boht**-shahft*	die ... Botschaft
my hotel	*main hoh-**tehl***	mein Hotel
the market	*dayn mahrkt*	den Markt
the museum	*dahs mu-**zay**-um*	das Museum
the police	*dee po-li-**tsai***	die Polizei
the post office	*dahs post-ahmt*	das Postamt
a public toilet	***ai**-neh **er**-fehnt-likh-eh to-ah-**leh**-teh*	eine öffentliche Toilette
the telephone centre	*dee teh-leh-**fohn**-tsehn-trah-leh*	die Telefonzentrale
the tourist information office	*dahs frehm-dehn-**fehr-kehrz**-bü-roh*	das Fremdenverkehrsbüro

What time does it open?
  *um vee-**feel** ur mahkht ehs owf?*   Um wieviel Uhr macht es auf?

What time does it close?
um vee-feel ur mahkht ehs tsu?

Um wieviel Uhr macht es zu?

What is the name of …?
vee haist …?

Wie heißt …?

| this street | *dee-zeh shtrah-seh* | diese Straße |
| this suburb | *dee-zehr for-ort* | dieser Vorort |

For directions, see the Getting Around section, page 190.

At the Bank

I want to exchange some money.
ikh merkh-teh ghehlt um-tow-shehn

Ich möchte Geld umtauschen.

I want to change some traveller's cheques.
ikh merkh-teh rai-zeh-sheks ain-ler-zehn

Ich möchte Reiseschecks einlösen.

What is the exchange rate?
vee ist dayr vehkh-sehl-kurs?

Wie ist der Wechselkurs?

How many marks per dollar?
vee-fee-leh mahrk für ai-nehn do-lahr?

Wieviele Mark für einen Dollar?

Can I have money transferred here from my bank?
kahn ikh ghehlt ows mai-nehr bahngk ü-behr-vai-zehn lah-sehn?

Kann ich Geld aus meiner Bank überweisen lassen?

GERMAN

When will it arrive?
*vahn virt ehs **ahn**-koh-mehn?* Wann wird es ankommen?

Has my money arrived yet?
*ist main ghehlt shon **ahn**-ghe-ko-mehn?* Ist mein Geld schon angekommen?

bank draft	*trah-teh*	Tratte
bank notes	*bahngk-noh-tehn*	Banknoten
cashier	*kah-seer-ehr-in*	Kassiererin (f)
	kah-seer-ehr	Kassierer (m)
coins	*mün-tsehn*	Münzen
commission	*gheh-bür*	Gebühr
credit card	*kreh-deet-kahr-teh*	Kreditkarte
exchange office	*vehkh-sehl-shtu-beh*	Wechselstube
loose change	*klain-ghehlt*	Kleingeld
signature	*un-tehr-shrift*	Unterschrift

At the Post Office

I would like to send …
*ikh **merkh**-teh … zehn-dehn* Ich möchte … senden.

a letter	*ai-nehn breef*	einen Brief
a postcard	*ai-neh pohst-kahr-teh*	eine Postkarte
a parcel	*ain pah-kayt*	ein Paket
a telegram	*ain teh-leh-ghrahm*	ein Telegramm

I would like some stamps.
*ikh **merkh**-teh breef-mahr-kehn kow-fehn* Ich möchte Briefmarken kaufen.

How much is the postage?
vee-feel kos-teht dahs por-to?

Wieviel kostet das Porto?

How much does it cost to send this to …?
vee-feel kos-teht ehs, dahs nahkh … tsu zehn-dehn?

Wieviel kostet es, das nach … zu senden?

an aerogram	*ai-nehn luft-post-laikht-breef*	einen Luftpost-leichtbrief
air mail	*pehr luft-post*	per Luftpost
envelope	*um-shlaak*	Umschlag
mailbox	*breef-kahs-tehn*	Briefkasten
parcel	*pah-kayt*	Paket
registered mail	*payr ain-shrai-behn*	per Einschreiben
surface mail	*gheh-vern-likh-eh pohst*	gewöhnliche Post

Telephone

I want to make a long-distance call to …
bi-teh ain fehrn-gheh-shprakh nahkh …

Bitte ein Ferngespräch nach …

The number is …
dee nu-mehr ist …

Die Nummer ist …

I want to speak for three minutes.
ikh merkh-teh drai mi-nu-tehn lahng shpreh-khen

Ich möchte drei Minuten lang sprechen.

How much does a three-
minute call cost?
> *vee-feel kos-teht ain drai
> mi-nu-tehn gheh-shprakh?*

Wieviel kostet ein drei
Minuten Gespräch?

How much does each extra
minute cost?
> *vee-feel kos-stet yay-deh
> tsu-zats-likh-eh mi-nu-teh?*

Wieviel kostet jede
zusätzliche Minute?

I would like to speak to Mrs
Schmidt.
> *ikh merkh-teh frow shmit
> shpreh-khen*

Ich möchte Frau Schmidt
sprechen.

I want to make a reverse-
charges phone call.
> *ikh merkh-teh ain
> air-gheh-shprakh*

Ich möchte ein R-Gespräch.

It's engaged.
> *ehs ist beh-zetst*

Es ist besetzt.

I've been cut off.
> *ikh bin un-tehr-bro-khen
> vor-dehn*

Ich bin unterbrochen
worden.

Sightseeing

Do you have a guidebook/
street map?
> *haa-behn zee ai-nehn rai-
> zeh-fü-rehr/shtaht-plahn?*

Haben Sie einen
Reiseführer/Stadtplan?

What are the main attractions?
> *vahs zint dee howpt-zay-
> ehns-vür-dikh-kai-tehn?*

Was sind die
Hauptsehenswürdigkeiten?

What is that?
vahs ist dahs? — Was ist das?

How old is it?
vee ahlt ist dahs? — Wie alt ist das?

Can I take photographs?
dahrf ikh foh-to-ghrah-fee-rehn? — Darf ich fotografieren?

What time does it open/close?
vahn mahkht ehs owf/tsu? — Wann macht es auf/zu?

ancient	*ahlt*	alt
archaeological	*ahr-kha-o-loh-ghish*	archäologisch
beach	*shtrahnt*	Strand
building	*gheh-boy-deh*	Gebäude
castle	*shlos*	Schloß
cathedral	*dohm*	Dom
church	*kir-kheh*	Kirche
concert hall	*kon-tsehrt-ha-leh*	Konzerthalle
library	*bi-bli-oh-tehk*	Bibliothek
main square	*howpt-plahts*	Hauptplatz
market	*mahrkt*	Markt
monastery	*klo-stehr*	Kloster
monument	*dehngk-mahl*	Denkmal
mosque	*mo-shay*	Moschee
old city	*ahlt-shtaht*	Altstadt
opera house	*oh-pehrn-hows*	Opernhaus
palace	*pah-lahst*	Palast
ruins	*ru-ee-nehn*	Ruinen
stadium	*shtaa-di-on*	Stadion
statues	*shtaa-tu-ehn*	Statuen
synagogue	*si-nah-ghoh-gheh*	Sinagoge

GERMAN

| temple | **tehm**-pehl | Tempel |
| university | u-ni-vehr-si-**tairt** | Universität |

Entertainment

What's there to do in the evenings?
   *vahs kahn mahn aa-behnts un-tehr-**nay**-mehn?*

Was kann man abends unternehmen?

Are there any discos?
   *ghipt ehs heer **dis**-kohs?*

Gibt es hier Discos?

Are there places where you can hear local folk music?
   *kahn mahn heer ir-**ghehnt**-voh **ert**-li-kheh folks-mu-zeek **her**-rehn?*

Kann man hier irgendwo örtliche Volksmusik hören?

How much does it cost to get in?
   *vee-**feel** ko-steht dayr **ain**-trit?*

Wieviel kostet der Eintritt?

cinema	**kee**-noh	Kino
concert	kon-**tsehrt**	Konzert
discotheque	**dis**-koh	Disco
theatre	tay-**aa**-tehr	Theater

In the Country
Weather

What's the weather like?
   *vee ist dahs **veh**-tehr?*

Wie ist das Wetter?

Will it rain?
   *virt ehs **raygh**-nehn?*

Wird es regnen?

Will it snow?
virt ehs shnai-yehn?   Wird es schneien?

The weather is ... today.
dahs veh-tehr ist hoy-teh ...   Das Wetter ist heute ...
Will it be ... tomorrow?
virt ehs mor-ghehn ... zain?   Wird es morgen ... sein?

cloudy	*vol-kikh*	wolkig
cold	*kahlt*	kalt
fine	*shern*	schön
foggy	*nay-blikh*	neblig
frosty	*fro-stikh*	frostig
hot	*hais*	heiß
windy	*vin-dikh*	windig

Camping

Am I allowed to camp here?
kahn ikh heer tsehl-tehn?   Kann ich hier zelten?
Is there a campsite nearby?
ghipt ehs in dayr nay-yeh   Gibt es in der Nähe einen
ai-nehn kehm-ping-plahts?   Campingplatz?

backpack	*ruk-zahk*	Rucksack
can opener	*doh-zehn-erf-nehr*	Dosenöffner
compass	*kom-pahs*	Kompaß
crampons	*shtaig-ai-zehn*	Steigeisen
firewood	*brehn-holts*	Brennholz
gas cartridge	*ghaas-flah-sheh*	Gasflasche
hammock	*hang-eh-mah-teh*	Hängematte
ice axe	*ais-pi-kehl*	Eispickel
mattress	*mah-trah-tseh*	Matratze

GERMAN

penknife	*tah-shehn-meh-sehr*	Taschenmesser
rope	*zail*	Seil
tent	*tsehlt*	Zelt
tent pegs	*tsehlt-hay-ring-eh*	Zeltheringe
torch (flashlight)	*tah-shehn-lahm-peh*	Taschenlampe
sleeping bag	*shlaaf-zahk*	Schlafsack
stove	*hayrt*	Herd
water bottle	*fehlt-flah-sheh*	Feldflasche

Food

Germans love a big breakfast. Wherever you stay in all German-speaking areas, breakfast will almost always be included as part of the price. Even at cheap hotels you may get ham, sausage, herrings, boiled eggs, bread rolls, and fresh fruit, as well as coffee, milk and fruit juice. Some Germans have a 'second breakfast' *(zweites Frühstück)* mid-morning, which can be like a smaller version of the earlier breakfast, only sometimes with beer; or it may be just a morning tea with cakes and coffee.

Traditionally lunch is the biggest meal of all, with dinner often being like a small breakfast – some eating places, in fact, have a main menu for lunch and a smaller one for the evening. However, at most restaurants (called a *Restaurant* or *Gaststätte*) you can get a large dinner if you want.

Ethnic German food tends to be filling – lots of meat, especially pork and chicken. Offal is quite common. Pickles (like sauerkraut-pickled cabbage), rather than fresh vegetables, are very popular. And of course sausage – you'll see lots of snack bars (called an *Imbiß* or *Schnellimbiß*) basically just selling a range of sausages. Now there are also all sorts of Asian and Turkish restaurants and takeaways; and, of course, the international fast-food chains.

GERMAN

Some areas, especially southern Germany and Austria, are renowned for their cakes and pastries – you are probably already familiar with apple strudel *(Apfelstrudel)* and Black Forest cake *(Schwarzwälder Kirschtorte)*. Vienna has been called the caff capital of the world, with an unbelievable array of elegant establishments to visit for coffee and cake.

Pubs (a *Bierstube)* are popular and similar to those in England or Australia. They generally sell snacks and light food.

Restaurants normally have a menu displayed outside, so you can figure out what it all means first! Many offer a good-value set menu (a *Gedeck* or *Tagesmenü)*. You do not usually wait to be seated when you enter, and it is common in less expensive restaurants for other people to sit at your table. The bill at the end of a meal always includes tax and service charge; however, you can leave a small tip – about 5% – if the service has been really good.

breakfast	*frü-shtük*	Frühstück
lunch	*mi-tahg-eh-sehn*	Mittagessen
dinner	*aa-behnt-eh-sehn*	Abendessen

Table for ..., please.
   ai-nehn tish für ..., bi-teh   Einen Tisch für ..., bitte.
Can I see the menu please?
   kahn ikh bi-teh dee shpai-   Kann ich bitte die
   zeh-kahr-teh haa-behn?   Speisekarte haben?
I would like the set lunch, please.
   ikh ha-teh ghehrn dahs   Ich hätte gern das
   taa-ghehs-meh-nü bi-teh   Tagesmenü bitte.
What does it include?
   vahs ehnt-halt dahs?   Was enthält das?

Is service included in the bill?
*ist dee beh-**dee**-nung*   Ist die Bedienung
*in-beh-**ghri**-fehn?*   inbegriffen?
Not too spicy please.
*bi-teh nikht zayr **vür**-tsikh*   Bitte nicht sehr würzig.

an ashtray	*ain **ah**-shehn-beh-khehr*	ein Aschenbecher
the bill	*dee **rehkh**-nung*	die Rechnung
a cup	*ai-neh **tah**-seh*	eine Tasse
dessert	*nahkh-**shpai**-zeh*	Nachspeise
a drink	*ain gheh-**trangk***	ein Getränk
a fork	*ai-neh **ghaa**-behl*	eine Gabel
fresh	*frish*	frisch
a glass	*ain ghlaas*	ein Glas
a knife	*ain **meh**-sehr*	ein Messer
a plate	*ain **teh**-lehr*	ein Teller
spicy	***vür**-tsikh*	würzig
a spoon	*ain **ler**-fehl*	ein Löffel
stale	*ahlt*	alt
sweet	*züs*	süß
teaspoon	*tay-**ler**-fehl*	Teelöffel
toothpick	*tsaan-**shto**-khehr*	Zahnstocher

Vegetarian Meals

I am a vegetarian.
*ikh bin veh-gheh-**taa**-ri-ehr-in*   Ich bin Vegetarierin. (f)
*ikh bin veh-gheh-**taa**-ri-ehr*   Ich bin Vegetarier. (m)
I don't eat meat.
*ikh **eh**-seh kain flaish*   Ich esse kein Fleisch.

I don't eat chicken, or fish, or ham.

ikh eh-seh kain hün-khehn, kai-nehn fish, unt kai-nehn shing-kehn

Ich esse kein Hühnchen, keinen Fisch, und keinen Schinken.

Breakfast
fried egg	*Spiegelei*
ham	*Schinken*
honey	*Honig*
jam	*Marmelade*
sausage	*Wurst*
scrambled eggs	*Rühreier*

Staples & Condiments
bread	*Brot*
butter	*Butter*
cheese	*Käse*
mustard	*Senf*
noodles	*Nudeln*
pepper	*Pfeffer*
rice	*Reis*
rolls	*Brötchen*
salt	*Salz*
tomato sauce	*Tomatenketchup*

Appetisers & Snacks — Vorspeisen
Belegtes Brot	open sandwich
Kleine/Kalte Gerichte	small/cold dishes
Pfannkuchen	pancake
Pilze	mushrooms

Rollmops	pickled herrings
Russische Eier	eggs with mayonnaise
Schnitten	selection of cold meats and vegetables
Wurst	sausage
Blutwurst	blood sausage
Bockwurst	pork sausage
Bratwurst	fried pork sausage
Leberwurst	liver sausage
Weißwurst	veal sausage
Zwiebelwurst	liver-and-onion sausage

Soups

Bauernsuppe	'farmer's soup', cabbage and sausage
Erbsensuppe	pea soup
Fleischbrühe	consommé
Gemüsesuppe or *Frühlingssuppe*	vegetable soup
Graupensuppe	barley soup
Hühnersuppe	chicken soup
Tomatensuppe	tomato soup

Meat & Seafood

Fischgerichte	fish dishes
Fleischgerichte	meat dishes
Hauptgerichte	main courses
Backhähnchen	fried chicken
Beefsteak	hamburger
Brathuhn	roast chicken
Fisch	fish
Frikadellen	meatballs
Hackbraten	meatloaf

Hasenpfeffer	hare stew with mushrooms and onions
Holsteiner Schnitzel	veal with fried egg, accompanied by seafood
Kalbfleisch	veal
Kohlroulade	cabbage leaves stuffed with minced meat
Königsberger Klops	meatballs in a sour-cream-and-caper sauce
Kotelette	chops
Kutteln	tripe
Labskaus	thick meat-and-potato stew
Leber	liver
Ragout	stew
Rindfleisch	beef
Schlachtplatte	selection of pork and sausage
Schmorbraten	beef pot roast
Schweinebraten	roast pork
Schweinefleisch	pork
Wiener Schnitzel	crumbed veal
Zunge	tongue

GERMAN

Vegetables	**Gemüse**
beans	*Bohnen*
beetroot	*rote Beete*
cabbage	*Kohl*
carrots	*Karotten*
cauliflower	*Blumenkohl*
chips (French fries)	*Pommes frites*
cucumber, gherkins	*Gurken*
lettuce	*Salat*
onions	*Zwiebeln*
peas	*Erbsen*

potato salad	*Kartoffelsalat*
potatoes	*Kartoffeln*
mashed potatoes	*Kartoffelbrei*
fried potatoes	*Bratkartoffeln*
pumpkin	*Kürbis*
red cabbage	*Rotkohl*
salad	*grüner Salat*
tomatoes	*Tomaten*

Methods of Cooking

baked	*gebacken*
boiled	*gekocht*
cooked (fried, roasted, grilled or baked)	*gebraten*
in the (Vienna) style	*(Wiener) Art*
rare	*englisch*
smoked	*geräuchert*
stuffed	*gefüllt*
well-done	*gut durchgebraten*
with	*... mit ...*

Dessert & Pastries — Nachspeisen und Kuchen

Apfelstrudel	apple strudel
Berliner Pfannkuchen	jam doughnut
Eis	ice cream
Königstorte	rum-flavoured fruit cake
Schwarzwälder Kirschtorte	Black Forest cake (chocolate layer cake filled with cream and cherries)
Spekulatius	almond biscuits
Torte	layer cake

Drinks – Nonalcoholic

apple juice	*Apfelsaft*
coffee	*Kaffee*
Vienna coffee (black, topped with whipped cream)	*Einspänner*
white coffee	*Milchkaffee*
fruit juice	*Fruchtsaft*
milkshake	*Milchshake*
mineral water (without bubbles)	*Mineralwasser (ohne Kohlensäure)*
peppermint tea	*Pfefferminztee*
tea	*Tee*
water	*Wasser*
with/without	*mit/ohne*
cream	*Sahne*
milk	*Milch*
sugar	*Zucker*

Drinks – Alcoholic

apple brandy	*Apfelschnaps*
apple cider	*Apfelwein*
beer	*Bier*
bitter	*Altbier*
malt beer, similar to stout	*Malzbier*
dark/strong	*Bock/Starkbier*
type of lager	*Pilsener*
made with wheat	*Weizenbier*
brandy	*Weinbrand*
champagne	*Sekt*
cherry brandy	*Kirschwasser*
spirit made from grain, often drunk after a meal	*Schnaps*

GERMAN

wine		Wein
chilled		gekühlt
dry		trocken
late harvest		Spätlese
mulled wine		Glühwein
red wine		Rotwein
sweet		süß
white wine		Weißwein
with ice		mit Eis

Shopping

How much is it?
*vee-**feel** ko-steht ehs?*   Wieviel kostet es?

bookshop	***bukh**-hahnt-lung*	Buchhandlung
camera shop	***foh**-to-gheh-shaft*	Fotogeschäft
clothing store	*beh-**klai**-dungs-gheh-shaft*	Bekleidungs-geschäft
delicatessen	*deh-li-kah-**teh**-sehn-gheh-shaft*	Delikatessen-geschäft
department store	***vaa**-rehn-hows*	Warenhaus
laundry	*va-sheh-rai*	Wäscherei
market	*mahrkt*	Markt
newsagency/ stationer's	***tsai**-tungs-hant-lehr/ **shraip**-vah-rehn-gheh-shaft*	Zeitungshändler/ Schreibwaren-geschäft
pharmacy	*ah-po-**tay**-keh*	Apotheke
shoeshop	***shu**-gheh-shaft*	Schuhgeschäft
souvenir shop	*zu-veh-**neer**-lah-dehn*	Souvenirladen

GERMAN

| supermarket | **zu**-pehr-markt | Supermarkt |
| vegetable shop | gheh-**mü**-zeh-hahnt-lung | Gemüsehandlung |

I would like to buy ...
   *ikh **merkh**-teh ... **kow**-fehn*   Ich möchte ... kaufen.
Do you have others?
   haa-behn zee nokh **ahn**-deh-reh?   Haben Sie noch andere?
I don't like it.
   *ehs gheh-**falt** mir nikht*   Es gefällt mir nicht.
Can I look at it?
   ker-nehn zee ehs mir **tsai**-ghehn?   Können Sie es mir zeigen?
I'm just looking.
   *ikh **show**-eh mikh nur um*   Ich schaue mich nur um.
Can you write down the price?
   ker-nehn zee dayn prais **owf**-shrai-behn?   Können Sie den Preis aufschreiben?
Do you accept credit cards?
   nay-mehn zee kreh-**deet**-kahr-tehn?   Nehmen Sie Kreditkarten?
Could you lower the price?
   ker-nehn zee dayn prais reh-du-**tsee**-rehn?   Können Sie den Preis reduzieren?
I don't have much money.
   *ikh **haa**-beh nur **vay**-nikh ghehlt*   Ich habe nur wenig Geld.

Can I help you?
   *kahn ikh **ee**-nehn **hehl**-fehn?*   Kann ich Ihnen helfen?

Anything else?
zonst nokh eht-vahs? Sonst noch etwas?

Would you like it wrapped?
*zoll ikh ehs ee-nehn
ain-vi-kehln?* Soll ich es Ihnen
einwickeln?

Sorry, this is the only one.
*ehnt-shul-di-ghung, dahs
ist dahs ain-tsi-gheh* Entschuldigung, das ist das
einzige.

How much/many do you want?
*vee-feel/vee-fee-leh
merkh-tehn zee?* Wieviel/Wieviele möchten
Sie?

Souvenirs

beer stein	*beer-kruk*	Bierkrug
cuckoo clock	*ku-kuks-ur*	Kuckucksuhr
earrings	*ohr-ring-eh*	Ohrringe
embroidery	*shti-keh-rai*	Stickerei
handicraft	*kunst-hahnt-vehrk*	Kunsthandwerk
necklace	*hahls-keh-teh*	Halskette
porcelain	*por-tseh-laan*	Porzellan
ring	*ring*	Ring

Clothing

clothing	*klai-dung*	Kleidung
coat	*mahn-tehl*	Mantel
dress	*klait*	Kleid
jacket	*yah-keh*	Jacke
jumper (sweater)	*pul-oh-vehr*	Pullover
shirt	*hehmt*	Hemd
shoes	*shu-eh*	Schuhe

skirt	*rok*	Rock
trousers	***hoh**-zeh*	Hose

It doesn't fit.
  ehs pahst nikht Es paßt nicht.

It is too …
  ehs ist tsu … Es ist zu …

big/small	*ghrohs/klain*	groß/klein
short/long	*kurts/lahng*	kurz/lang
tight/loose	*ehng/vait*	eng/weit

Materials

brass, of	*ows **meh**-sing*	aus Messing
cotton	***bowm**-vo-leh*	Baumwolle
gold, of	*ows gholt*	aus Gold
handmade	*hahnt-gheh-**ahr**-bai-teht*	handgearbeitet
leather	***lay**-dehr*	Leder
silk	***zai**-deh*	Seide
silver, of	*ows **zil**-behr*	aus Silber
wool	***vo**-leh*	Wolle

Toiletries

comb	*kahm*	Kamm
condoms	*kon-**doh**-meh*	Kondome
deodorant	*day-oh-do-**rahnt***	Deodorant
hairbrush	***haar**-bür-steh*	Haarbürste
moisturising cream	***foykh**-tikh-kaits-**kray**-meh*	Feuchtig-keitscreme
razor	*rah-**zeer**-meh-sehr*	Rasiermesser
sanitary napkins	***daa**-mehn-bin-dehn*	Damenbinden
shampoo	***shahm**-pu*	Shampoo

GERMAN

shaving cream	*rah-**zeer**-kray-meh*	Rasiercreme
soap	***zai**-feh*	Seife
sunblock cream	***sahn**-blok-kray-meh*	Sunblockcreme
tampons	***tahm**-pons*	Tampons
tissues	*pah-**peer**-tü-khehr*	Papiertücher
toilet paper	*to-ah-**leh**-tehn-pah-peer*	Toilettenpapier
toothbrush	***tsahn**-bür-steh*	Zahnbürste
toothpaste	***tsahn**-pah-stah*	Zahnpasta

Stationery & Publications

map	***kahr**-teh*	Karte
newspaper	***tsai**-tung*	Zeitung
newspaper in English	***tsai**-tung owf **ehng**-lish*	Zeitung auf Englisch
novels in English	*roh-**maa**-neh owf **ehng**-lish*	Romane auf Englisch
paper	*pah-**peer***	Papier
pen (ballpoint)	*ku-**ghehl**-shrai-behr*	Kugelschreiber
scissors	***shay**-reh*	Schere

Photography

When will the photos be ready?

*vahn **wehr**-dehn dee **foh**-tohs **fehr**-tikh zain?*

Wann werden die Fotos fertig sein?

I'd like a film for this camera.

*ikh **merkh**-teh ai-nehn film für **dee**-zeh **kah**-meh-rah*

Ich möchte einen Film für diese Kamera.

B&W (film)	*shvahrts-vais*	schwarzweiß
camera	*kah-meh-rah*	Kamera
colour (film)	*fahrp-film*	Farbfilm
film	*film*	Film
flash	*blits*	Blitz
lens	*lin-zeh*	Linse
light meter	*beh-likh-tungs-meh-seh*	Belichtungsmesse

Smoking

A packet of cigarettes, please.

ai-neh shahkh-tehl tsi-ghah-reh-tehn bi-teh

Eine Schachtel Zigaretten bitte.

Are these cigarettes strong/mild?

zint dee-zeh tsi-ghah-reh-tehn shtahrk/milt?

Sind diese Zigaretten stark/mild?

Do you have a light?

haa-behn zee foy-ehr?

Haben Sie Feuer?

cigarette papers	*tsi-ghah-reh-tehn-pah-pee-reh*	Zigarettenpapiere
cigarettes	*tsi-ghah-reh-tehn*	Zigaretten
filtered	*mit fil-tehr*	mit Filter
lighter	*foy-ehr-tsoyk*	Feuerzeug
matches	*shtraikh-herl-tsehr*	Streichhölzer
menthol	*mehn-tol*	Menthol
pipe	*pfai-feh*	Pfeife
tobacco (pipe)	*taa-bahk (pfai-fehn-taa-bahk)*	Tabak (Pfeifen-tabak)

GERMAN

Colours

black	*shvahrts*	schwarz
blue	*blow*	blau
brown	*brown*	braun
green	*ghrün*	grün
orange	*o-r-zheh*	orange
pink	*roh-zah*	rosa
purple	*lee-lah*	lila
red	*roht*	rot
white	*vais*	weiß
yellow	*ghelp*	gelb

Sizes & Comparisons

small	*klain*	klein
big	*ghrohs*	groß
heavy	*shvehr*	schwer
light	*laikht*	leicht
more	*mayr*	mehr
less (not as much/ not as many)	*nikht zoh feel/nikht zoh fee-leh*	nicht so viel/nicht so viele
too much/many	*tsu feel/tsu fee-leh*	zu viel/zu viele
many	*fee-leh*	viele
enough	*gheh-nuk*	genug
also	*owkh*	auch
a little bit	*ain bis-khehn*	ein bißchen

Health

Where is …?	*voh ist …?*	Wo ist …?
the doctor	*dayr ahrtst*	der Arzt
the hospital	*dahs krahng-kehn-hows*	das Krankenhaus

| the chemist | *dee ah-po-tay-keh* | die Apotheke |
| the dentist | *dayr tsaan-ahrtst* | der Zahnarzt |

I am sick.
  ikh bin krahngk   Ich bin krank.
My friend is sick.
  mai-neh froyn-din/main   Meine Freundin (f)/Mein
  froynt ist krahngk   Freund (m) ist krank.
Could I see a female doctor?
  kahn ikh ai-neh arts-tin   Kann ich eine Ärztin
  shpreh-khehn?   sprechen?
What's the matter?
  voh faylt ehs?   Wo fehlt es?
Where does it hurt?
  voh haa-behn zee   Wo haben Sie Schmerzen?
  shmehr-tsehn?
It hurts here.
  ehs tut mir heer vay   Es tut hier weh.
My … hurts.
  mir tut … vay   Mir tut … weh.

GERMAN

Parts of the Body

arm	*dayr ahrm*	der Arm
back	*dayr rü-kehn*	der Rücken
chest	*dayr brust-korp*	der Brustkorb
ear	*dahs korp*	das Ohr
eye	*dahs ow-gheh*	das Auge
finger	*dayr fing-ehr*	der Finger
foot	*dayr fus*	der Fuß
hand	*dee hahnt*	die Hand
head	*dayr kopf*	der Kopf
heart	*dahs hehrts*	das Herz

knee	*dahs knee*	das Knie
leg	*dahs bain*	das Bein
liver	*dee lay-behr*	die Leber
nose	*dee naa-zeh*	die Nase
skin	*dee howt*	die Haut
teeth	*dee tsair-neh*	die Zähne

Ailments

I have …

ikh haa-beh …   Ich habe …

an allergy	*ai-neh ah-lehr-ghee*	eine Allergie
anaemia	*ah-na-mee*	Anämie
a blister	*ai-neh blaa-zeh*	eine Blase
a cold	*ai-neh ehr-kal-tung*	eine Erkältung
constipation	*fehr-shtop-fung*	Verstopfung
a cough	*hu-stehn*	Husten
diarrhoea	*durkh-fahl*	Durchfall
fever	*fee-behr*	Fieber
a headache	*kopf-shmehr-tsehn*	Kopfschmerzen
indigestion	*ai-neh maa-ghehn-fehr-shti-mung*	eine Magenver-stimmung
an infection	*ai-neh in-fek-tsi-ohn*	eine Infektion
influenza	*dee ghri-peh*	die Grippe
lice	*loy-zeh*	Läuse
low/high blood pressure	*nee-dri-ghehn/how-ehn blut-druk*	niedrigen/hohen Blutdruck
a pain	*shmehr-tsehn*	Schmerzen
sore throat	*hahls-shmehr-tsehn*	Halsschmerzen
sprain	*ai-neh mus-kehl-tseh-rung*	eine Muskel-zerrung
sunburn	*zo-nehn-brahnt*	Sonnenbrand

| a venereal disease | *ai-neh gheh-shlehkhts-krahngk-hait* | eine Geschlechts-krankheit |
| worms | *vür-mehr* | Würmer |

Some Useful Words & Phrases

I'm ...
ikh bin ...   Ich bin ...

diabetic	*di-ah-bay-ti-kehr-in*	Diabetikerin (f)
	di-ah-bay-tik	Diabetiker (m)
epileptic	*eh-pi-lehp-ti-keh-rin*	Epileptikerin (f)
	eh-pi-lehp-ti-kehr	Epileptiker (m)
asthmatic	*ahst-maa-ti-keh-rin*	Asthmatikerin (f)
	ahst-maa-ti-kehr	Asthmatiker (m)

I'm allergic to antibiotics/
penicillin.
   *ikh bin **ghay**-ghehn ahn-ti-bi-oh-ti-kah/peh-ni-tsi-lin ah-**lehr**-ghish*   Ich bin gegen Antibiotika/ Penizillin allergisch.

I'm pregnant.
   *ikh bin **shvahng**-ehr*   Ich bin schwanger.

I'm on the pill.
   *ikh **nay**-meh dee pi-leh*   Ich nehme die Pille.

I haven't had my period for
... months.
   *ikh **haa**-beh zait ... **moh**-nah-tehn **mai**-neh peh-ri-**oh**-deh nikht gheh-**hahbt***   Ich habe seit ... Monaten meine Periode nicht gehabt.

I have been vaccinated.
   *ikh bin gheh-**impft***   Ich bin geimpft.

GERMAN

I feel better/worse.

ikh fü-leh mikh beh-sehr/
shli-mehr

Ich fühle mich besser/
schlimmer.

accident	*un-fahl*	Unfall
addiction	*zukht*	Sucht
antibiotics	*ahn-ti-bi-oh-ti-kah*	Antibiotika
antiseptic	*ahn-ti-sehp-ti-kum*	Antiseptikum
bandage	*fehr-bahnt*	Verband
blood test	*blut-proh-beh*	Blutprobe
contraceptive	*fehr-hü-tungs-mi-tehl*	Verhütungsmittel
injury	*fehr-leh-tsung*	Verletzung
medicine	*meh-di-tseen*	Medizin
menstruation	*mehn-stru-ah-tsi-ohn*	Menstruation
nausea	*ü-behl-kait*	Übelkeit
vitamins	*vi-tah-mee-neh*	Vitamine

GERMAN

At the Chemist

I need medication for ...

ikh brow-kheh eht-vahs
ghay-ghehn ...

Ich brauche etwas gegen ...

I have a prescription.

ikh haa-beh ain reh-tsehpt

Ich habe ein Rezept.

At the Dentist

I have a toothache.

ikh haa-beh tsaan-shmehr-
tsehn

Ich habe Zahnschmerzen.

I've lost a filling.

ikh haa-beh ai-ne fü-lung
fehr-lo-rehn

Ich habe eine Füllung
verloren.

I've broken a tooth.
   mir ist ain tsaan ahp-gheh-   Mir ist ein Zahn
   bro-khehn   abgebrochen.
My gums hurt.
   *dahs **tsaan-flaish** tut mir*   Das Zahnfleisch tut mir weh.
   vay
I don't want it extracted.
   ikh vil een nikht tsee-yehn Ich will ihn nicht ziehen
   lah-sehn   lassen.
Please give me an anaesthetic.
   *ghay-behn zee mir **bi**-teh* Geben Sie mir bitte eine
   ai-neh shpri-tseh   Spritze.

Time & Dates

What date is it today?
   *dayr vee-**feel**-teh ist*   Der wievielte ist heute?
   hoy-teh?

What time is it?
   vee shpayt ist ehs?   Wie spät ist es?
It is ... o'clock.
   ehs ist ... ur   Es ist ... Uhr.

in the morning	*mor-ghehns*	morgens
in the afternoon	*nahkh-mi-tahks*	nachmittags
in the evening	*aa-behnts*	abends

Days of the Week

Monday	*mohn-taak*	Montag
Tuesday	*deens-taak*	Dienstag
Wednesday	*mit-vokh*	Mittwoch

GERMAN

Thursday	*do-nehrs-taak*	Donnerstag
Friday	*frai-taak*	Freitag
Saturday	*zahms-taak*	Samstag
Sunday	*zon-taak*	Sonntag

Months

January	*yah-nu-aar*	Januar
February	*feh-bru-aar*	Februar
March	*marts*	März
April	*ah-**pril***	April
May	*mai*	Mai
June	*yu-ni*	Juni
July	*yu-li*	Juli
August	*ow-ghust*	August
September	*zehp-**tehm**-behr*	September
October	*ok-**toh**-behr*	Oktober
November	*noh-**vehm**-behr*	November
December	*day-**tsehm**-behr*	Dezember

Seasons

summer	*zo-mehr*	Sommer
autumn	*hehrpst*	Herbst
winter	*vin-tehr*	Winter
spring	*frü-ling*	Frühling

Present

today	*hoy-teh*	heute
this morning	*hoy-teh **mor**-ghehn*	heute morgen
tonight	*hoy-teh aa-behnt*	heute abend
this week	*dee-zeh vo-kheh*	diese Woche
year	*dee-zehs yaar*	dieses Jahr
now	*yehtst*	jetzt

GERMAN

Past

yesterday	*gheh-stehrn*	gestern
day before yesterday	*for-gheh-stehrn*	vorgestern
yesterday morning	*gheh-stehrn mor-ghehn*	gestern morgen
last night	*leht-steh nahkht*	letzte Nacht
last week	*leht-steh vo-kheh*	letzte Woche
last year	*leht-stehs yaar*	letztes Jahr

Future

tomorrow	*mor-ghehn*	morgen
day after tomorrow	*ü-behr-mor-ghehn*	übermorgen
tomorrow morning	*mor-ghehn frü*	morgen früh
tomorrow afternoon/evening	*mor-ghehn nahkh-mi-tahk/aa-behnt*	morgen nachmittag/abend
next week	*nakh-steh vo-kheh*	nächste Woche
next year	*nakh-stehs yaar*	nächstes Jahr

During the Day

afternoon	*nahkh-mi-tahk*	Nachmittag
day	*taak*	Tag
early	*frü*	früh
midnight	*mi-tehr-nahkht*	Mitternacht
morning	*mor-ghehn*	Morgen
night	*nahkht*	Nacht
noon	*mi-tahk*	Mittag
sundown	*zo-nehn-un-tehr-ghahng*	Sonnenuntergang
sunrise	*zo-nehn-owf-ghahng*	Sonnenaufgang

Numbers & Amounts

0	*nul*	null
1	*ains*	eins
2	*tsvai (tsvoh)*	zwei (zwo on the telephone)
3	*drai*	drei
4	*feer*	vier
5	*fünf*	fünf
6	*zehkhs*	sechs
7	*zee-behn*	sieben
8	*ahkht*	acht
9	*noyn*	neun
10	*tsayn*	zehn
11	*ehlf*	elf
12	*tsverlf*	zwölf
13	*drai-tsayn*	dreizehn
14	*feer-tsayn*	vierzehn
15	*fünf-tsayn*	fünfzehn
16	*zehkh-tsayn*	sechzehn
17	*zeep-tsayn*	siebzehn
18	*ahkht-tsayn*	achtzehn
19	*noyn-tsayn*	neunzehn
20	*tsvahn-tsikh*	zwanzig
30	*drai-sikh*	dreißig
40	*feer-tsikh*	vierzig
50	*fünf-tsikh*	fünfzig
60	*zehkh-tsikh*	sechzig
70	*zeep-tsikh*	siebzig
80	*ahkht-tsikh*	achtzig
90	*noyn-tsikh*	neunzig
100	*hun-dehrt*	hundert

1000	*tow-zehnt*	tausend
one million	*ai-neh mi-li-ohn*	eine Million
1st	*ehr-steh*	erste
2nd	*tsvai-teh*	zweite
3rd	*dri-teh*	dritte
¼	*ain feer-tehl*	ein Viertel
⅓	*ain dri-tehl*	ein Drittel
½	*ai-neh half-teh*	eine Hälfte
¾	*drai feer-tehl*	drei Viertel

Some Useful Words

a little (amount)	*ain bis-khehn*	ein bißchen
double	*nokh ain-mahl zoh*	noch einmal so (literally: 'the same again')
a dozen	*ain du-tsehnt*	ein Dutzend
Enough!	*gheh-nuk!*	Genug!
a few	*ain paar*	ein paar
less	*vay-ni-ghehr*	weniger
a lot, much	*feel*	viel
many	*fee-leh*	viele
more	*mayr*	mehr
once	*ain-mahl*	einmal
a pair	*ain paar*	ein Paar
percent	*proh-tsehnt*	Prozent
some	*ai-ni-gheh*	einige
too much	*tsu feel*	zu viel
twice	*tsvai-mahl*	zweimal

GERMAN

Abbreviations

A.A.	AA
Ausw.	ID
Bhf	Station
BRD	Federal Republic of Germany (old)
DB	German Federal Railways
DDR	German Democratic Republic (old)
DJH	Youth Hostel (name of association)
DM	German Mark
EG	EC
GB	UK
HPA or HA	GPO (Main Post Office)
Hr./Fr.	Mr/Mrs
KW	Short Wave
n. Chr./v. Chr.	AD/BC
N/S	Nth/Sth
p. Adr.	c/o
Str.	St/Rd/etc
U	Underground (Railway)
usw.	etc
vorm./nachm.	am/pm
z.B.	eg

Irish

Irish

Introduction

Irish (the correct legal and linguistic term) is the national and first official language of Ireland, and the ancestral language of the 70-million-strong Irish diaspora, and of most Scots, throughout the world. It belongs, together with Scottish Gaelic, Manx, Welsh, Breton and Cornish, to the Celtic branch of the Indo-European language family, once spoken across Europe from Ireland to Anatolia (modern Turkey). Irish and Scottish Gaelic shared a common literary language from the 6th to the late 18th centuries. Indeed the Latin word *Scotus* meant simply an Irish speaker, whether from Ireland or Scotland.

Irish largely inspired the movement that brought about Ireland's national independence in the early 20th century. It has thus been an obligatory subject at all first and second level schools since independence in 1922, and the number of Irish-medium schools has been rapidly growing in recent years. Since 1913 it has been essential for matriculation at the National University of Ireland. The 1986 census showed a total of 1.04 million Irish speakers in the Irish state. There are an estimated 100,000 Irish speakers in Northern Ireland. Irish is now the everyday language in *Gaeltacht*, or traditional Irish-speaking areas, and is increasingly heard in urban areas, particularly in Dublin and Belfast. Its literature is flourishing. Irish has been included in the European Community LINGUA program, an ambitious project to promote the teaching of European languages throughout the Member States, and is one of the languages on the common EC passport.

The usual word order in Irish is verb–subject–object.

The initial consonant of feminine nouns changes after the definite article, for example, 'woman: the woman', *bean: an bhean*, (pronounced *ban: on van*). The verb is inflected for tense:

kiss	*pohg*	póg
she kissed	*fohg shee*	phóg sí
she kisses	*pohg-an shee*	pógann sí
she will kiss	*pohg-hee shee*	pógfaidh sí
she would kiss	*fohg-hokh shee*	phógfadh sí
she used to kiss	*fohg-okh shee*	phógadh sí
kissing	*eh pohg-a*	ag pógadh
kissed	*pohg-ha*	pógtha

Some well-known English words have been borrowed from Irish:

whiskey	*ish-keh ba-ha*	uisce beatha – 'water of life'
slogan	*sloo-a gorr-im*	slua-ghairm – 'crowd call'
glen	*glyan*	gleann – 'a valley'
colleen	*col-yeen*	cailín – 'a girl'
cairn	*corr-an*	carn – 'a pile of stones'
clan	*klon*	clann – 'people with common ancestor'
shamrock	*sham-rohg*	seamróg
tory	*tohr-ee*	tóraí – 'a pursuer, an outlaw'

IRISH

Pronunciation

There are a number of Irish sounds not found in English, and an approximation to these will be given. Stress is normally on the first syllable. In Irish, as in Russian, the palatalised consonants are separate phonemes, for instance, the words for 'day' and 'to melt', *lá* and *leá*, (pronounced *laa* and *lyaa*), are distinguished only by the two varieties of the letter **l**. Long vowels are marked by the acute accent: 'a poem', *dán* (pronounced *daan*).

bh, mh	'v'
ch	before **i** and **e**, like the 'h' in Hugh, or the German *ich*
ch	before **a**, **o**, and **u**, like the Scottish *loch*
dh, gh	a 'y' sound before **i** and **e**
dh, gh	a 'g' sound before **a**, **o** and **u** (approximately)
fh	silent
ph	'f'
sh, th	'h'
r	trilled
mb	'm'
gc	'g'
nd	'n'
bhf	'v'
ng	'ng' as in 'sing', occurs initially, as in Japanese
bp	'b'
ts	't'

Vowel sounds are as in many Continental European languages, and are not diphthongised. The four Irish diphthong sounds are written and pronounced as follows:

IRISH

'ay'	sice	saghas – 'a kind'
	ay-rk	adharc – 'a horn'
'ow'	ow-in	abhainn – 'a river'
	down	domhan – 'world'
	bour	bodhar – 'deaf'
	row	rogha – 'choice'
'oo-a'	foo-ar	fuar – 'cold'
'ee-a'	shee-ad	siad – 'they'

Greetings & Civilities
Greetings
Hi!/Good morning./Good
afternoon.
 dee-a gwit   Dia duit. (lit. 'God to you')
Good night.
 ee-ha vo   Oíche mhaith.
How are you?
 kunas taa too?   Conas tá tú?
Well.
 go mo   Go maith.
Very well, thanks.
 go hon vo, go-ra mo ogot   Go han-mhaith, gura maith
                              agat.

What's new?
 kayn shkay-al?   Cén scéal?

Goodbyes
Goodbye.
 slaan   Slán.
See you later.
 slaan go foh-il   Slán go fóill.

Take care.
toor ara   Tabhair aire.

Important Civilities
Please.
lyeh do hull   Le do thoil.
Thank you.
go-ra mo ogot   Gura maith agat.
Thank you very much.
go-ra myee-la mo ogot   Gura míle maith agat.
You're welcome.
taa faa-il-tyeh roht   Tá fáilte romhat.
I'd like to present you to ...
sho ...   Seo ...
I'm pleased to meet you.
taa aa-hass o-rom boo-la lyat   Tá áthas orm bualadh leat.

Forms of Address
Sir/Mr ...!
a gwin-a oo-as-il!   A dhuine uasail!
Madame/Mrs ...!
a van oo-as-al!   A bhean uasal!

Small Talk
What's your name?
kod iss an-im dit?   Cad is ainm duit?
I'm ...
iss mish-a ...   Is mise ...
Who is that?
kyay hay shin?   Cé hé sin?

I don't know.
   nyeel iss ogom Níl a fhios agam.
Where are you from?
   kod oss dit? Cad as duit?

I'm from …
   oss … As …

Australia	*on os-traa-il*	an Astráil
Canada	*kyan-ada*	Ceanada
England	*soss-ana*	Sasana
New Zealand	*on noo-a hay-lin*	an Nua-Shéalainn
Scotland	*ol-bwin*	Albain
Wales	*an mrat-in vyug*	an mBreatain Bheag
the USA	*mer-ik-aa … dum*	Meiriceá … dom

More Useful Phrases

How do you say that in Irish?
   kunas a dyair-faa shin oss gwayl-gyeh? Conas a déarfá sin as Gaeilge?
Excuse me.
   gov mo lyeh-shkay-al Gabh mo leithscéal.
Where's the toilet, please?
   kaa will on lyeh-aras, lyeh do hull? Cá bhfuil an leithreas, le do thoil?

On the left.	*ehr klay*	Ar clé.
On the right.	*ehr yesh*	Ar dheis.
Straight on.	*dyee-rokh ehr ay*	Díreach ar aghaidh.

Food

Waiter!
a rass-tal-ee!   A fhreastalaí!

What will you drink/eat?
kod a ohl-hee/ees-hee too?   Cad a ólfaidh/íosfaidh tú?

I'd like ...
bo vo lyum ...   Ba mhaith liom ...

A little bread, please.
byug-aan a-raan, lyeh do hull   Beagán aráin, le do thoil.

a beer	*byohr*	beoir
a drop of ...	*breen*	braon
apple juice	*soo ool*	sú úll
dessert	*myil-shohg*	milseog
fish	*ee-ask*	iasc
meat	*fyoh-il*	feoil
mineral water	*ish-keh myee-an-ree*	uisce mianraí
orange juice	*soo or-aash-teh*	sú oráiste
potatoes	*praa-tee*	prátaí
salmon and brown bread	*brad-aan og-as a-raan don*	bradán agus arán donn
soup	*on-ra*	anraith
vegetables	*gloss-ree*	glasraí
water	*ish-keh*	uisce
wine	*fee-on*	fíon
whiskey	*ish-keh ba-ha*	uisce beatha

IRISH

Signs & Irish Words Commonly Heard in English

NO SMOKING	NÁ CAITEAR TOBAC
CITY CENTRE (on buses)	AN LÁR
LADIES/GENTLEMEN	MNÁ/FIR

A hundred thousand welcomes.	Céad míle fáilte.
Lower House of Parliament	Dáil Éireann
Prime Minister	An Taoiseach
Presidential Residence	Áras an Uachtaráin

IRISH

Portuguese

Portuguese

Introduction

Like French, Italian, Spanish and Romanian, Portuguese is a Romance language, that is, one closely derived from Latin. It is spoken by over 10 million in Portugal, 130 million in Brazil, and it is also the official language of five African nations (Angola, Mozambique, Guinea-Bissau, Cape Verde and São Tomé & Príncipe). In Asia it is still spoken in the former Portuguese territory of East Timor, and in enclaves around Malacca, Goa, Damão and Diu. Visitors to Portugal are often struck by the strangeness of the language, which some say sounds like Arabic. However, those who understand French or Spanish are often surprised to see how similar written Portuguese is to the other Romance languages.

The obscure indigenous people who inhabited the Iberian Peninsula before the arrival of the Romans are considered responsible for the most striking traits of the Portuguese language. The first Roman troops arrived in the Peninsula in the 3rd century BC, with the invasion proper beginning in 197 BC. By 27 BC it was totally under Roman domination. Roman soldiers and merchants brought their language with them: Vulgar Latin soon took over the indigenous languages, more slowly so in the west of the Peninsula, the Lusitanian territory that is now Portugal.

From 409 AD the Iberian Peninsula was successively invaded by Barbarians of Teutonic origin, and from the 6th to the 8th century by the Visigoths, who all left their imprint on the language, but their influence was not strong enough to change its by then well-established neo-Latin character.

The Arab invasion began in 711 AD, and Arabic soon became the prestige cultural language in the Peninsula. Portugal became an independent kingdom in 1139, Lisbon being reconquered from the Moors in 1147. The Moors were finally expelled from the south of Portugal in 1249, and that was the end of the last significant influence on the formation of the Portuguese language. During the Middle Ages, Portuguese underwent mostly French and Provençal influences; later, in the 16th and 17th centuries, Italian and Spanish were above all responsible for innovations in vocabulary.

Portuguese is the language of a very rich literature, which begins in the dark medieval period. In the 16th century Luis Vaz de Camões wrote the epic poem *The Lusiads*, which many foreigners know in translation. Twentieth-century Portuguese literature has not been widely read abroad, due to the lack of good translations. However, since the 1974 democratic revolution in Portugal, Europe has begun to pay more attention to Portuguese literature, and, though not always easily available, there are now good translations into English of at least the best Portuguese poet of the 20th century, Fernando Pessoa, and of some outstanding contemporary novelists, namely José Cardoso Pires and José Saramago.

Pronunciation

Pronunciation of Portuguese is difficult, given that, as in English, vowels and consonants have more than one sound, depending on position in the syllable and word stress. Moreover, there are nasal vowels and diphthongs in Portuguese which have no equivalent in English. It is therefore important to become

PORTUGUESE

familiar with the following simplified phonetic symbols, which are used in the pronunciation guide in this book.

Vowels	Pronunciation Guide	Sounds
a	ah	open **a**, as in 'cut'
a	ă	closed **a**, as in 'courtesy', 'her'
e	eh	open **e**, as in 'bet', 'bury'
e	e	closed **e**, as in French *été*, and similar to 'laird'
e	'	silent final **e**, as in 'these'. Also silent in unstressed syllables.
i	ee	stressed **i**, as in 'see'
o	oh	open **o**, as in 'pot', 'sorry'
o	o	closed **o**, as in 'caught', 'awful'
o, u	u	an 'oo' sound, as in 'good', 'pull'

Nasal Vowels

Nasalisation can be represented in Portuguese by an **n** or an **m** after the vowel, or by a tilde, ~, over it. The nasal **i** exists in English, as the 'ing' sound in 'sing'. For other vowels, try to pronounce a long **a** or **e** *(ah, eh)* holding your nose, as if you had a head cold. In this book nasal vowels are represented as: *ã, ẽ, ing* (nasal **i**), *oong* (nasal **u**).

Diphthongs

au	ow	as in 'now', 'out'
ai	ay	as in 'pie', 'dive', 'eye'
ei	ey	as in 'day', 'pay'
eu	e-w	pronounced together
oi	oy	similar to 'boy'

Nasal Diphthongs

Try the same technique as for nasal vowels. To say 'no', *não*, pronounce English 'now' through your nose.

ão	*õw*	nasal 'now' *(nowng)*
ãe	*ẽy*	nasal 'day' *(eing)*
õe	*õy*	nasal 'boy' *(oing)*
ui	*ũy*	similar to 'ensu*ing*', 'issu*ing*'.

Consonants

The letters **b, d, f, l, m, n, p, s, t, v** and **z** are similar enough to their English counterparts.

c	*k*	before **a, o** or **u**
c	*s*	before **e** or **i**, as in 'see'
ç	*s*	as in 'see'
g	*g*	before **a, o** or **u**, as in 'garden'
g	*zh*	before **e** or **i**, as in 'treasure'
gu	*g*	before **e** or **i**, as in 'get'
h		never pronounced at the beginning of a word
nh	*ny*	as in 'onion'
lh	*ly*	as in 'million'
j	*zh*	as in 'treasure'
m	*m*	in final position is not pronounced, it simply nasalises the previous vowel: um *(oong)*, bom *(bõ)*
qu	*k*	before **e** or **i**
qu	*kw*	before **a** or **o**, as in 'quack'

r (**rr** in the middle of a word)	*rr*	is a harsh, guttural sound similar to the French *rue*, Scottish *loch*, or German *Bach*. In some areas of Portugal this **r** is not guttural, but strongly rolled.
r	*r*	in the middle or at the end of a word it's a rolled sound, stronger than the English 'r'
s (**ss** in the middle of a word)	*s*	at the beginning of a word is pronounced like the 's' in 'send'
s	*z*	between vowels is pronounced 'z' as in 'zeal'
s	*sh*	before another consonant or at the end of a word is pronounced 'sh', as in 'she'
x	*sh*	as in 'ship': taxa *(tah-shă)*
x	*z*	as in 'zeal': exame *(ee-ză-m')*
x	*ks*	'ks', as in 'taxi'

Word stress is important in Portuguese, as it can change the meaning of the word. Many Portuguese words have a written accent. The stress must fall on that syllable when you pronounce it. Stressed syllables are in bold print in this chapter, for example: 'thanks', obrigado, *o-bree-**gah**-du.*

Portuguese, like the other Romance languages, has masculine and feminine word forms. In this chapter, the masculine word is indicated first, the feminine word or variant syllable after and separated by a slash: /. When using a verb or adjectival form in the first person, remember that the masculine and feminine forms vary according to you, the speaker. Thus, if you are a male, you will say 'thank you', *obrigado*; if you are female, say 'thank you', *obrigada*.

Greetings & Civilities
Top Useful Phrases

Hello.
  oh-lah   Olá.
Goodbye.
  ă-dewsh   Adeus.
Yes.
  sing   Sim.
No.
  nõw   Não.
Excuse me.
  d'sh-kul-p'/kõ lee-sẽ-să   Desculpe./Com licença.
May I? Do you mind?
  poh-su?   Posso?
Please.
  s'fahsh fă-vor   Se faz favor.
Thank you.
  o-bree-gah-du/dă   Obrigado/a.
That's fine. You're welcome.
  d' nah-dă   De nada.

Greetings

Good morning.
  bõ dee-ă   Bom dia.
Good afternoon.
  bo-ă tahr-d'   Boa tarde.
Good evening/night.
  bo-ă tahr-d'/noy-t'   Boa tarde/noite.
How are you?
  ko-moo shtah?   Como está?

Well, thanks.

běy, o-bree-gah-du/da Bem, obrigado/a.

Forms of Address

Madam/Mrs	**mee-nyǎ s'nyo-rǎ/ s'nyo-rǎ do-nǎ**	Minha senhora/ Senhora Dona
Sir/Mr	**s'nyor**	Senhor
Miss	**m'-nee-nǎ**	Menina
companion,	**kō-pǎ-nyey-ru/-rǎ**	companheiro/a
friend	**ǎ-mee-gu/-gǎ**	amigo/a

Small Talk
Meeting People

What is your name?

ko-mu s'shǎ-mǎ? Como se chama?

My name is …

shǎ-mu-m' … Chamo-me …

I'm pleased to meet you.

mŭy-tu prǎ-zer Muito prazer.

Nationalities

Where are you from?

dy õ dy eh? De onde é?

I am from …

so …		Sou …
Australia	**dǎ owsh-trah-lee-ǎ**	da Austrália
Canada	**du kǎ-nǎ-dah**	do Canadá
England	**d' ing-glǎ-teh-rrǎ**	de Inglaterra
Ireland	**dǎ eer-lǎ-dǎ**	da Irlanda
New Zealand	**dǎ noh-vǎ z'-lǎ-dee-ǎ**	da Nova Zelândia
Scotland	**dǎ sh-koh-see-ǎ**	da Escócia

| the USA | *duz'sh-**tah**-du-zu-**nee**-dush* | dos Estados Unidos |
| Wales | *du pǎ-**eesh** d' **gah**-l'sh* | do País de Gales |

Age

How old are you?
*kwã-tu-zǎ-nush-**têy**?* — Quantos anos tem?
I am ... years old.
***te**-nyu ... ǎ-nush* — Tenho ... anos.

Occupations

What (work) do you do?
*êy ky **eh** k' trǎ-**bah**-lya?* — Em que é que trabalha?
I am (a/an) ...
so ... — Sou ...

business person	*ee-z'-ku-**tee**-vu, ê-pr'-**zah**-ree-u/-ǎ, **oh**-mêy d' n'-**goh**-cee-ush*	executivo, empresário/a, homem de negócios
farmer	*ǎ-gree-kul-**tor**/-ǎ*	agricultor/a
journalist	*zhur-nǎ-**leesh**-tǎ*	jornalista
manual worker	*o-p'-**rah**-ree-u/-ǎ*	operário/a
nurse	*ê-f'r-**mey**-ru/-rǎ*	enfermeiro/a
office worker	*ê-pr'-**gah**-du/-dǎ d'sh-kree-**toh**-ree-u*	empregado/a de escritório
scientist	*see-ê-**teesh**-tǎ*	cientista
student	*shtu-**dã**-t'*	estudante
teacher	*pru-f'-**sor**/-ǎ*	professor/a
waiter	*ê-pr'-**gah**-du/-dǎ d' **me**-zǎ*	empregado/a de mesa
writer	*shkree-**tor**/-rǎ*	escritor/a

PORTUGUESE

Religion

What is your religion?

kwah-leh ă su-ă   Qual é a sua religião?
rr'lee-zhee-õw?

I am not religious.

nõw so rr'-lee-zhee-   Não sou religioso/a.
o-zu/-ză

I am …		Sou …
so …		
Buddhist	*bu-deesh-tă*	budista
Catholic	*kă-toh-lee-ku/-kă*	católico/a
Christian	*kreesh-tõw/kreesh-tã*	cristão/cristã
Hindu	*ing-du*	hindu
Jewish	*zhu-de-w/zhu-dee-ă*	judeu/judia
Muslim	*mu-sul-mă-nu/-nă*	muçulmano/a

Family

Are you married?

eh kă-zah-du/-dă?   É casado/a?

I am single.

so sol-tey-ru/-ră   Sou solteiro/a.

I am married.

so kă-zah-du/-dă   Sou casado/a.

How many children do you
have?

kwă-tush fee-lyush tẽy?   Quantos filhos tem?

I don't have any children.

nõw te-nyu fee-lyush   Não tenho filhos.

Is your husband/wife here?
*u se-w mă-**ree**-du/ă su-ă*
*mu-**lyehr** shtah ă-kee*
kõ-see-gu?

O seu marido/A sua mulher
está aqui consigo?

Do you have a boyfriend/
girlfriend?
*têy nă-mu-**rah**-du/-dă?*

Tem namorado/a?

brother	*eer-**mõw***	irmão
children	*fee-lyush*	filhos
daughter	*fee-lyă*	filha
family	*fă-**mee**-lee-ă*	família
father	*pay*	pai
grandfather	*ă-**vo***	avô
grandmother	*ă-**voh***	avó
husband	*mă-**ree**-du*	marido
mother	*mẽy*	mãe
sister	*eer-**mã***	irmã
son	*fee-lyu*	filho
wife	*mu-**lyehr**/**shpo**-ză*	mulher/esposa

Feelings

I (don't) like …
*(nõw) **gohsh**-tu d' …*

(Não) Gosto de …

I am sorry. (condolence)
***sing**-tu **mũy**-tu/lă-mẽ-tu*
***mũy**-tu*

Sinto muito/Lamento muito.

I am grateful.
***mũy**-tu ă-gră-d'-**see**-du/-dă*

Muito agradecido/a.

PORTUGUESE

I am …
te-nyu …   Tenho …

cold/hot	*free-u/kă-lor*	frio/calor
hungry/thirsty	*foh-m'/se-d'*	fome/sede
in a hurry	*preh-să*	pressa
right	*rră-zõw*	razão
sleepy	*so-nu*	sono

I am …
sh-to …   Estou …

angry	*ză-gah-du/-dă*	zangado/a
happy/sad	*kõ-tẽ-t'/treesh-t'*	contente/triste
tired	*kă-sah-du/-dă*	cansado/a
well	*bẽy*	bem
worried	*pree-oh-ku-pah-du/ -dă*	preocupado/a

Language Difficulties

Do you speak English?
  fah-lă ing-glesh?   Fala Inglês?

Does anyone speak English?
  ah ă-kee ahl-gẽy k'fahl' ing-glesh?   Há aqui alguém que fale Inglês?

I speak a little Portuguese.
  fah-lu oong bu-kă-dee-nyu d' pur-tu-gesh   Falo um bocadinho de Português.

I (don't) speak …
  (nõw) fah-lu …   (Não) Falo …

I (don't) understand.
  (nõw) p'r-se-bu/ẽ-tẽ-du   (Não) Percebo/Entendo.

Could you speak more slowly please?

   *pu-**dee**-ă fă-**lahr** maysh d'-vă-**gahr**, s'fash fă-**vor**?* — Podia falar mais devagar, se faz favor?

Could you repeat that?

   *pu-**dee**-ă rr'-p'-teer?* — Podia repetir?

How do you say …?

   *ko-mu eh k's'**deesh** …?* — Como é que se diz …?

What does … mean?

   *k' see-gnee-**fee**-kă …?* — Que significa …?

I speak …

   fah-lu … — Falo …

English	*ing-**glesh***	Inglês
French	*fră-**sesh***	Francês
German	*ă-l'-**mõw***	Alemão
Italian	*ee-tă-lee-ă-nu*	Italiano
Spanish	*shpă-**nyohl***	Espanhol

Some Useful Phrases

Sorry. (excuse me, forgive me)

   *d'sh-**kul**-p'* — Desculpe.

Sure.

   *kõ s'r-te-ză/**klah**-ru (k'sing)* — Com certeza/Claro (que sim)!

Just a minute.

   *oong mu-**mẽ**-tu* — Um momento.

Good luck!

   *bo-ă **sohr**-t'* — Boa sorte.

PORTUGUESE

Signs

BAGGAGE COUNTER	BALCÃO DE BAGAGENS
CHECK-IN COUNTER	ENTREGA DE BAGAGENS/ CHECK-IN
CUSTOMS	ALFÂNDEGA
EMERGENCY EXIT	SAÍDA DE EMERGÊNCIA
ENTRANCE	ENTRADA
EXIT	SAÍDA
FREE ADMISSION	ENTRADA GRATIS
HOT/COLD	QUENTE/FRIO
INFORMATION	INFORMAÇÕES
NO ENTRY	PROIBIDA A ENTRADA
NO SMOKING	PROIBIDO FUMAR
OPEN	ABERTO
CLOSED	ENCERRADO/FECHADO
PROHIBITED	PROIBIDO
RESERVED	RESERVADO
TELEPHONE	TELEFONE
TOILETS	W.C.

Emergencies

POLICE	POLÍCIA
POLICE STATION	ESQUADRA DA POLÍCIA

Help!
su-ko-rru!

Socorro!

There's been an accident!
*o-v' oong ă-see-dē-t'/
d'-zahsh-tr'!*

Houve um acidente/desastre!

Call a doctor!
shă-m' oong meh-dee-ku!

Chame um médico!

Call an ambulance!
shă-mu-mă-bu-lā-see-ă!

Chame uma ambulância!

I've been raped.
fuy vee-u-lah-dă/vee-u-lah-rõw-m'

Fui violada./Violaram-me.

I've been robbed.
fuy rro-bah-du/-dă

Fui roubado/a.

Call the police!
shă-mă pu-lee-see-ă!

Chame a polícia!

Where is the police station?
*õ-dy eh ă sh-kwah-dră dă
pu-lee-see-ă?*

Onde é a esquadra da
polícia?

Go away!
dey-sh'-mē pahsh!

Deixe-me em paz!

Thief!
lă-drõw!

Ladrão!

I am ill.
shto du-ē-t'

Estou doente.

My friend is ill.
*u me-w ă-mee-gu/ă mee-
nyă ă-mee-gă shtah du-ē-t'*

O meu amigo/A minha
amiga está doente.

I am lost.
shto p'r-dee-du/-dă

Estou perdido/a.

Where are the toilets?
õ-dy eh ă kah-ză d' bă-nyu? Onde é a casa de banho?

Could you help me please?
ing-pohr-tă-s' d' mă-zhu-dahr? Importa-se de me ajudar?

Could I please use the telephone?
poh-su t'l'fu-nahr? Posso telefonar?

I'm sorry. I apologise.
d'sh-kul-p'/p'r-dõw Desculpe./Perdão.

I didn't realise I was doing anything wrong.
nõw să-bee-ă k' shtah-vă ă fă-zer mahl Não sabia que estava a fazer mal.

I didn't do it.
e-w nõw fee-zee-su Eu não fiz isso.

I wish to contact my embassy/consulate.
keh-ru fă-lahr kõ ă mee-nya ē-bay-shah-dă/kõ u me-w kõ-su-lah-du Quero falar com a minha embaixada/o meu consulado.

I speak English.
fah-lu ing-glesh Falo Inglês.

I have medical insurance.
te-nyu s'gu-ru meh-dee-ku Tenho seguro médico.

My possessions are insured.
te-nyu s'gu-ru (kõ-tră rro-bu) Tenho seguro (contra roubo).

My ... was stolen.
rro-bah-rõw-m' u/ă ... Roubaram-me o/a ...

I've lost …
p'r-dee …		Perdi …
my bags	*ăsh **mah**-lăsh*	as malas
my handbag	*ă **mah**-lă/ă kăr-**tey**-ră*	a mala/a carteira
my money	*u dee-**nyey**-ru*	o dinheiro
my travellers' cheques	*ush me-w-sh **sheh**-k'sh d' vee-**ah**-gēy*	os meus cheques de viagem
my passport	*u pah-să-**pohr**-t'*	o passaporte

Paperwork

name/surname	*no-m'/ă-p'-lee-du*	nome/apelido
address	*mu-**rah**-dă/dee-reh-**sōw***	morada/direcção
date of birth	***dah**-tă d' năsh-see-**mē**-tu*	data de nascimento
place of birth	*lu-**gahr** d' năsh-see-**mē**-tu*	lugar de nascimento
age	*ee-**dah**-d'*	idade
sex	***seh**-ksu*	sexo
nationality	*nă-see-u-nă-lee-**dah**-d'*	nacionalidade
religion	*rr'-lee-gee-**ōw***	religião
reason for travel	*mu-**tee**-vu dă vee-**ah**-zhēy*	motivo da viagem
profession	*pru-fee-**sōw***	profissão
marital status	***shtah**-du see-**veel***	estado civil
passport	*pah-să-**pohr**-t'*	passaporte
passport number	***nu**-m'-ru du pah-să-**pohr**-t'*	número do passaporte
visa	*vee-**ză**/**veesh**-tu*	visa/visto

tourist card	*kăr-tṓw d' tu-reesh-tă*	cartão de turista
identification	*du-ku-mē-tu /bee-lye-t' dee-dē-tee-dah-d'*	documento/bilhete de identidade
birth certificate	*s'r-tee-dṓw d' năsh-see-mē-tu*	certidão de nascimento
driver's licence	*kahr-tă d' kō-du-sṓw*	carta de condução
car owner's title	*lee-vre-t'/du-ku-mē-tush du kah-rru*	livrete/documentos do carro
car registration	*mă-tree-ku-lă du kah-rro*	matrícula do carro
customs	*ahl-fă-d'-gă*	alfândega
immigration	*ee-mee-gră-sṓw*	imigração
border	*frō-tey-ră*	fronteira

Getting Around

ARRIVALS	CHEGADAS
BUS STOP	PARAGEM DO AUTOCARRO
DEPARTURES	PARTIDAS
STATION	ESTAÇÃO
TICKET OFFICE	BILHETEIRA
TIMETABLE	HORÁRIO
TRAIN STATION	ESTAÇÃO FERROVIÁRIA/ ESTAÇÃO DE COMBÓIOS

What time does ... arrive/
leave?

ă ky oh-răsh she-gă/ *pahr-t' ...?*		A que horas chega/parte ...?
the (air)plane	*u ă-vee-õw*	o avião
the boat	*u bahr-ku*	o barco
the bus	*u ow-toh-kah-rru*	o autocarro
the intercity bus	*ă kah-mee-u-neh-tă*	a camioneta
the train	*u kõ-boy-u*	o comboio
the tram	*u ee-leh-tree-ku*	o eléctrico

Directions

Where is ...?
    õ-dy eh ...?/õ-d'fee-kă ...?   Onde é ...?/Onde fica ...?

How do I get to ...?
    ko-mu vo pă-ră ...?   Como vou para ...?

Is it far from/near here?
    eh lõ-zh'/pehr-tu dăkee?   É longe/perto daqui?

Can I walk there?
    poh-su eer ă peh?   Posso ir a pé?

Can you show me (on the
map)?
    poh-d'-m' mush-trahr nu   Pode-me mostrar (no mapa)?
    mah-pă?

I want to go to ...
    keh-ru eer ă ...   Quero ir a ...

Go straight ahead.
    see-gă sẽ-pr' ă dee-rey-tu/   Siga sempre a direito/
    sẽ-pr' ẽy frẽ-t'   sempre em frente.

PORTUGUESE

It's two blocks down.
eh ă doysh kwăr-tey-rõysh dă-kee
É a dois quarteirões daqui.

Turn left ...
vee-rahsh-ker-dă ...
Vire à esquerda ...

Turn right ...
vee-rah dee-rey-tă ...
Vire à direita ...

at the next corner
nă proh-see-măsh-kee-nă
na próxima esquina

at the traffic lights
nu s'mah-fu-ru/nush see-naysh d' tră-see-tu
no semáforo/nos sinais de trânsito

behind	*ă-trahsh d'*	atrás de
in front of	*ẽy frẽ-t' d'*	em frente de
far	*lõ-zh'*	longe
near	*pehr-tu*	perto
opposite	*du o-tru lah-du/ ẽy frẽ-t'-d'*	do outro lado/ em frente de

Booking Tickets

Where is the ticket office?
fahsh fă-vor, õ-dy eh ă bee-ly'tey-ră?
Faz favor, onde é a bilheteira?

Where can I buy a ticket?
õ-dy eh k' kõ-pru u bee-lye-t'?
Onde é que compro o bilhete?

I want to go to ...
keh-ru eer pă-ră ...
Quero ir para ...

Do I need to book?
eh pr'-see-zu rr'-z'r-vahr?
É preciso reservar?

You need to book.
tēy d' fā-zer rr'-zehr-vă Tem de fazer reserva.

I'd like to book a seat to …
k'-ree-ă rr'-z'r-vahr Queria reservar lugar
lu-gahr pă-ră … para …

It is full.
shtah shey-u Está cheio.

Is it completely full?
shtah shgu-tah-du? Está esgotado?

Can I get a stand-by ticket?
poh-su kō-prahr oong Posso comprar um bilhete de
bee-lye-t' d' stehnd-bay stand-by (um bilhete sem
(oong bee-lye-t' sēy dee-rey- direito a reserva antecipada)?
tu ă rr'zehr-vă ā-t'-see-
pah-dă)?

Can I have a refund?
poh-dē-m' rree-ē-bol-sahr/ Podem-me reembolsar/
d'-vol-ver u dee-nyey-ru? devolver o dinheiro?

I would like …
k'-ree-ă … Queria …

a one-way ticket	*oong bee-lye-t' d'* *ee-dă/sing-pl'sh*	um bilhete de ida/ simples
a return ticket	*oong bee-lye-t' d'* *ee-dă ee vohl-tă*	um bilhete de ida e volta
two tickets	*doysh bee-lye-t'sh*	dois bilhetes
tickets for all of us	*bee-lye-t'sh pă-ră* *to-dush nohsh*	bilhetes para todos nós
a student's fare	*bee-lye-t' d'* *shtu-dā-t'*	bilhete de estudante
1st class	*pree-mey-ră klah-s'*	primeira classe
2nd class	*s'-gŭ-dă klah-s'*	segunda classe

Bus

BUS STOP	PARAGEM DE AUTOCARRO
TRAM STOP	PARAGEM DE ELÉCTRICO

Where is the bus/tram stop?
*õ-dy **eh** ă pă-**rah**-gēy du ow-toh-**kah**-rru/du ee-**leh**-tree-ku?*

Onde é a paragem do autocarro/do eléctrico?

Which bus goes to …?
***kwah-leh** u ow-toh-**kah**-rru pă-**ră** …?*

Qual é o autocarro para …?

Does this bus go to …?
***esh**-tow-toh-**kah**-rru **vay** pă-**ră** …?*

Este autocarro vai para …?

How often do buses pass by?
*u ow-toh-**kah**-rru pah-**să** kõ fr'-**kwē**-see-ă?*

O autocarro passa com frequência?

Could you let me know when we get to …?
*poh-d'-ma-vee-**zahr** kwă-du sh'-**gahr**-mush ă …?*

Pode-me avisar quando chegarmos a …?

I want to get off!
***keh**-ru d'sh-**ser**!*

Quero descer!

What time is the … bus?
*ă ky oh-**ră** **eh** u … ow-toh-**kah**-rru?*

A que hora é o … autocarro?

next	*proh-see-mu*	próximo
first	*pree-mey-ru*	primeiro
last	*ool-tee-mu*	último

Train

DINING CAR	VAGÃO-RESTAURANTE
EXPRESS	EXPRESSO
PLATFORM NO	PLATAFORMA No.
SLEEPING CAR	VAGÃO-CAMA

Is this the right platform
for …?
  eh dehsh-tă plah-tă-fohr-mă k' say u kŏ-boy-u pă-ra …?
    É desta plataforma que sai o combóio para …?

The train leaves from
platform …
  u kŏ-boy-u say/pahr-t' dă plah-tă-fohr-mă nu-m'ru …
    O combóio sai/parte da plataforma número …

Passengers must …
  ush pă-să-zhey-rush deh-vēy …
    Os passageiros devem …

| change trains | *mu-dahr d' kŏ-boy-u* | mudar de combóio |
| change platforms | *mu-dahr d' plah-tă-fohr-mă* | mudar de plataforma |

The train is delayed/cancelled.
  u kŏ-boy-u shtah ă-tră-zah-du/foy ă-nu-lah-du
    O combóio está atrasado/foi anulado.

PORTUGUESE

How long will it be delayed?

u ă-trah-zu eh d' kwā-tu tē-pu? — O atraso é de quanto tempo?

There is a delay of … hours.

u ă-trah-zu eh d' … oh-rash — O atraso é de … horas.

dining car	*vah-gõw rr'sh-tow-rã-t'*	vagão-restaurante
express	*shpreh-su*	expresso
local	*lu-kahl/rr'-zhee-u-nahl*	local/regional
sleeping car	*vah-gõw kă-mă*	vagão-cama

Metro

METRO/UNDERGROUND	METROPOLITANO

Which line takes me to …?

kwah-leh ă lee-nyă pă-ră …? — Qual é a linha para …?

What is the next station?

kwah-leh ă proh-see-mă shtă-sõw? — Qual é próxima estação?

Taxi

Please take me to …

leh-v'-m'ă …, s'fahsh fă-vor — Leve-me a …, se faz favor.

How much does it cost to go to …?

kwā-tu kush-tă eer ă …? — Quanto custa ir a …?

Instructions

Here is fine, thank you.
ă-kee shtah bĕy, o-bree-gah-du/-ă
Aqui está bem, obrigado/a.

The next corner, please.
nă proh-see-mă shkee-nă, s' fahsh fă-vor
Na próxima esquina, se faz favor.

Continue!
vah ă-dă-du!/see-gă!
Vá andando!/Siga!

The next street to the left/right.
ă proh-see-mă rru-ă ah shker-dă/ah dee-rey-tă
A próxima rua à esquerda/ à direita.

Stop here!
pah-r' a-kee!
Pare aqui!

Car

DETOUR	DESVIO
GARAGE	GARAGEM
GIVE WAY	DAR PRIORIDADE
MECHANIC	MECÂNICO
NO ENTRY	PROIBIDA A ENTRADA
NO PARKING	PROIBIDO ESTACIONAR
NORMAL	NORMAL
ONE WAY	SENTIDO ÚNICO
REPAIRS	CONSERTOS/ REPARAÇÕES
SELF SERVICE	AUTO-SERVIÇO
STOP	STOP
SUPER	SUPER
UNLEADED	SEM CHUMBO

I'd like to hire a car.
k'-ree-ă ă-lu-gahr oong kah-rru | Queria alugar um carro.

daily/weekly
pur dee-ă/pur s'-mă-nă | por dia/por semana

Where's the next petrol station?
ő-dy eh ă proh-see-mă shtă-sőw d's'r-vee-su? | Onde é a próxima estação de serviço?

Please fill the tank.
ē-shă u d'-poh-see-tu, s'fahsh fă-vor | Encha o depósito, se faz favor.

I want … litres of petrol (gas).
keh-ru … lee-trush d'gă-zu-lee-nă | Quero … litros de gasolina.

Please check the oil and water.
v'-ree-fee-ku oh-lee-u ee ă ah-gwă, s'fahsh fă-vor | Verifique o óleo e a água, se faz favor.

air (for tyres)	*ahr (pă-ră p-ne-wsh)*	ar (para pneus)
battery	*bă-t'-ree-ă*	bateria
brakes	*tră-vőysh*	travões
clutch	*ē-bray-ah-zhĕy*	embraiagem
driver's licence	*kahr-tă d' kő-du-sőw*	carta de condução
engine	*mu-tor*	motor
lights	*fă-roysh*	faróis
oil	*oh-lee-u*	óleo
puncture	*oong fu-ru*	um furo
radiator	*rră-dee-ă-dor*	radiador
road map	*mah-pă dăz'-sh-trah-dăsh*	mapa das estradas

PORTUGUESE

| tyres | *p-ne-wsh* | pneus |
| windscreen | ***pah-ră bree-***zăsh | pára-brisas |

Car Problems

The battery is flat.
   ă bă-t'-ree-ă shtah   A bateria está descarregada.
   d'sh-kă-rr'-gah-dă

The radiator is leaking.
   u rră-dee-ă-dor shtah ă   O radiador está a perder
   p'r-der ah-gwă   água.

I have a flat tyre.
   te-nyu oong p'ne-w   Tenho um pneu furado.
   fu-rah-du

It's overheating.
   shtah ah-keh-ser d'-maysh   Está a aquecer demais.

It's not working.
   nŏw fŭ-see-o-nă   Não funciona.

Accommodation

CAMPING GROUND	PARQUE DE CAMPISMO
GUESTHOUSE	PENSÃO
YOUTH HOSTEL	ALBERGUE DE JUVENTUDE

I am looking for ...
   ă-du ah pro-ku-ră d'...   Ando à procura de ...
Where is a ... hotel?
   ŏ-dy ah oong oh-tehl ...?   Onde há um hotel ...?

cheap	*bă-rah-tu*	barato
nearby	*pehr-tu*	perto
clean	*ling-pu*	limpo

What is the address?
   kwah-leh ă mu-rah-dă/
   dee-reh-sõw   Qual é a morada/direcção?
Could you write the address,
please?
   pu-dee-ă shkr'-ver ă
   mu-rah-dă/dee-reh-sõw?   Podia escrever a
                             morada/direcção?

At the Hotel
Do you have any rooms
available?
   tẽy kwahr-tush lee-vr'sh?   Tem quartos livres?

I would like …		
k'-ree-ă …		Queria …
a single room	*oong kwahr-tu ing-dee-vee-du-ahl*	um quarto indivi-dual
a double room	*oong kwahr-tu du-plu/ oong kwahr-tu d' kă-zahl*	um quarto duplo/ um quarto dè casal
a room with a bathroom	*oong kwahr-tu kõ kah-ză d' bă-nyu*	um quarto com casa de banho
to share a dorm	*fee-kahr noong dur-mee-toh-ree-u*	ficar num dormitório
a bed	*u-mă kă-mă*	uma cama

I'm going to stay for …
vo fee-kahr …

	Vou ficar …	
one day	*oong dee-ă*	um dia
two days	*doysh dee-ăsh*	dois dias
one week	*u-mă s'mă-nă*	uma semana

Do you have identification?
*têy ahl-**goong** du-ku-mē-tu
dee-dē-tee-**dah**-d'?*

Tem algum documento de
identidade?

Sorry, we're full.
*d'sh-**kul**-p', shtă-mush
shey-ush*

Desculpe, estamos cheios.

How long will you be staying?
*kwă-tu tê-pu vay fee-**kahr**?*

Quanto tempo vai ficar?

How many nights?
kwă-tăsh noy-t'sh?

Quantas noites?

It's … per day/per person.
*sôw … pur dee-ă/pur
p'-so-ă*

São … por dia/por pessoa.

How much is it per night/per
person?
*kwă-tu eh pur noy-t'/pur
p'-so-ă?*

Quanto é por noite/por
pessoa?

Can I see it?
poh-su ver?

Posso ver?

Are there any others?
ah o-trush kwahr-tush?

Há outros quartos?

Are there any cheaper rooms?
*ah kwahr-tush mayzh
bă-**rah**-tush?*

Há quartos mais baratos?

PORTUGUESE

Can I see the bathroom?
poh-su ver ă kah-ză d'bă-nyu?

Posso ver a casa de banho?

Is there a reduction for students/children?
ah d'sh-kŏ-tu pă-ră shtu-dā-t'sh/kree-ā-săsh?

Há desconto para estudantes/crianças?

Does it include breakfast?
u p'ke-nu ahl-mo-su shtah ing-klu-ee-du?

O pequeno almoço está incluído?

It's fine, I'll take it.
shtah bĕy fee-ku kŏ e-l'

Está bem, fico com ele.

I'm not sure how long I'm staying.
nŏw te-nyu ă s'r-te-ză d' kwă-tu tĕ-pu vo fee-kahr

Não tenho a certeza de quanto tempo vou ficar.

Where is the bathroom?
ŏ-dy eh ă kah-ză d' bă-nyu?

Onde é a casa de banho?

Is there hot water all day?
ah ah-gwă kĕ-t' du-rā-t' to-du u dee-ă?

Há água quente durante todo o dia?

Do you have a safe where I can leave my valuables?
tĕy oong koh-fr'ŏ-d' poh-să dey-shahr koy-săsh d'vă-lor?

Tem um cofre onde possa deixar coisas de valor?

Is there somewhere to wash clothes?
ah ŏ-d' lă-vahr rro-pă?

Há onde lavar roupa?

Can I use the kitchen?
   poh-su u-zahr ă *ku-zee-nyă?*   Posso usar a cozinha?

Can I use the telephone?
   poh-su t'l'fu-nahr?   Posso telefonar?

Some Useful Phrases

I am/We are leaving (now).
   vo-m'/vă-mu-nush ě-boh-ră   Vou-me/Vamo-nos embora.

I would like to pay the bill.
   k'-ree-ă pă-gahr ă *kõ-tă*   Queria pagar a conta.

Some Useful Words

bathroom	*kah-ză d' bă-nyu*	casa de banho
bed	*kă-mă*	cama
bill	*kõ-tă*	conta
blanket	*ku-b'r-tor*	cobertor
candle	*veh-lă*	vela
clean	*ling-pu*	limpo
dirty	*su-zhu*	sujo
double bed	*kă-mă d' kă-zahl*	cama de casal
electricity	*ee-leh-tree-cee-dah-d'*	electricidade
excluded	*nõw (shtah) ing-klu-ee-du*	não (está) incluído
fan	*vě-tu-ee-nyă*	ventoinha
included	*ing-klu-ee-du*	incluído
key	*shah-v'*	chave
lift (elevator)	*ee-l'vă-dor*	elevador
light bulb	*lã-pă-dă*	lâmpada

lock (n)	*f'shă-du-ră*	fechadura
mirror	*shpe-lyu*	espelho
pillow	*ahl-mu-fah-dă*	almofada
quiet	*su-s'-gah-du*	sossegado
sheet	*lē-sohl*	lençol
shower	*shu-vey-ru/du-sh'*	chuveiro/duche
soap	*să-bu-ne-t'*	sabonete
toilet	*rr'-treh-t'*	retrete
toilet paper	*pă-pehl ee-zhee-eh-nee-ku*	papel higiénico
towel	*tu-ah-lyă*	toalha
water	*ah-gwă*	água
cold water	*ah-gwă free-ă*	água fria
hot water	*ah-gwă kĕ-t'*	água quente
window	*zhă-neh-lă*	janela

Around Town

I'm looking for …

ã-du ah pro-ku-ră …	Ando à procura …
a bank	*doong bā-ku*	dum banco
the city centre	*du cĕ-tru dă see-dah-d'/dă bay-shă*	do centro da cidade/da baixa
the … embassy	*dă ē-bay-shah-dă d' …*	da embaixada de …
my hotel	*du me-w oh-tehl*	do meu hotel
the market	*du m'r-kah-du/dă prah-să*	do mercado/da praça
the police	*dă pu-lee-see-ă*	da polícia
the post office	*dush ku-rrey-ush*	dos correios
a public toilet	*du-mă kah-ză d' bă-nyu pu-blee-kă*	duma casa de banho pública

| the telephone centre | *dă sē-**trahl** d' t'l'-**foh**-n'sh* | da central de telefones |
| the tourist information office | *du tu-**reesh**-mu/du s'r-**vee**-su ding-fur-mă-**sõysh** pă-ră tu-**reesh**-tăsh* | do turismo/do serviço de informações para turistas |

What time does it open?
   *ă ky **oh**-răsh **ah**-br'?*   A que horas abre?
What time does it close?
   *ă ky **oh**-răsh **fey**-shă?*   A que horas fecha?
What street is this?
   *k'-**rru**-ă eh **ehsh**-tă?*   Que rua é esta?
What suburb is this?
   *k'-**bay**-rru eh **esh**-t'?*   Que bairro é este?

For directions, see the Getting Around section, page 269.

At the Bank

I want to exchange some
money/traveller's cheques.
   *k'-**ree**-ă tru-**kahr** dee-**nyey**-ru/*   Queria trocar dinheiro/uns
   *oongsh **sheh**-k'sh d' vee-ah-*   cheques de viagem.
   gёy
What is the exchange rate?
   ***kwah**-leh ă **tah**-shă d'*   Qual é a taxa de câmbio?
   *kã-**bee**-u?*
How many escudos per dollar?
   *kwã-tuz' **shku**-dush vah-l'*   Quantos escudos vale um
   *oong **doh**-lar?*   dólar?

banknotes	***noh**-tăsh d' **bā**-ku*	notas de banco
cashier	***kay**-shă*	caixa
coins	*mu-**eh**-dăsh*	moedas
credit card	*kăr-**tōw** d' **kreh**-dee-tu*	cartão de crédito
exchange	***kā**-bee-u*	câmbio
loose change	***troh**-kush*	trocos
signature	*ă-see-nă-**tu**-ră*	assinatura

At the Post Office

I would like to send …
*k'-**ree**-ă mā-**dahr** …* — Queria mandar …

a letter	*u-mă **kahr**-tă*	uma carta
a postcard	*oong push-**tahl***	um postal
a parcel	*u-mă ĕ-ku-**mē**-dă*	uma encomenda
a telegram	*oong t'l'-**gră**-mă*	um telegrama

I would like some stamps.
*k'-**ree**-ă se-lush* — Queria selos.

How much is the postage?
*kwā-tu eh ă frā-**kee**-ă?* — Quanto é a franquia?

How much does it cost to send this to …?
*kwā-tu kush-tă mā-**dahr** eesh-tu pă-ră …?* — Quanto custa mandar isto para …?

an aerogram	*oong ă-eh-roh-**gră**-mă*	um aerograma
air mail	*ku-**rrey**-u ă-**eh**-ree-u*	correio aéreo
envelope	*ē-v'**loh**-p'*	envelope
mailbox	***kay**-shă du ku-**rrey**-u*	caixa do correio

parcel	*ē-ku-mē-dǎ*	encomenda
registered mail	*rr'geesh-tah-du*	registado
surface mail	*vee-ǎ su-p'r-fee-cee*	via superfície

Telephone

I want to ring …
k'-ree-ǎ t'l'-fu-nahr pǎ-rǎ …

Queria telefonar para …

The number is …
u nu-m'ru eh …

O número é …

I want to speak for three minutes.
keh-ru fǎ-lahr du-rã-t' tresh mee-nu-tush

Quero falar durante três minutos.

How much does a three-minute call cost?
kwã-tu kush-tǎ oong t'l'-fu-ne-mǎ d' tresh mee-nu-tush?

Quanto custa um telefonema de três minutos?

How much does each extra minute cost?
kwã-tu kush-tǎ kǎ-dǎ mee-nu-tu ǎ maysh?

Quanto custa cada minuto a mais?

I would like to speak to Mr Perez.
k'-ree-ǎ fǎ-lahr kõ u s'nyor peh-r'sh

Queria falar com o Senhor Peres.

It's engaged.
shtah ing-p'-dee-du/shtah ǎ fǎ-lahr

Está impedido./Está a falar.

I've been cut off.
d'sh-lee-go-s'   Desligou-se.

I want to make a reverse-
charges phone call.
keh-ru fă-zer oong t'l'-fu-   Quero fazer um telefonema
ne-mă pă-ră pă-gahr lah/u-   para pagar lá/uma chamada
mă shă -mah-dă pah-gă   paga no destino.
nu d'sh-tee-nu

Sightseeing

Do you have a guidebook/
local map?
tĕy oong gee-ă/oong   Tem um guia/um mapa do
mah-pă du see-tee-u?   sítio?

What are the main attractions?
kwaysh sŏw ăz ă-trah-   Quais são as atracções
sŏysh pring-see-paysh?   principais?

What is that?
ky eh ă-kee-lu?   Que é aquilo?

How old is it?
eh ă-tee-gu? d'kwă-du eh?   É antigo?/De quando é?

Can I take photographs?
poh-su tee-rahr fu-tu-gră-   Posso tirar fotografias?
fee-ăsh?

What time does it open/close?
ă ky oh-r˜ashah-br'/fey-shă?   A que horas abre/fecha?

the university library   a biblioteca da universidade
St Francis church   a igreja de São Francisco
the Alcobaça monastery   o mosteiro de Alcobaça
the monastery of Batalha   o mosteiro da Batalha

the monastery of Jerónimos — o mosteiro dos Jerónimos
the Gulbenkian museum — o museu Gulbenkian
the Sé Cathedral — a Sé Catedral
the Tower of Belém — a Torre de Belém
the zoo — o Jardim Zoológico

In the Country
Weather

What's the weather like?
*ko-mu **shtah** u tē-pu?* — Como está o tempo?

The weather is … today.
*u tē-pu **shtah** … o-zh'* — O tempo está … hoje.
Will it be … tomorrow?
*ah-mǎ-**nyā** shtǎ-**rah** …?* — Amanhã estará …?

cloudy	*nu-**blah**-du*	nublado
cold	***free**-u*	frio
hot	*kǎ-**lor***	calor
raining	*ǎ shu-**ver***	a chover
snowing	*ǎ n'**vahr***	a nevar
sunny	***sohl***	sol
windy	*vē̃-tu*	vento

Camping

Am I allowed to camp here?
***poh**-su ǎ-kǎ-**pahr** ǎ-**kee**?* — Posso acampar aqui?
Is there a campsite nearby?
*ah oong **pahrk**' d' — Há um parque de campismo
kǎ-**peesh**-mu ǎ-**kee pehr**-tu?* — aqui perto?

backpack	*mu-**shee**-lǎ*	mochila
can opener	*ah-br' **lah**-tǎsh*	abre-latas

compass	*bu*-su-lǎ	bússola
firewood	*le*-nyǎ	lenha
gas cartridge	*bu-tee*-zhǎ d'*gahsh*	botija de gás
mattress	*kol-shōw*	colchão
penknife	*kǎ-nee-veh-t'*	canivete
rope	*kohr-*dǎ	corda
tent	*tē-*dǎ	tenda
tent pegs	*shtah-*kǎsh	estacas
torch (flashlight)	*lǎ-tehr-*nǎ	lanterna
sleeping bag	*sah-*ku kǎ-mǎ	saco-cama
stove	*fu-gōw/fu-ga-rey-*ru	fogão/fogareiro
water bottle	*gǎ-rrah-*fǎ *dah-*gwǎ	garrafa de água

Food

breakfast	*p'ke-*nu ahl-*mo-*su	pequeno almoço
lunch	ahl-*mo-*su	almoço
afternoon tea	*lǎ-sh'*	lanche
dinner	*jǎ-tahr*	jantar

Table for ..., please.
  *u-*mǎ *me-*zǎ pǎ-rǎ ...,
  s'fahsh fǎ-*vor*

Uma mesa para ..., se faz favor.

Can I see the menu please?
  *k'-ree-*ǎ *ver* ǎ *leesh-*tǎ

Queria ver a lista.

I'd like the set lunch, please.
  *k'-ree-*a u ahl-*mo-*su dǎ
  kah-zǎ/u ahl-*mo-*su ǎ *pre-*su fee-*ksu, s'fahsh* fǎ-*vor*

Queria o almoço da casa/o almoço a preço fixo, se faz favor.

What does it include?
  ing-*kluy* u *ke?*

Inclui o quê?

Is service included in the bill?

u s'r-vee-su shtah ing-klu-ee-du nă kõ-tă?

O serviço está incluído na conta?

Not too spicy please.

po-ku pee-kă-t', s'fahsh fă-vor

Pouco picante, se faz favor.

ashtray	*sing-zey-ru*	cinzeiro
the bill	*ă kõ-tă*	a conta
a cup	*u-mă shah-v'nă*	uma chávena
a drink	*u-mă b'-bee-dă*	uma bebida
a fork	*oong gahr-fu*	um garfo
a glass	*oong koh-pu*	um copo
a knife	*u-mă fah-kă*	uma faca
a plate	*oong prah-tu*	um prato
a spoon	*u-mă ku-lyehr*	uma colher

Vegetarian Meals

I am a vegetarian.

so v'zh'-tă-ree-ă-nu/-nă

Sou vegetariano/a.

I don't eat meat.

nõw ko-mu kahr-n'

Não como carne.

Soups & Staples

Arroz

Rice. Typical Portuguese dishes made with rice are *arroz de cabidela* (with duck or chicken) and *arroz de pato* (with duck and several local spicy sausages). *Arroz de polvo* (octopus) is characteristic of the Algarve. *Arroz de marisco* (shellfish) can be found all along the coast.

Caldo verde
  Potato and green cabbage soup with spicy sausage *(chouriço)*.
Canja de galinha
  Chicken broth.
Caril
  Curry – relatively common in Portuguese restaurants because of contact with Indian cuisine in Portugal's former colonies. Most common are *caril de camarão* (seafood curry) and *caril de galinha* (chicken curry). Often more spicy than hot.
Creme de camarão
  Shrimp soup.
Sopa de legumes
  Mixed vegetable soup.
Sopa de tomate com ovo
  Fresh tomato soup, served with a whole poached egg, or with an egg stirred into it at the end.

Meat

Bifes de cebolada
  Beef slices stewed with onions, garlic, tomatoes and parsley.
Bife com ovo a cavalo/Bitoque
  Portuguese steaks are usually thinly cut and well done. These are fried and served with a fried egg and chips. If you want a thick steak, you must ask for *um bife alto*.
Cabrito assado
  Kid is widely eaten in Portugal, usually roasted in wine with garlic and laurel.
Carne de porco com amêijoas
  Pork casserole with clams and fresh coriander.
Coelho à caçadora
  Rabbit casserole in red wine and tomato sauce.

Cozido à portuguesa
A stew of beef, pork and chicken meats, spicy sausages (*chouriço, linguiça, farinheira, morcelas,* etc) and vegetables (potatoes, turnips, carrots, cabbages).

Croquetes
Fried patties made from minced roast beef and *chouriço* sausage with bechamel sauce.

Ervilhas com ovos
A stew of fresh peas, spicy sausages and fresh herbs, with poached eggs.

Favada
Similar to the above, but made with broad beans instead of peas. No eggs added.

Febras de porco
Grilled, thinly cut pork steaks.

Frango
Chicken. *Frango assado* (roast chicken) is available everywhere. More exotic are *frango na púcara*, where the chicken portions are cooked in an earthenware pot with tomato, onion, Port wine and sultanas; and *frango de churrasco*, spiced charcoal-grilled chicken.

Iscas à portuguesa
Beef liver steaks cooked with onion slices.

Leitão da Bairrada
Suckling pig, roasted in wall ovens.

Lombo de porco assado
Pork loin roasted in white wine. In the Alentejo province it is often served with clams (*amêijoas*), elsewhere with a variety of sauces.

Rojões
    Marinated, then fried, pork cubes, served together with fried
    pieces of pork liver and tripe.
Sarrabulho
    Lean pork cubes, pieces of pork liver and tripe cooked in the
    pig's previously cooked blood.
Torresmos
    Fatty pork cubes, fried in pig's fat, then braised in white wine.
    Served with potatoes fried in the pig's fat.
Vitela assada
    Roast veal.

Seafood

Açorda de mariscos
    A main course that resembles a very thick soup, made with
    shellfish (or sometimes fish) and soaked bread and eggs.
Bacalhau
    Codfish, the dried, salted, non-smoked variety, that must be
    soaked before cooking. It is the traditional Portuguese dish
    for Christmas Eve, served with boiled potatoes and chick-
    peas: *bacalhau com grão* or *bacalhau da consoada*. It is often
    served in *bolinhos* or *pastéis de bacalhau*, small fried potato,
    codfish and parsley patties. It can be prepared in hundreds of
    other ways. Best known are:
Bacalhau assado
    Charcoal-grilled.
Bacalhau à Brás
    With finely-cut potato chips (French fries), scrambled eggs
    and olives.
Bacalhau no forno
    Cooked in the oven, either with cream or tomatoes.

Bacalhau à Gomes de Sá
 With slices of boiled potato and egg.
Bacalhau à Zé do Pipo
 With mayonnaise and potato purée.
Caldeirada
 A fish stew, with several different types of fish and sometimes
 also shellfish, cooked with olive oil, wine, tomatoes and
 onions.
Filetes de pescada/de tamboril
 Lightly battered, fried fillets of fish. *Pescada* and *tamboril*
 make good, large fish fillets, usually bone-free.
Rissóis
 Rissoles of shellfish (*rissóis de camarão*) or fish (*rissóis de
 peixe*).
Sardinhas assadas
 Fresh sardines, traditionally charcoal-grilled in the open air.
 Served with charcoal-grilled green peppers and boiled
 potatoes.

Vegetables

artichoke	*ahl-kǎ-**shoh**-frǎ*	alcachofra
asparagus	***shpahr**-gush*	espargos
beetroot	*b'-t'-**rrah**-bǎ*	beterraba
broad beans	***fah**-vǎsh*	favas
broccoli	***broh**-ku-lush*	brócolos
Brussel sprouts	*ko-v'sh d' bru-**sheh**-lǎsh*	couves de Bruxelas
cabbage	*ko-v'*	couve
capsicum	*pee-**mẽ**-tu*	pimento
carrot	*s'-**no**-rǎ*	cenoura
cauliflower	*ko-v' flor*	couve-flor

celery	*ah-pee-u*	ápio
chick peas	*grõw*	grão
cucumber	*p'-pee-nu*	pepino
eggplant	*b'-ring-zheh-lă*	beringela
garlic	*ah-lyu*	alho
green beans	*fey-zhõw ver-d'*	feijão verde
green peas	*er-vee-lyăsh*	ervilhas
leeks	*ah-lyu po-rru/frā-sesh*	alho porro/francês
lentils	*lē-tee-lyăsh*	lentilhas
lettuce	*ahl-fah-s'*	alface
mushroom	*ku-gu-meh-lu*	cogumelo
onion	*s'-bo-lă*	cebola
parsley	*sahl-să*	salsa
potato	*bă-tah-tă*	batata
pumpkin	*ă-boh-bu-ră*	abóbora
radish	*rră-bă-ne-t'*	rabanete
spinach (often listed as *esparre-gado*, a spinach purée)	*sh-pee-nah-fr'sh*	espinafres
sweet potato	*bă-tah-tă do-s'*	batata doce
tomato	*tu-mah-t'*	tomate
turnip	*nah-bu*	nabo
zucchini	*kur-zheh-t'*	courgette

Fruit

apple	*mă-să*	maçã
apricot	*ahl-pehr-s'/dă-mahsh-ku*	alperce/damasco
banana	*bă-nă-nă*	banana

canteloupe	*m'-lo-ă*	meloa
cherry	*s'-rey-zhă*	cereja
currants	*gro-ze-lyă*	groselha
date	*tă-mă-ră*	tâmara
fig	*fee-gu*	figo
grapes	*u-văsh*	uvas
grapefruit	*tu-rõ-zha*	toronja
lemon	*lee-mõw*	limão
loquat	*nesh-p'-răsh*	nêsperas
mandarine	*tă-zh'-ree-nă*	tangerina
melon	*m'-lõw*	melão
mulberries	*ă-moh-răsh*	amoras
orange	*lă-rã-zhă*	laranja
pear	*pe-ră*	pera
plum	*ă-mey-shă*	ameixa
pineapple	*ă-nă-nahsh*	ananás
pomegranate	*rru-mã*	romã
raspberries	*frã-bu-e-săsh*	framboesas
strawberries	*mu-rã-gush*	morangos
watermelon	*m'-lă-see-ă*	melancia

Sweets & Desserts

Arroz-doce
  Cinnamon-flavoured rice pudding (cooked in milk).
Bolo de amêndoa
  Almond cake.
Bolo-rei
  A dry, light cake, with dry and crystalised fruits, especially made for Christmas.
Barriga-de-freira, Encharcada, Sericá
  These are different types of egg-yolk and sugar-syrup sweets.

PORTUGUESE

Farófias
  Egg-white sweet with milk-based sauce.
Leite-creme
  Milk-and-egg-yolk sweet with burnt-sugar crust.
Ovos-moles
  Egg-yolk-and-sugar sweet, traditionally served in small wooden barrels or in paper-like pastry.
Papos de anjo
  Small egg cakes in sugar syrup.
Pastéis de nata
  Small custard tarts in puff pastry.
Pudim flan
  Creme caramel.
Queijadas
  Cheese tartlets. Their texture and taste vary from region to region.
Rabanadas
  Sweet egg-yolk-and-bread slices, traditionally served with syrup at Christmas.
Torta de laranja
  Light, moist, almost flourless, orange 'Swiss' roll.
Toucinho do céu
  Moist almond and cinnamon cake.
Trouxas de ovos
  Small egg-yolk-and-sugar rolls, cooked and served in syrup.

Drinks – Nonalcoholic

coffee	*kă-feh*	café
small black	*bee-kă*	bica
long white (cup)	*kă-feh kō ley-t'*	café com leite
long white (glass)	*gă-lõw*	galão

fruit juice	*su-*mu d'*fru-*tă	sumo de fruta
mineral water	*ah-*gwă mee-n'-*rahl*	água mineral
sparkling	*kŏ* gahsh	com gás
still	*sē* gahsh	sem gás
soft drinks	rre-*fresh-*kush	refrescos
coffee-flavoured syrup and water	kă-pee-*leh*	capilé
tea	shah	chá
water	*ah-*gwă	água

Drinks – Alcoholic

beer	s'r-*vey-*zhă	cerveja
port	*vee-*nyu du *por-*tu	vinho do Porto
wine	*vee-*nyu	vinho
dry	*se-*ku	seco
sparkling	shpu-*mā-*t'	espumante
sweet	*do-*s'	doce

Shopping

How much does it cost?

| *kwă-*tu *kush-*tă? | | Quanto custa? |

general store, shop	m'r-see-ă-*ree-*ă/ shahr-ku-tă-*ree-*ă	mercearia/ charcutaria
laundry	lă-vă-dă-*ree-*ă	lavandaria
market	m'r-*kah-*du/*prah-*să	mercado/praça
newsagency/ stationers	pă-p'-lă-*ree-*ă/ tă-bă-kă-*ree-*ă	papelaria/tabacaria
pharmacy	făr-*mah-*see-ă	farmácia
supermarket	su-pehr-m'r-*kah-*du	supermercado
vegetable shop	lu-*gahr/*fru-tă-*ree-*ă	lugar/frutaria

I would like to buy …
k'-ree-ă kō-**prahr** …

Queria comprar …

Do you have others?
těy o-trush?

Tem outros?

I don't like it.
nõw gohsh-tu

Não gosto.

I'm just looking.
shto soh a **ver**

Estou só a ver.

Can you write down the price?
pu-dee-ă shkr-ver u pre-su?

Podia escrever o preço?

Do you accept credit cards?
ă-sey-tõw kăr-**tõysh**
d' **kreh**-dee-tu?

Aceitam cartões de crédito?

Can I help you?
zhah shtah ă-tě-dee-du/dă ?
d'-**zey**-zhă ahl-**gu**-mă
koy-ză?

Já está atendido/da?
Deseja alguma coisa?

Will that be all?
eh tu-du?
may-zahl-**gu**-mă **koy**-ză?

É tudo?
Mais alguma coisa?

How much/many do you want?
kwã-tu/**kwã**-tush k'-**ree**-ă?

Quanto/Quantos queria?

Souvenirs

cork souvenirs	ăr-**tee**-gush d' kur-**tee**-să	artigos de cortiça
earthenware	**lo**-să d' **bah**-rru	louça de barro
carpets and handwoven wall-hangings	tă-**pe**-t'sh dă-rray-**oh**-lush	tapetes de Arraiolos

embroidered napkins, hand-kerchiefs, etc. from Madeira	*bur-**dah**-dush dă mă-**dey**-ră*	bordados da Madeira
'fado' cassettes and records	*kah-**seh**-t'sh ee deesh-kush d' **fah**-du*	cassettes e discos de fado
filigree jewellery	*fee-lee-**gră**-nă*	filigrana
handpainted pottery	*lo-să dahl-ku-**bah**-să/d'sh-tr'-mosh*	louça de Alcobaça/de Estremoz, etc
lace	*rrĕ-dăsh*	rendas
leathergoods (jackets, wallets, belts)	*ăr-**tee**-gush d' kă-b'-**dahl** (blu-zōysh, kăr-**tey**-răsh, **sing**-tush)*	artigos de cabedal (blusões, car-teiras, cintos)
linen, napery	*ă-tu-ă-**lyah**-dush/tu-ah-lyăsh d' me-ză*	atoalhados/toalhas de mesa
painted porcelain roosters	*gah-lush d' băr-**seh**-lush*	galos de Barcelos
shoes and handbags	*să-**pah**-tush ee mah-lăsh*	sapatos e malas
tiles	*ă-zu-**ley**-zhush*	azulejos
windmills	*mu-ee-nyush d'vē-tu*	moinhos de vento

Clothing

clothing	*rro-pă*	roupa
coat (women's)	*kă-zah-ku kō-**pree**-du*	casaco comprido
coat (men's)	*su-br'-**tu**-du*	sobretudo
dress	*v'sh-**tee**-du*	vestido
jacket	*kă-**zah**-ku*	casaco
jumper (sweater)	*kă-mee-**zoh**-lă*	camisola
shirt	*kă-**mee**-ză*	camisa

shoes	să-**pah**-tush	sapatos
skirt	**say**-yă	saia
trousers	**kahl**-săsh	calças

It doesn't fit.
   *nŏw m' **sehr**-v'*   Não me serve.

It is too ...
   eh d'mă-zee-ah-du ...   É demasiado ...

big	**gră**-d'	grande
small	p'**ke**-nu	pequeno
short	**kur**-tu	curto
long	kŏ-**pree**-du	comprido
tight	ă-p'r-**tah**-du	apertado
loose	**lahr**-gu	largo

Materials

cotton	ahl-gu-**dŏw**	algodão
handmade	**fey**-tu ah mŏw	feito à mão
leather	kă-b'-**dahl**/**ko**-ru	cabedal/couro
silk	se-dă	seda
wool	lã	lã

Toiletries

comb	**pẽ**-t'	pente
conditioner	**kreh**-m' ă -mă -**see**-ă -**dor**	creme amaciador
condoms	pr'-z'r-vă-**tee**-vush	preservativos
deodorant	d'zo-du-ree-**zã**-t'	desodorizante
moisturing cream	**kreh**-m' ee-dră-**tã**-t'	desodorizante
razor	**mah**-kee-nă/**lã**-mee-nă d' bărbee-**ahr**	máquina/lâmina de barbear

sanitary napkins	*pē-sush ee-zhee-eh-nee-kush*	pensos higiénicos
shampoo	*shã-po*	shampô
shaving cream	*kreh-m'/shpu-mă d' băr-bee-ahr*	creme/espuma de barbear
soap	*să-bu-ne-t'*	sabonete
tampons	*tã-põysh*	tampões
tissues	*lē-sush d' pă-pehl*	lenços de papel
toilet paper	*pă-pehl ee-zhee-eh-nee-ku*	papel higiénico
toothbrush	*shko-vă d' dē-t'sh*	escova de dentes
toothpaste	*pahsh-tă d' dē-t'sh*	pasta de dentes

Stationery & Publications

map	*mah-pă*	mapa
newspaper	*zhur-nahl*	jornal
newspaper in English	*zhur-nahl ẽy ing-glesh*	jornal em Inglês
paper	*pă-pehl*	papel
pen (ballpoint)	*shfeh-roh-grah-fee-ka*	esferográfica

Photography

How much is it to process this film?
kwă-tu kush-tă rr'v'-lahr esh-t' rro-lu?
Quanto custa revelar este rolo?

When will it be ready?
kwā-du eh k' fee-kă prõ-tu?
Quando é que fica pronto?

I'd like a film for this camera.
k'-ree-ă oong rro-lu pă-ră ehsh-tă mah-kee-nă
Queria um rolo para esta máquina.

PORTUGUESE

B&W (film)	ă *pre-tu* ee *brã-ku*	a preto e branco
camera	*mah-kee-nă*	máquina
	fu-tu-grah-fee-kă	fotográfica
colour (film)	ă *ko-r'sh*	a cores
film	*rro-lu*	rolo
flash	*flahsh*	flash
lens	*lē-t'*	lente
light meter	*ing-dee-kă-dor* dă *lush*	indicador da luz

Smoking

A packet of cigarettes, please.

*oong **mah**-su d' see-**gah**-rrush, s'**fahsh** fă-**vor*** — Um maço de cigarros, se faz favor.

Do you have a light?

tēy lu-m'? — Tem lume?

Are these cigarettes strong/mild?

*esh-t'sh see-**gah**-rrush sõw fohr-t'sh/su-ah-v'sh* — Estes cigarros são fortes/suaves?

cigarette papers	pă-**pehl** dē-rru-**lahr** see-**gah**-rrush	papel de enrolar cigarros
cigarettes	see-**gah**-rrush	cigarros
filtered	kõ **feel**-tru	com filtro
lighter	eesh-**key**-ru	isqueiro
matches	**fohsh**-fu-rush	fósforos
menthol	d' mē-**tohl**	de mentol
tobacco	tă-**bah**-ku	tabaco

Colours

black	*pre-tu*	preto
blue	*ă-zool*	azul
brown	*kăsh-tă-nyu*	castanho
green	*ver-d'*	verde
red	*ě-kăr-nah-du/*	encarnado/
	v'r-me-lyu	vermelho
white	*brã-ku*	branco
yellow	*ă-mă-reh-lu*	amarelo

Sizes & Comparisons

small	*p'ke-nu*	pequeno
big	*grã-d'*	grande
heavy	*p'-zah-du*	pesado
light	*leh-v'*	leve
more	*maysh*	mais
less	*me-nush*	menos
too much/many	*d'-maysh/d'-mă-zee-ah-dush*	demais/demasiados

Health

Where is …?
  õ-deh ky ah …?   Onde é que há …?

a doctor	*oong meh-dee-ku*	um médico
a hospital	*oong osh-pee-tahl*	um hospital
a chemist	*u-mă făr-mah-see-ă*	uma farmácia
a dentist	*oong dě-teesh-tă*	um dentista

Could I see a female doctor?
  pr'-f'-ree-ă u-mă   Preferia uma médica.
  meh-dee-kă

What's the matter?
    d'k's'key-shă?   De que se queixa?
Where does it hurt?
    ŏ-deh k'ly'doy?   Onde é que lhe dói?
It hurts here.
    doy-m'ă-kee   Dói-me aqui.

Parts of the Body

arm	**brah-su**	braço
back	**kohsh-tăsh**	costas
chest	**pey-tu**	peito
ear	**o-re-lyă**	orelha
eye	**o-lyu**	olho
finger	**de-do**	dedo
foot	**peh**	pé
hand	**mŏw**	mão
head	**kă-be-să**	cabeça
heart	**ku-ră-sŏw**	coração
leg	**pehr-nă**	perna
mouth	**bo-kă**	boca
nose	**nă-reesh**	nariz
ribs	**kus-teh-lăsh**	costelas
skin	**peh-l'**	pele
spine	**shpee-nyă/ku-lu-nă**	espinha/coluna
stomach	**shto-mă-gu**	estômago
teeth	**dē-t'sh**	dentes
throat	**găr-gă-tă**	garganta

Ailments

I have ...
te-nyu ...   Tenho ...

an allergy	*u-mah-lehr-gee-ă*	uma alergia
a cold	*u-mă kŏsh-tee-pă-sŏw*	uma constipação
constipation	*pree-zŏw d' vĕ-tr'*	prisão de ventre
diarrhoea	*dee-ă-rrey-ă*	diarreia
fever	*feh-br'*	febre
a headache	*u-mă dor d' kă-be-să*	uma dor de cabeça
indigestion	*ing-dee-zh'sh-tŏw*	indigestão
influenza	*gree-p'*	gripe
low/high blood pressure	*ă tĕ-sŏw bay-shă/ ahl-tă*	a tensão baixa/alta
a pain	*u-mă dor*	uma dor
sore throat	*dor d' găr-gā-tă*	dor de garganta
sprain	*u-ma tur-sŏw mush-ku-lahr*	uma torsão muscular
a stomachache	*dor d'sh-to-mă-gu*	dor de estômago
sunburn	*u-mă key-mă-du-ră du sohl*	uma queimadura do sol
a toothache	*dor d' dĕ-t'sh*	dor de dentes
a venereal disease	*u-mă du-ĕ-să v'-neh-ree-ă*	uma doença venérea

Some Useful Words & Phrases

I'm ...
so ...   Sou ...

diabetic	*dee-ă-beh-tee-ku/ă*	diabético/a
epileptic	*e-pee-leh-tee-ku/ă*	epiléptico/a
asthmatic	*azh-mah-tee-ku/ă*	asmático/a

I'm allergic to …
   so ă-lehr-gee-ku/-ă   Sou alérgico/a a …
   ă …

antibiotics   *ă-tee-bee-oh-tee-kush*   antibióticos
penicillin   *ah peh-nee-see-lee-nă* à penicilina

I'm pregnant.
   shto grah-vee-dă   Estou grávida.
I'm on the pill.
   e-w toh-mu ă pee-lu-lă   Eu tomo a pílula.
I haven't had my period for
  … weeks.
   ah … s'-mă-năsh k'nõw m' Há … semanas que não me
   vẽy ă mẽsh-tru-ă-sõw   vem a menstruação.
I have been vaccinated.
   fuy vă-cee-nah-du/-a   Fui vacinado/a.
I have my own syringe.
   te-nyu ă mee-nyă proh-   Tenho a minha própria
   pree-ă s'-ring-gă   seringa.
I feel better/worse.
   sing-tu-m' m'-lyohr/pee-ohr Sinto-me melhor/pior.

accident	*ă-see-dē-t'*	acidente
addiction	*vee-see-u*	vício
antiseptic	*ă-tee-seh-tee-ku*	antisséptico
bandage	*lee-gă-du-ră*	ligadura
blood test	*ă-nah-lee-z'd'să-g'*	análise de sangue
contraceptive	*ă-tee-kõ-seh-see-u-nahl*	anticoncepcional
medicine	*rr'-meh-dee-u/ m'-dee-kă-mē-tu*	remédio/medica-mento
menstruation	*mẽsh-tru-ă-sõw*	menstruação

| nausea | **now**-zee-ă/**voh**-mee-tush | náusea/vómitos |
| vitamins | vee-tă-**mee**-năsh | vitaminas |

At the Chemist

I need medication for ...
   pr'-**see**-zu doong
   m'-dee-kă-**mē**-tu pă-ră ...

Preciso dum medicamento para ...

I have a prescription.
   te-nyu rr'-**sey**-tă
   meh-dee-kă

Tenho receita médica.

At the Dentist

I have a toothache.
   doy-m' oong **dē**-t'

Dói-me um dente.

I've lost a filling.
   kă-**eew**-m' oong **shoong**-bu

Caiu-me um chumbo.

I've broken a tooth.
   păr-**tee** oong **dē**-t'

Parti um dente.

My gums hurt.
   doh-ēy-măsh zhē-**zhee**-văsh

Dóem-me as gengivas.

I don't want it extracted.
   nõw keh-ru k' mu ă-**rrã**-k'

Não quero que mo arranque.

Please give me an anaesthetic.
   de-mă-n'sh-t'-**zee**-ă,
   s'**fahsh** fă-**vor**

Dê-me anestesia, se faz favor.

Time & Dates

What time is it?
   ky-**oh**-răsh sõw?

Que horas são?

What date is it today?
   k' **dee**-ă eh o-zh?

Que dia é hoje?

It is … am/pm.

sōw … oh-răsh dă   São … horas da manhã/da
mă-nyã/dă **tahr**-d'   tarde.

in the morning	d' ma-**nyã**	de manhã
in the afternoon	d' **tahr**-d'/ah **tahr**-d'	de tarde/à tarde
in the evening	ow **fing** dă **tahr**-d'/	ao fim da tarde/
	ah **noy**-t'	à noite

Days of the Week

Monday	s'-**goong**-dă fey-ră	Segunda-feira
Tuesday	ter-să fey-ră	Terça-feira
Wednesday	kwahr-tă fey-ră	Quarta-feira
Thursday	king-tă fey-ră	Quinta-feira
Friday	seysh-tă fey-ră	Sexta-feira
Saturday	sah-bă-du	Sábado
Sunday	du-**ming**-gu	Domingo

Months

January	zhă-**ney**-ru	Janeiro
February	f'-v'-**rey**-ru	Fevereiro
March	**mahr**-su	Março
April	ă-**breel**	Abril
May	**may**-u	Maio
June	zhu-nyu	Junho
July	zhu-lyu	Julho
August	ă-**gosh**-tu	Agosto
September	s'-**tē**-bru	Setembro
October	o-tu-bru	Outubro
November	nu-**vē**-bru	Novembro
December	d'-**zē**-bru	Dezembro

Seasons

summer	*v'-rõw*	verão
autumn	*o-to-nu*	outono
winter	*ing-vehr-nu*	inverno
spring	*pree-mă-veh-ră*	primavera

Present

today	*o-zh*	hoje
this morning	*o-zh d' mă-nyã*	hoje de manhã
tonight	*o-zh ah noy-t'*	hoje à noite
this week	*ehsh-tă s'-mă-nă*	esta semana
this year	*esh-ty ănu*	este ano
now	*ă-goh-ră*	agora

Past

yesterday	*õ-tẽy*	ontem
day before yesterday	*ã-tee-õ-tẽy*	anteontem
last night	*õ-tẽy ah noy-t'*	ontem à noite
(two) days ago	*ah (doysh) dee-ăsh*	há (dois) dias

Future

tomorrow	*ah-mă-nyã*	amanhã
day after tomorrow	*d'-poysh dah-mă-nyã*	depois de amanhã
in (two) days	*dẽ-tru d' (doysh) dee-ăsh*	dentro de (dois) dias
next week	*nă proh-see-mă s'-mă-nă*	na próxima semana

During the Day

afternoon	*tahr*-d'	tarde
day	*dee*-ă	dia
midnight	*mey*-ă *noy*-t'	meia-noite
morning	mă-*nyā*	manhã
night	*noy*-t'	noite
noon	*mey*-u *dee*-ă	meio-dia
sundown	*por* du *sohl*	pôr do sol
sunrise	nă-sh-*ser* du *sohl*/	nascer do sol/
	mă-dru-*gah*-dă	madrugada

Numbers & Amounts

0	*zeh*-ru	zero
1	*oong/u*-mă	um/uma
2	*doysh/du*-ăsh	dois/duas
3	tresh	três
4	*kwah*-tru	quatro
5	*sing*-ku	cinco
6	seysh	seis
7	*seh*-t'	sete
8	*oy*-tu	oito
9	*noh*-v'	nove
10	dehsh	dez
11	*õ*-z'	onze
12	*do*-z'	doze
13	*tre*-z'	treze
14	kă-*tor*-z'	catorze
15	*king*-z'	quinze
16	d'-ză-*seysh*	dezasseis
17	d'-ză-*seh*-t'	dezassete
18	d'-*zoy*-tu	dezoito
19	d'-ză-*noh*-v'	dezanove

20	*ving-t'*	vinte
100	*sẽy*	cem
1000	*meel*	mil
one million	*oong mee-lyõw d'*	um milhão de

Some Useful Words

a little (amount)	*oong po-ku/oong bu-kă-dee-nyu*	um pouco/um bocadinho
Enough!	*bahsh-tă! she-gă!*	Basta! Chega!
few	*po-kush/po-kăsh*	poucos/as
more	*maysh*	mais
some	*ahl-goongsh/ahl-gu-măsh*	alguns/algumas
too much	*d'-mă-zee-ah-du/ d'maysh*	demasiado/demais

Abbreviations

AD/a.C.	AD/BC
A/c	Care of (used in addresses)
AE (auto-estrada)	freeway
Av.	Avenue, Ave.
B.I. (Bilhete de Identidade)	ID (Identity card)
B.N.	National Library
B.T.	Traffic Police
CE	EC
C.M. (L.)	City Council (Lisbon, etc)
CP	Portuguese Trains
CTT	P.O.
D^o	right-hand side (used in flat addresses
Esq^o	left-hand side (used in flat addresses

EN	National Broadcaster
EUA	USA
FMI	IMF
GNR	National Republican Guard (police outside cities)
IVA	VAT
Lx.	Lisbon
M	Underground (Metro)
Nº	No.
ONU	UN
OTAN	NATO
PALOP	African countries with Portuguese as official language
Pr.	town square (used in adresses)
PSP	Police (cities)
R.	Street (used in addresses)
r/c	ground floor
RN/R/Rodoviária	Portuguese coach lines
RTP	Portuguese television
SIDA	AIDS
Sr./Sra. D.	Mr/Mrs
TAP	Portuguese airlines

Spanish (Castilian)

Spanish

Introduction

Spanish, or Castilian, as it is often and more precisely called, is the most widely spoken of the Romance languages. Outside Spain, it is the language of all of South America, except Brazil and the Guianas; of Mexico, Central America, and most of the West Indies; and, to some extent, of the Philippines and Guam, as well as of some areas of the African coast. In Spain itself, three Romance languages are spoken: Castilian, the main one, in the north, centre and south; Catalan, in the east and south-east; and Galician (a dialect of Portuguese), in the north-west. There is another language, of obscure, non-Latin origin: Basque, spoken in the north-east. Castilian, or Spanish, covers by far the largest territory. Within Spanish there are yet three dialectal divisions (Castilian-Andalusian, Leonese-Asturian, and Navarro-Aragonese), but these involve mainly differences in pronunciation and need not be considered separately here. The other main Romance language in the Peninsula is, of course, Portuguese.

Spanish is the neo-Latin language derived from the Vulgar Latin which Roman soldiers and merchants brought to the Iberian Peninsula during the period of the Roman conquest (3rd to 1st century BC). By 19 BC Spain had become totally Roman, and popular Latin became the language of the Peninsula in the four centuries of Romanisation which followed. Latin completely obliterated the languages of the Celtic and Iberian indigenous tribes.

In 711 AD an African Berber army invaded the Peninsula.

Soon many more Arabs came from the African Maghreb, and it was not until the 9th century that the reconquest of Spain began, led by the Christians who had taken refuge in the mountains of the north. As the reconquest advanced southwards, the Latin spoken by those Christians was progressively brought back to central and, eventually, southern Spain. Although the Arabs were not completely driven from the south for centuries yet, and although many people spoke Arabic as well as Vulgar Latin during that period, the influence of the Arabic language on Spanish is limited to vocabulary innovations.

With Columbus's discovery of the New World in 1492 began an era of Spanish expansion in America, which is reflected in the language. *Patata, tomate, cacao* and *chocolate* are a few examples of accretions from the American Indian languages. But fundamentally Spanish lexicon, syntax, phonology and morphology has always remained neo-Latin.

Spanish literature begins in the 12th century with the famous epic poem *Cantar de mío Cid*. Cervantes's 17th century *Don Quijote* is universally known. Nowadays Spain has an equally thriving literature, some of which is available in English translation – although not as much as that of the celebrated Latin American boom. Novelists such as Ana María Matute, Carmen Martín Gaite, Juan Goytisolo, Miguel Delibes and the 1989 Nobel Prize winner, José Camilo Cela, have had some of their works translated into English, and these will give visitors a valuable insight into contemporary Spanish society.

Pronunciation

Pronunciation of Spanish is not difficult, given that many Spanish sounds are similar to their English counterparts, and there is a clear and consistent relationship between pronunciation and spelling. If you stick to the following rules you should have very few problems being understood.

Vowels

Unlike English, each of the vowels in Spanish has a uniform pronunciation which does not vary. For example, the Spanish 'a' has one pronunciation rather than the numerous pronunciations we find in English, such as the 'a's in 'cake', 'art' and 'all'. Vowels are pronounced clearly even in unstressed positions or at the end of a word.

a	as the 'u' in 'nut', or a shorter sound than the 'a' in 'art'; represented in our pronunciation guide by *ah*
e	as the 'e' in 'met'
i	similar to the 'i' sound in 'marine' but not so drawn out or strong; between that sound and that of the 'i' in 'flip'
o	similar to the 'o' in 'hot'
u	as the 'oo' in 'fool'

Consonants

Some Spanish consonants are the same as their English counterparts. Pronunciation of other consonants varies according to which vowel follows, and also according to what part of Spain you're in. The Spanish alphabet also contains three consonants which are not found in the English alphabet: **ch**, **ll** and **ñ**.

b	when initial, or preceded by a nasal, as the 'b' in 'book'; elsewhere, and most often in Spanish, a much softer **b** than the English one

c	a hard 'c' as in 'cat' when followed by **a, o, u** or a consonant; as the 'th' in 'thin' before **e** or **i**
ch	as the 'ch' in 'choose'
d	in an initial position, as the 'd' in 'dog'; elsewhere as the 'th' in 'then', represented here by *TH*
g	in an initial position, as the 'g' in 'gate' before **a, o** and **u**; everywhere else, the Spanish **g** is much softer than the English one. Before **e** or **i** it is a harsh, breathy sound, similar to the 'h' in 'hit'.
h	never pronounced, silent
j	a harsh, guttural sound similar to the 'ch' in the Scottish 'loch', represented here by *h*.
ll	as the 'lli' in 'million'; some people pronounce it rather like the 'y' in 'yellow'; represented here by *ly*
ñ	this is a nasal sound like the 'ni' in 'onion', represented here by *ny*
q	as the 'k' in 'kick'; **q** is always followed by a silent **u** and is only combined with **e** as in *que* and **i** as in *qui*
r	a rolled 'r' sound; a longer and stronger sound when it is a double **rr** or when a word begins with **r**
s	as the 's' in 'send'
v	the same sound as **b**
x	as the 'ks' in 'taxi',when between two vowels; as the 's' in 'say' when the **x** precedes a consonant
z	as the 'th' in 'thin'

Semiconsonant

y	**y** is a semiconsonant. It is pronounced as the Spanish **i** when it is at the end of a word or when it stands alone as a conjunction. As a consonant, its sound is somewhere between 'y' in 'yonder' and 'g' in 'beige', depending on the region.

SPANISH

Greetings & Civilities
Top Useful Phrases

Hello.
o-lah! — ¡Hola!

Goodbye.
ah-THios! — ¡Adiós!

Yes./No.
si/no — Sí./No.

Excuse me.
*per-**mi**-so* — Permiso.

May I? Do you mind?
*pwe-**THo**?/me per-**mi**-te?* — ¿Puedo?/¿Me permite?

Sorry. (excuse me, forgive me)
*lo **sien**-to/dis-**kool**-pe-me/ per-**THo**-ne-me* — Lo siento. Discúlpeme. Perdóneme.

Please.
*por fah-**bor*** — Por favor.

Thank you.
***grah**-thiahs* — Gracias.

Many thanks.
*moo-chahs/moo-**chi**-si- mahs **grah**-thi-ahs* — Muchas/Muchísimas gracias.

That's fine. You're welcome.
*de **nah**-THah* — De nada.

Greetings

Good morning.
*bwe-nos **THi**-ahs* — Buenos días.

Good afternoon.
*bwe-nahs tahr-**THes*** — Buenas tardes.

Good evening/night.
   bwe-nahs no-ches   Buenas noches.
How are you?
   ko-mo es-tah?/ko-mo le   ¿Cómo está? ¿Cómo le va?
   bah?/ke tahl?   ¿Qué tal?
Well, thanks.
   bien, grah-thiahs   Bien, gracias.

Forms of Address

Madam/Mrs	*se-nyo-rah/do-nya*	Señora/Doña
Sir/Mr	*se-nyor/don*	Señor/Don
Miss	*se-nyo-ri-tah*	Señorita
companion	*kom-pah-nye-ro/ah*	compañero/a
friend	*ah-mi-go/ah*	amigo/a

Small Talk
Meeting People

What is your name?
   ko-mo se lyah-mah   ¿Cómo se llama usted?
   oos-teTH?
My name is …
   me lyah-mo …   Me llamo …
I'd like to introduce you to …
   ki-sie-rah pre-sen-tahr-le Quisiera presentarle a …
   ah …
I'm pleased to meet you.
   moo-cho goos-to   Mucho gusto.
Where are you from?
   de THon-de es oos-teTH? ¿De dónde es usted?

Nationalities

I am from …
soy de …

		Soy THe …
Australia	*ahoos-trah-li-ah*	Australia
Canada	*kah-nah-THah*	Canadá
England	*in-glah-te-rrah*	Inglaterra
Ireland	*ir-lahn-dah*	Irlanda
New Zealand	*nwe-bah the-lahn-diah/the-lahn-dah*	Nueva Zelandia/Zelanda
Scotland	*es-ko-thiah*	Escocia
South America	*ah-me-ri-kah THel soor/soo-THah-me-ri-kah*	América del Sur/Sudamérica
the USA	*los es-tah-THos oo-ni-THos*	Los Estados Unidos
Wales	*pah-is THe gah-les*	País de Gales

Age

How old are you?
kwahn-tos ah-nyos tie-ne?   ¿Cuántos años tiene?
I am … years old.
ten-go … ah-nyos   Tengo … años.

Occupations

What do you do?
ke ah-the oos-teTH?   ¿Qué hace usted?
I am a/an …
soy …   Soy …

artist	*ahr-tis-tah*	artista
business person	*ko-mer-thi-ahn-te*	comerciante
doctor	*dok-tor/-ah, me-di-ko/-ah*	doctor/a, médico/a

engineer	*in-he-**nie**-ro/-ah*	ingeniero/a
factory worker	*o-**bre**-ro/-ah*	obrero/a
farmer	*ah-gri-cool-**tor**/-ah,*	agricultor/a,
	*grahn-**he**-ro/-ah*	granjero/a
journalist	*pe-ri-o-**THis**-tah*	periodista
lawyer	*ah-bo-**gah**-THo/-ah*	abogado/a
manual worker	*o-**bre**-ro/ah,*	obrero/a,
	*trah-bah-hah-**dor**/-ah*	trabajador/a
mechanic	*me-**kah**-ni-ko/-ah*	mecánico/a
nurse	*en-fer-**me**-ro/-ah*	enfermero/a
office worker	*o-fi-thi-**nis**-tah,*	oficinista,
	*em-ple-**ah**-do/-ah*	empleado/a
scientist	*thien-ti-fi-ko/-ah*	científico/a
student	*es-tu-**THi**-ahn-te*	estudiante
teacher	*pro-fe-**sor**/-ah*	profesor/a
waiter	*kah-mah-**re**-ro/-ah*	camarero/a
writer	*es-kri-**tor**/-ah*	escritor/a

Religion

What is your religion?

*kwahl es soo rre-li-**hion**?* ¿Cuál es su religión?

I am not religious.

no soy rre-li-hi-o-so/ah No soy religioso/a.

I am …

soy …		Soy …
Buddhist	*bu-**THis**-tah*	budista
Catholic	*kah-to-li-ko/-ah*	católico/a
Christian	*kris-ti-**ah**-no/-ah*	cristiano/a
Hindu	*in-**doo***	hindú
Jewish	*hoo-**THi**-o/-ah*	judío/a
Muslim	*moo-sool-**mahn**/-ah*	musulmán/a

Family

Are you married?
es kah-sah-THo/-ah? ¿Es casado/a?

I am single.
soy sol-te-ro/-ah Soy soltero/a.

I am married.
soy kah-sah-THo/-ah Soy casado/a.

How many children do you
have?
kwahn-tos i-hos tie-ne? ¿Cuántos hijos tiene?

I don't have any children.
no ten-go i-hos No tengo hijos.

I have a daughter/a son.
ten-go oo-nah i-hah/oon i-ho Tengo una hija/un hijo.

How many brothers/sisters do
you have?
kwahn-tos/-ahs er-mah- ¿Cuántos/as hermanos/as
nos/-ahs tie-ne? tiene?

Is your husband here?
su es-po-so/mah-ri-THo ¿Su esposo/marido está
es-tah ah-ki? aquí?

Is your wife here?
su es-po-sah/mu-her es-tah ¿Su esposa/mujer está aquí?
ah-ki?

Do you have a boyfriend/
girlfriend?
tie-ne no-bio/-ah? ¿Tiene novio/a?

brother	*er-mah-no*	hermano
children	*i-hos*	hijos
daughter	*i-hah*	hija
family	*fah-mi-liah*	familia

father	**pah-THre pah-pah**	padre, papá
grandfather	ah-**bwe**-lo	abuelo
grandmother	ah-**bwe**-lah	abuela
husband	es-po-so, mah-**ri**-THo	esposo, marido
mother	**mah-THre, mah-mah**	madre, mamá
sister	er-**mah**-nah	hermana
son	**i**-ho	hijo
wife	es-po-sah, mu-**her**	esposa, mujer

Feelings

I (don't) like …
  (no) me goos-tah …   (No) Me gusta …
I am sorry. (condolence)
  *lo **sien**-to **moo**-cho*   Lo siento mucho.
I am grateful.
  *le ah-grah-**deth**-ko moo-cho*   Le agradezco mucho.

(I am …)
  ***ten**-go …*   Tengo …

hot	**kah-lor**	calor
cold	**fri**-o	frío
hungry	**ahm**-bre	hambre
thirsty	seTH	sed
in a hurry	**pri**-sah	prisa
right	rrah-**thon**	razón
sleepy	**swe**-nyo	sueño

I am …
  *es-**toy** …*   Estoy …

| angry | e-no-**hah**-THo/-ah | enojado/a |
| happy | fe-**lith** | feliz |

sad	*tris*-te	triste
tired	*kahn-sah-THo/-ah*	cansado/a
well	*bien*	bien
worried	*pre-o-koo-pah-THo/-ah*	preocupado/a

Language Difficulties

Do you speak English?
ah-blah in-gles? — ¿Habla inglés?

Does anyone speak English?
ahy ahl-gien ke ah-ble in-gles? — ¿Hay alguien que hable inglés?

I speak a little Spanish.
ah-blo oon po-ki-to de kahs-te-lyah-no/es-pah-nyol — Hablo un poquito de castellano/español.

I don't speak …
no ah-blo … — No hablo …

I (don't) understand.
(no) en-tien-do — (No) Entiendo.

Could you speak more slowly please?
pwe-THe ah-blahr mahs des-pah-thio, por fah-bor? — ¿Puede hablar más despacio, por favor?

Could you repeat that?
pwe-THe rre-pe-tir-lo? — ¿Puede repetirlo?

How do you say …?
ko-mo se di-the …? — ¿Cómo se dice …?

What does … mean?
ke si-gni-fi-kah …? — ¿Qué significa …?

I speak …
  ah-blo …   Hablo …

English	*in-gles*	inglés
French	*frahn-thes*	francés
German	*ah-le-mahn*	alemán
Italian	*i-tah-li-ah-no*	italiano

Some Useful Phrases

Sure.
  por su-pwes-to! ko-mo no!   ¡Por supuesto! ¡Cómo no!
  klah-ro!   ¡Claro!
Just a minute.
  oon mo-men-to   Un momento.
It's (not) important.
  (no) es im-por-tahn-te   (No) Es importante.
It's (not) possible.
  (no) es po-si-ble   (No) Es posible.
Wait!
  es-pe-re!   ¡Espere!
Good luck!
  bwe-nah swer-te! swer-te!   ¡Buena suerte! ¡Suerte!

Signs

CHECK-IN COUNTER	FACTURACION DE EQUIPAJE/CHECK-IN
CUSTOMS	ADUANA
EMERGENCY EXIT	SALIDA DE EMERGENCIA
ENTRANCE	ENTRADA
EXIT	SALIDA

FREE ADMISSION	ENTRADA GRATIS
HOT/COLD	CALIENTE/FRIO
INFORMATION	INFORMACION
NO ENTRY	PROHIBIDO EL PASO
NO SMOKING	PROHIBIDO FUMAR
OPEN/CLOSED	ABIERTO/CERRADO
PROHIBITED	PROHIBIDO
RESERVED	RESERVADO
TELEPHONE	TELEFONO
TOILETS	SERVICIOS/ASEOS

Emergencies

POLICE	POLICIA
POLICE STATION	ESTACION DE POLICIA

Help!
  so-ko-rro! ahoo-si-lio!   ¡Socorro! ¡Auxilio!
It's an emergency!
  es oo-nah e-mer-hen-thiah!   ¡Es una emergencia!
There's been an accident!
  oo-bo oon ahk-thi-THen-te!   ¡Hubo un accidente!
Call a doctor!
  lyah-me ah oon dok-tor!   ¡Llame a un doctor!
Call an ambulance!
  *lyah-me oo-nah ahm-boo-
  lahn-thiah!*   ¡Llame una ambulancia!

I've been raped.
  e si-do bio-lah-THah/me
  bio-lah-ron

He sido violada./Me
violaron.

I've been robbed!
  me ahn rro-bah-THo!

¡Me han robado!

Call the police!
  lyah-me ah lah po-li-thi-ah!

¡Llame a la policía!

Where is the police station?
  don-de ke-THah lah es-tah-
  thion de po-li-thi-ah?

¿Dónde queda la estación
de policía?

Go away!
  bah-yah-se!

¡Váyase!

I'll call the police!
  boy ah lyah-mahr ah lah
  po-li-thi-ah!

¡Voy a llamar a la policía!

Thief!
  oon lah-THron!

¡Un ladrón!

I am ill.
  es-toy en-fer-mo/-ah

Estoy enfermo/a.

My friend is ill.
  mi ah-mi-go/-ah es-tah
  en-fer-mo/-ah

Mi amigo/a está enfermo/a.

I am lost.
  es-toy per-THi-THo/-ah

Estoy perdido/a.

Where are the toilets?
  don-de ke-THahn los
  ser-bi-thios?

¿Dónde quedan los
servicios?

Could you help me please?
  pwe-THe ahy-oo-THahr-
  me por fah-bor?

¿Puede ayudarme, por
favor?

Could I please use the telephone?

pwe-THo oo-sahr el te-le-fo-no, por fah-vor?

¿Puedo usar el teléfono, por favor?

I'm sorry. (I apologise)

lo sien-to/dis-kool-pe-me

Lo siento./Discúlpeme.

I didn't realise I was doing anything wrong.

no sah-bi-ah ke no es-tah-bah per-mi-ti-THo

No sabía que no estaba permitido.

I didn't do it.

no lo i-the

No lo hice.

I wish to contact my embassy/consulate.

de-se-o ko-moo-ni-kahr-me con mi em-bah-hah-dah/kon-soo-lah-THo

Deseo comunicarme con mi embajada/consulado.

I speak English.

ah-blo in-gles

Hablo inglés.

I have medical insurance.

ten-go se-goo-ro me-THi-ko

Tengo seguro médico.

My possessions are insured.

ten-go se-goo-ro kon-trah rro-bo

Tengo seguro contra robo.

My ... was stolen.

me rro-bah-ron mi ...

Me robaron mi ...

I've lost ...

e per-THi-THo .../per-THi ...

He perdido .../Perdí ...

| my bags | *mis mah-le-tahs* | mis maletas |
| my handbag | *mi bol-so* | mi bolso |

my money	*mi THi-ne-ro*	mi dinero
my travellers' cheques	*mis che-kes biah-he-ros, che-kes de biah-he*	mis cheques viajeros, cheques de viaje
my passport	*mi pah-sah-por-te*	mi pasaporte

Paperwork

name and surname	*nom-bre i ah-pe-lyi-THo*	nombre y apellido
address	*di-rek-thion*	dirección
date of birth	*fe-chah de nah-thi-mien-to*	fecha de nacimiento
place of birth	*loo-gahr de nah-thi-mien-to*	lugar de nacimiento
age	*e-THahTH*	edad
sex	*se-kso*	sexo
nationality	*nah-thi-o-nah-li-THahTH*	nacionalidad
religion	*rre-li-hion*	religión
reason for travel	*mo-ti-bo del biah-he*	motivo del viaje
profession	*pro-fe-sion*	profesión
marital status	*es-tah-THo thi-bil*	estado civil
passport	*pah-sah-por-te*	pasaporte
passport number	*noo-me-ro del pah-sah-por-te*	número del pasaporte
visa	*bi-sah-THo*	visado
tourist card	*tahr-he-tah de tu-riz-mo*	tarjeta de turismo
identification	*kahr-ne de i-den-ti-THahTH*	carnet de identidad

SPANISH

birth certificate	*pahr-ti-THah de nah-thi-mien-to*	partida de nacimiento
driver's licence	*kahr-ne de kon-doo-thir*	carnet de conducir
car owner's title	*ti-too-lo de pro-pie-THahTH*	título de propiedad
car registration	*mah-tri-koo-lah*	matrícula
customs	*ah-THoo-ah-nah*	aduana
immigration	*in-mi-grah-thion*	inmigración
border	*fron-te-rah*	frontera

Getting Around

ARRIVALS	LLEGADAS
BUS STOP	PARADA DE AUTOBUS
DEPARTURES	PARTIDAS
STATION	ESTACION
SUBWAY	METRO
TICKET OFFICE	TAQUILLA
TIMETABLE	HORARIO
TRAIN STATION	ESTACION DE TRENES/FERROCARRIL

What time does ... leave/arrive?

ah ke o-rah sah-le/lye-gah ...? — ¿A qué hora sale/llega ...?

the (air)plane	*el bwe-lo*	el vuelo
the boat	*el boo-ke/bahr-ko*	el buque/barco
the bus (city)	*el ahoo-to-boos*	el autobús
	el boos	el bus
the bus (intercity)	*el ahoo-to-kahr*	el autocar

| the train | el **tren** | el tren |
| the tram | el **trahm**-*bi*-ah | el tranvía |

Directions

Where is …?
don-de es-**tah** … ?/**don**-de ke-**THah** … ?
¿Dónde está …?/¿Dónde queda …?

How do I get to …?
ko-mo pwe-**THo** lye-**gahr** ah … ?
¿Cómo puedo llegar a …?

Is it far from/near here?
es-**tah** le-hos/**ther**-kah de ah-**ki**?
¿Está lejos/cerca de aquí?

Can I walk there?
se pwe-**THe** kah-mi-**nahr** ahs-tah ah-**lyi**/ah-**lyah**?
¿Se puede caminar hasta allí/allá?

Can you show me (on the map)?
me pwe-**THe** mos-**trahr**/ indi-**kahr** en el mah-pah?
¿Me puede mostrar/indicar (en el mapa)?

Are there other means of getting there?
ahy o-tros me-**THios** pah-**rah** ir ah-**lyi**/ah-**lyah**?
¿Hay otros medios para ir allí/allá?

I want to go to …
kie-ro ir ah …
Quiero ir a …

Turn left …
do-ble ah lah ith-**kier**-THah …
Doble a la izquierda …

Turn right …
do-ble ah lah
THe-re-chah …

Doble a la derecha …

at the next corner   *en lah pro-ksi-mah*   en la próxima
   es-ki-nah   esquina

at the traffic   *en el se-mah-fo-ro*   en el semáforo
lights

Go straight ahead.
si-gah/bahy-ah to-THo
THe-re-cho

Siga/Vaya todo derecho.

It's two streets down.
es-tah ah THos kah-lyes
THe ah-ki

Está a dos calles de aquí.

behind	*de-trahs THe*	detrás de
near	*ther-kah*	cerca
far	*le-hos*	lejos
in front of	*en-fren-te THe/*	enfrente de/
	de-lahn-te THe	delante de
opposite	*fren-te ah*	frente a

Booking Tickets

Excuse me, where is the ticket
office?
per-THon don-de ke-THah
lah tah-ki-lyah?

¿Perdón, dónde queda la
taquilla?

Where can I buy a ticket?
don-de pwe-THo kom-prahr
el bi-lye-te/pah-sah-he?

¿Dónde puedo comprar el
billete/pasaje?

I want to go to …
kie-ro ir ah …

Quiero ir a…

Do I need to book?
ten-go ke rre-ser-bahr? ¿Tengo que reservar?
You need to book.
tie-ne/ahy ke rre-ser-bahr Tiene/Hay que reservar.
I would like to book a seat to …
ki-sie-rah rre-ser-bahr Quisiera reservar una plaza
oo-nah plah-thah para …
pah-rah …

I would like …		
ki-sie-rah …		Quisiera …
a one-way ticket	*oon bi-lye-te sen-thi-lyo*	un billete sencillo
a return ticket	*oon bi-lye-te de i-THah i bwel-tah*	un billete de ida y vuelta
two tickets	*dos bi-lye-tes*	dos billetes
tickets for all of us	*bi-lye-tes pah-rah to-THos no-so-tros*	billetes para todos nosotros
a student fare	*oon bi-lye-te THe es-tu-THi-ahn-te*	un billete de estudiante
a child's/ pensioner's fare	*oon bi-lye-te THe ni-nyo/pen-si-o-nis-tah*	un billete de niño/pensionista
1st class	*pri-me-rah klah-se*	primera clase
2nd class	*se-goon-dah klah-se*	segunda clase

It is full.
es-ta kom-ple-to Está completo.
Is it completely full?
es-tah kom-ple-tah-men-te lye-no? ¿Está completamente lleno?

Can I get a stand-by ticket?
*pwe-THo kom-prahr oon
es-tahnd-bahy ti-ket
(pah-sah-he soo-he-to ah
es-pah-thio)?*

¿Puedo comprar un
'standby ticket' (pasaje
sujeto a espacio)?

Air

CHECKING IN	FACTURACION/ CHECK-IN
LUGGAGE PICKUP	RECOGIDA DE EQUIPAJE
REGISTRATION	REGISTRO

Is there a flight to ...?
ahy oon bwe-lo pah-rah ...?
¿Hay un vuelo para ...?

When is the next flight to ...?
*kwahn-do sah-le el pro-ksi-
mo bwe-lo pah-rah ...?*
¿Cuándo sale el próximo
vuelo para ...?

How long does the flight take?
*kwahn-to tiem-po
THoo-rah el bwe-lo?*
¿Cuánto tiempo dura el
vuelo?

What is the flight number?
*kwahl es el noo-me-ro THel
bwe-lo?*
¿Cuál es el número del
vuelo?

You must check in at ...
*tie-ne ke fahk-too-rahr el
e-ki-pah-he/pre-sen-tahr-se
en ...*
Tiene que facturar el equi-
paje/presentarse en ...

airport tax	*tah-sah ah-e-ro-por-too-ah-riah*	tasa aeroportuaria
boarding pass	*tahr-he-tah THe em-bahr-ke*	tarjeta de embarque
customs	*ah-THoo-ah-nah*	aduana

Bus

BUS/TRAM STOP	PARADA DE AUTOBUS/ TRANVIA

Where is the bus/tram stop?
don-de es-tah lah pah-rah-THah THe ahoo-to-boos/ trahm-bi-ah

¿Dónde está la parada de autobús/tranvía?

Which bus goes to ...?
kwahl es el ahoo-to-boos ke bah ah ...?

¿Cuál es el autobus que va a ...?

Does this bus go to ...?
es-te ahoo-to-boos bah ah ...?

¿Este autobus va a ...?

How often do buses pass by?
kwahn-tahs be-thes pah-sah el ahoo-to-boos?

¿Cuántas veces pasa el autobus?

Could you let me know when we get to ...?
pwe-THe ah-bi-sahr-me/ in-di-kahr-me kwahn-do lye-ge-mos ah ...?

¿Puede avisarme/indicarme cuando lleguemos a ...?

I want to get off!
  kie-ro bah-hahr-me!   ¡Quiero bajarme!

What time is the ... bus?
  *ah ke o-rah **sah**-le el ...*   ¿A qué hora sale el ...
  *ahoo-to-**boos**/boos?*   autobús/bus?

next	*pro-ksi-mo*	próximo
first	*pri-mer*	primer
last	*ool-ti-mo*	último

Train

DINING CAR	COCHE-COMEDOR/
	VAGON RESTAURANTE
EXPRESS	RAPIDO
PLATFORM NO	ANDEN Nº

Is this the right platform
for ...?
  *el tren **pah**-rah ... **sah**-le*   ¿El tren para ... sale de este
  *THe es-te ahn-**den**?*   andén?
The train leaves from
platform ...
  *el tren **sah**-le THel ahn-**den***   El tren sale del andén
  noo-me-ro ...   número ...
Passengers must change
trains/platforms.
  *los pah-sah-**he**-ros*   Los pasajeros deben
  *THe-ben kahm-bi-**ahr** THe*   cambiar de tren/andén.
  *tren/ahn-**den***

dining car	*ko-che ko-me-**THor**/ bah-**gon** res-tahoo-**rahn**-te*	coche-comedor/ vagón restaurante
express	*es-**pre**-so*	expreso
local	*de ther-kah-**ni**-ahs*	de cercanías
sleeping car	*ko-che **kah**-mah*	coche-cama

Metro

METRO/UNDERGROUND	METRO
CHANGE (for coins)	CAMBIO (MONEDA SUELTA)
THIS WAY TO ...	DIRECCION ...
WAY OUT	SALIDA

Which line takes me to ...?
*ke **li**-neah ko-ho pah-rah ...?*   ¿Qué línea cojo para ...?

What is the next station?
*kwahl es lah pro-ksi-mah es-tah-**thion**?*   ¿Cuál es la próxima estación?

Taxi

Can you take me to ...?
*pwe-**THe** lye-**bahr**-me ah ...?*   ¿Puede llevarme a ...?

Please take me to ...
*por fah-**bor** lye-be-me ah ...*   Por favor, lléveme a ...

How much does it cost to go to …?
> **kwahn**-to **kwes**-tah/**bah**-le ir ah …?

¿Cuánto cuesta/vale ir a …?

Instructions

Here is fine, thank you.
> ah-**ki** es-**tah** bien, **grah**-thiahs

Aquí está bien, gracias.

The next corner, please.
> lah **pro**-ksi-mah es-**ki**-nah, por fah-**bor**

La próxima esquina, por favor.

Continue!
> si-**gah**!

¡Siga!

The next street to the left/right.
> lah **pro**-ksi-mah **cah**-lye ah lah ith-**kier**-THah/THe-re-chah

La próxima calle a la izquierda/derecha.

Stop here!
> **pah**-re ah-**ki**

¡Pare aquí!

Please slow down.
> por fah-**bor** bahy-ah mahs des-**pah**-thio

Por favor vaya más despacio.

Please wait here.
> por fah-**bor** es-pe-re ah-**ki**

Por favor espere aquí.

Some Useful Phrases

The train is delayed/cancelled.
> el tren **tie**-ne rre-**trah**-so/ fu-e kahn-the-**lah**-THo

El tren tiene retraso/fue cancelado.

How long will it be delayed?
   kwahn-to lye-bah THe
   rre-trah-so?

¿Cuánto lleva de retraso?

There is a delay of ... hours.
   lye-bah ... o-rahs THe
   rre-trah-so

Lleva ... horas de retraso.

Can I reserve a place?
   pwe-THo rre-ser-bahr
   oo-nah plah-thah/oon
   ah-sien-to?

¿Puedo reservar una
plaza/un asiento?

How long does the trip take?
   kwahn-to tiem-po
   THoo-rah el biah-he?

¿Cuánto tiempo dura el
viaje?

Is it a direct route?
   biah-hah THi-rek-to?

¿Viaja directo?

Is that seat taken?
   es-tah o-koo-pah-THo es-te
   ah-sien-to?

¿Está ocupado este asiento?

I want to get off at ...
   kie-ro ah-pe-ahr-me en ...

Quiero apearme en ...

Excuse me. (when making
your way to the door)
   per-mi-so

Permiso.

Where can I hire a bicycle?
   don-de pwe-THo ahl-ki-
   lahr oo-nah bi-thi-kle-tah?

¿Dónde puedo alquilar una
bicicleta?

Car

DETOUR	DESVIO
FREEWAY	AUTOPISTA
GARAGE	GARAJE/TALLER
GIVE WAY	CEDA EL PASO
MECHANIC	MECANICO
NO ENTRY	DIRECCION PROHIBIDA
NO PARKING	PROHIBIDO ESTACIONAR
NORMAL	NORMAL
ONE WAY	SENTIDO UNICO
REPAIRS	REPARACIONES
SELF SERVICE	AUTOSERVICIO
STOP	STOP/PARE
SUPER	SUPER
UNLEADED	SIN PLOMO

Where can I rent a car?
don-de pwe-THo ahl-ki-lahr oon ko-che/ahoo-to?
¿Dónde puedo alquilar un coche/auto?

How much is it daily/weekly?
kwahn-to kwes-tah por THi-ah/por se-mah-nah?
¿Cuánto cuesta por día/por semana?

Does that include insurance/mileage?
in-kluy-e el se-goo-ro/el ki-lo-me-trah-he
¿Incluye el seguro/el kilometraje?

Where's the next petrol station?

*ahy oo-nah gah-so-li-**ne**-rah por ah-**ki**?*

¿Hay una gasolinera por aquí?

Please fill the tank.

*por fah-**bor**, lye-ne-me el de-po-**si**-to*

Por favor, lléneme el depósito.

I want … litres of petrol (gas).

*kie-ro … **li**-tros THe gah-so-li-nah*

Quiero … litros de gasolina.

Please check the oil and water.

*por fah-**bor**, rre-**bi**-se el ni-**bel** THel ah-**thei**-te i THel **ah**-gwah*

Por favor, revise el nivel del aceite y del agua.

How long can I park here?

*kwahn-to **tiem**-po pwe-THo es-tah-thio-**nahr** ah-**ki**?*

¿Cuánto tiempo puedo estacionar aquí?

Does this road lead to?

se bah ah … por es-tah kah-rre-te-rah?

¿Se va a … por esta carretera?

air (for tyres)	*ahi*-re (*pah-rah neoo-**mah**-ti-kos*)	aire (para neumáticos)
battery	*bah-te-**ri**-ah/ah-koo-moo-lah-**THor***	batería/acumulador
brakes	*fre-nos*	frenos
clutch	*em-**brah**-ge*	embrague
driver's licence	*kahr-**ne**/per-**mi**-so THe kon-doo-**thir***	carnet/permiso de conducir
engine	*mo-**tor***	motor
lights	*fah-ros*	faros

oil	*ah-**thei**-te*	aceite
puncture	*pin-**chah**-tho*	pinchazo
radiator	*rrah-**THi**-ah-**THor***	radiador
road map	***mah**-pah THe cah-rre-te-rahs*	mapa de carreteras
tyres	*neoo-**mah**-ti-kos*	neumáticos
windscreen	***pah**-rah-**bri**-sahs*	parabrisas

Car Problems

I need a mechanic.
| *ne-the-**si**-to oon me-**kah**-ni-ko* | Necesito un mecánico. |

What make is it?
| *de ke **mahr**-kah es?* | ¿De qué marca es? |

The battery is flat.
| *el ah-koo-moo-lah-**THor**/ lah bah-te-**ri**-ah es-**tah** des-kahr-**gah**-THo/ah* | El acumulador/La batería está descargado/a. |

The radiator is leaking.
| *el rrah-**THi**-ah-**THor** tie-ne oo-nah foo-gah* | El radiador tiene una fuga. |

I have a flat tyre.
| ***ten**-go oon pin-**chah**-tho* | Tengo un pinchazo. |

It's overheating.
| *es-**tah** re-kah-len-**tahn**-do-se* | Está recalentándose. |

It's not working.
| *no foon-thi-o-nah* | No funciona. |

Accommodation

CAMPING GROUND	TERRENO DE CAMPING
GUEST HOUSE	PENSION/CASA DE HUESPEDES
YOUTH HOSTEL	ALBERGUE PARA JOVENES

I am looking for a …
   ahn-do boos-kahn-do oon …   Ando buscando un …

cheap hotel	*o-tel bah-rah-to*	hotel barato
good hotel	*bwen o-tel*	buen hotel
nearby hotel	*o-tel ther-kah-no*	hotel cercano
clean hotel	*o-tel-lim-pio*	hotel limpio

What is the address?
   kwahl es lah di-rek-thion?   ¿Cuál es la dirección?
Could you write the address, please?
   pwe-THe es-kri-bir lah   ¿Puede escribir la dirección,
   di-rek-thion por fah-bor?   por favor?

At the Hotel
Do you have any rooms available?
   tie-ne ah-bi-tah-thi-o-nes   ¿Tiene habitaciones libres?
   li-bres?

SPANISH

I would like …
*ki-**sie**-rah* …   Quisiera …

a single room	*oo-nah*	una habitación
	*ah-bi-tah-**thion***	individual
	*in-di-bi-**THoo-ahl***	
a double room	*oo-nah ah-bi-tah-*	una habitación
	***thion do**-ble*	doble
a room with a	*oo-nah ah-bi-tah-*	una habitación
bathroom	***thion** kon **bah**-nyo*	con baño
to share a dorm	*kom-pahr-**tir** oon*	compartir un
	dor-mi-to-rio	dormitorio
a bed	*oo-nah **kah**-mah*	una cama

I want a room with a …
kie-ro oo-nah ah-bi-tah-   Quiero una habitación
***thion** kon* …   con …

bathroom	***bah**-nyo*	baño
shower	***doo**-chah*	ducha
television	*te-le-bi-**sion***	televisión
window	*ben-**tah**-nah*	ventana

I'm going to stay for …
*me boy ah ke-**THahr*** …   Me voy a quedar …

one day	*oon **di**-ah*	un día
two days	*dos **THi**-ahs*	dos días
one week	*oo-nah se-**mah**-nah*	una semana

Do you have identification?
***tie**-ne kahr-**ne** THe i-THen-*   ¿Tiene carnet de identidad?
*ti-**THahTH**?*

Your membership card, please.
   *su tahr-**he**-tah de **so**-thio, por fah-**bor***

Su tarjeta de socio, por favor.

Sorry, we're full.
   *lo **sien**-to, no te-**ne**-mos **nah**-THah **li**-bre*

Lo siento, no tenemos nada libre.

How long will you be staying?
   ***kwahn**-to **tiem**-po se ke-THah?*

¿Cuánto tiempo se queda?

How many nights?
   ***kwahn**-tahs **no**-ches?*

¿Cuántas noches?

It's ... per day/per person.
   *son ... por **THi**-ah/por **per**-so-nah*

Son ... por día/por persona.

How much is it per night/per person?
   ***kwahn**-to **kwes**-tah por **no**-che/por **per**-so-nah?*

¿Cuánto cuesta por noche/por persona?

Can I see it?
   *pwe-**THo ber**-lah?*

¿Puedo verla?

Are there any others?
   *ahy **o**-trahs?*

¿Hay otras?

Are there any cheaper rooms?
   *ahy ah-bi-tah-thi-o-nes mahs bah-**rah**-tahs?*

¿Hay habitaciones más baratas?

Can I see the bathroom?
   *pwe-**THo ber** el **bah**-nyo?*

¿Puedo ver el baño?

Is there a reduction for
students/children?

*ahy ahl-**goon** des-**kwen**-to/
pre-thio es-pe-thi-**ahl**
pah-rah es-too-**THi**-ahn-tes/
ni-nyos?*

¿Hay algún descuento/
precio especial para es-
tudiantes/niños?

Does it include breakfast?

*in-**kluy**-e el de-sahy-oo-no?*

¿Incluye el desayuno?

It's fine, I'll take it.

***bah**-le, lah ahl-**ki**-lo*

Vale, la alquilo.

I'm not sure how long I'm
staying.

*no es-**toy** se-**goo**-ro
kwahn-to **tiem**-po me boy
ah ke-**THahr***

No estoy seguro cuánto
tiempo me voy a quedar.

Is there hot water all day?

*ahy **ah**-gwah kah-**lien**-te
to-**THo** el **di**-ah?*

¿Hay agua caliente todo el
día?

Do you have a safe where I
can leave my valuables?

***tie**-ne oo-nah kah-**hah**
fwer-te **THon**-de pwe-
THah de-**hahr** mis
ko-sahs THe bah-**lor**?*

¿Tiene una caja fuerte
donde pueda dejar mis
cosas de valor?

Where is the bathroom?

*don-de es-**tah** el **bah**-nyo?*

¿Dónde está el baño?

Is there somewhere to wash
clothes?

*ahy ahl-**goon** loo-**gahr**
THon-de pwe-**THah**
lah-**bahr** lah rro-**pah**?*

¿Hay algún lugar donde
pueda lavar la ropa?

Can I use the kitchen?
pwe-THo oo-sahr lah
ko-thi-nah?

¿Puedo usar la cocina?

Can I use the telephone?
pwe-THo oo-sahr el
te-le-fo-no?

¿Puedo usar el teléfono?

Is there a lift?
ahy ahs-then-sor?

¿Hay ascensor?

Requests & Complaints

Please wake me up at …
por fah-bor, des-pier-te-me
ah lahs …

Por favor, despiérteme
a las …

The room needs to be cleaned.
ahy ke lim-pi-ahr lah
ah-bi-tah-thion

Hay que limpiar la
habitación.

Please change the sheets.
por fah-bor, kahm-bie lahs
sah-bah-nahs

Por favor, cambie las
sábanas.

I can't open/close the window.
no pwe-THo ah-brir/
the-rrahr lah ben-tah-nah

No puedo abrir/cerrar la
ventana.

I've locked myself out of my
room.
the-rre lah pwer-tah i se me
ol-bi-dah-ron lahs
lyah-bes THen-tro

Cerré la puerta y se me
olvidaron las llaves dentro.

The toilet won't flush.
lah THes-kahr-gah THe lah
rre-tre-te no foon-thi-o-nah

La descarga de la retrete no
funciona.

I don't like this room.
  *no me **goos**-tah **es**-tah
  ah-bi-tah-**thion***

No me gusta esta
habitación.

It's too small.
  *es de-mah-si-**ah**-THo
  chi-**ki**-tah/pe-ke-nyah*

Es demasiado chiquita/
pequeña.

It's noisy.
  *es rrwi-**TH**o-sah*

Es ruidosa.

It's too dark.
  *es de-mah-si-**ah**-THo
  os-**koo**-rah*

Es demasiado oscura.

It's expensive.
  *es **kah**-rah*

Es cara.

Some Useful Phrases

I am/We are leaving now.
  *me boy/nos **bah**-mos
  ah-o-rah*

Me voy/Nos vamos ahora.

I would like to pay the bill.
  ***kie**-ro pah-**gahr** lah
  kwen-tah*

Quiero pagar la cuenta.

name	***nom**-bre*	nombre
surname	*ah-pe-**lyi**-THo*	apellido
room number	***noo**-me-ro THe lah
ah-bi-tah-**thion***	número de la
habitación

Some Useful Words

address	*di-rek-**thion***	dirección
air-conditioned	*kon **ahi**-re ah-kon-
di-thi-o-**nah**-THo*	con aire
acondicionado
balcony	*bahl-**kon***	balcón

bathroom	***bah**-nyo*	baño
bed	***kah**-mah*	cama
bill	***kwen**-tah*	cuenta
blanket	***mahn**-tah/frah-**thah**-THah/ ko-ber-**tor***	manta/frazada/ cobertor
candle	*be-**lah***	vela
chair	*si-**lyah***	silla
clean	***lim**-pio/ah*	limpio/a
cupboard	*ahr-**mah**-rio*	armario
dark	*os-koo-**ro**/ah*	oscuro/a
dirty	*soo-**thio**/ah*	sucio/a
double bed	***kah**-mah THe mah-tri-mo-nio*	cama de matrimonio
electricity	*e-lek-tri-thi-**THahTH***	electricidad
excluded	*no in-kloo-**i**-THo*	no incluido
fan	*ben-ti-lah-**THor***	ventilador
included	*in-kloo-**i**-THo*	incluido
key	***lyah**-be*	llave
lift (elevator)	*ahs-then-**sor***	ascensor
light bulb	*bom-**bi**-lyah*	bombilla
lock (n)	*the-rrah-**THoo**-rah*	cerradura
mattress	*kol-**chon***	colchón
mirror	*es-pe-**ho***	espejo
padlock	*kahn-**dah**-THo*	candado
pillow	*ahl-mo-**ah**-THah*	almohada
quiet	*trahn-**ki**-lo/ah*	tranquilo/a
room (in hotel)	*ah-bi-tah-**thion***	habitación
sheet	***sah**-bah-nah*	sábana
shower	***doo**-chah*	ducha
soap	*hah-**bon***	jabón

suitcase	*mah-le-tah*	maleta
swimming pool	*pis-thi-nah*	piscina
table	*me-sah*	mesa
toilet	*rre-tre-te/bah-ter*	retrete/wáter
toilet paper	*pah-pel i-hi-e-ni-ko*	papel higiénico
towel	*to-ah-lyah*	toalla
water	*ah-gwah*	agua
cold water	*ah-gwah fri-ah*	agua fría
hot water	*ah-gwah kah-lien-te*	agua caliente
window	*ben-tah-nah*	ventana

Around Town

I'm looking for …
   ahn-do boos-kahn-do …   Ando buscando …

the art gallery	*el moo-se-o/lah gah-le-ri-ah THe be-lyahs ahr-tes*	el museo/la galería de bellas artes
a bank	*oon bahn-ko*	un banco
the church	*lah i-gle-si-ah*	la iglesia
the city centre	*el then-tro THe lah thiu-THahTH*	el centro de la ciudad
the … embassy	*lah em-bah-hah-THah …*	la embajada …
my hotel	*mi o-tel*	mi hotel
the museum	*el moo-se-o*	el museo
the police	*lah po-li-thi-ah*	la policía
the post office	*ko-rre-os*	Correos
a public toilet	*ser-bi-thios/ah-se-os poo-bli-kos*	servicios/aseos públicos

| the telephone centre | *lah then-**trahl** te-le-fo-ni-kah* | la central telefónica |
| the tourist information office | *lah o-fi-**thi**-nah THe too-**riz**-mo* | la oficina de turismo |

What time does it open?
ah ke o-rah ah-bren? ¿A qué hora abren?
What time does it close?
*ah ke o-rah **thie**-rrahn?* ¿A qué hora cierran?

What ... is this?
ke ... es es-tah/es-te? ¿Qué ... es ésta/éste?
street **kah**-lye calle
suburb **bah**-rrio, soo-**boor**-bio barrio, suburbio

For directions, see the Getting Around section, page 331.

At the Bank

I want to exchange some money/traveller's cheques.
*kie-ro kahm-bi-**ahr** THi-**ne**-ro/ che-kes THe **biah**-he* Quiero cambiar dinero/ cheques de viaje.
What is the exchange rate?
*kwahl es el **ti**-po THe **kahm**-bio?* ¿Cuál es el tipo de cambio?
How many pesetas per dollar?
kwahn-tahs pe-se-tahs por THo-lahr? ¿Cuántas pesetas por dólar?

SPANISH

Can I have money transferred here from my bank?

pwe-THen trahns-fe-rir-me THi-ne-ro THe mi bahn-ko ah es-te?

¿Pueden transferirme dinero de mi banco a éste?

How long will it take to arrive?

kwahn-to tiem-po tar-THa-rah en lye-gahr?

¿Cuánto tiempo tardará en llegar?

Has my money arrived yet?

yah ah lye-gah-THo mi THi-ne-ro?

¿Ya ha llegado mi dinero?

bankdraft	*le-trah bahn-kah-riah*	letra bancaria
bank notes	*bi-lye-tes THe bahn-ko*	billetes (de banco)
cashier	*kah-hah*	caja
coins	*mo-ne-THahs*	monedas
credit card	*tahr-he-tah THe kre-THi-to*	tarjeta de crédito
exchange	*kahm-bio*	cambio
loose change	*mo-ne-THahs swel-tahs*	monedas sueltas
signature	*fir-mah*	firma

At the Post Office

I would like to send ...

ki-sie-rah em-bi-ahr ...

Quisiera enviar ...

a letter	*oo-nah kahr-tah*	una carta
a postcard	*oo-nah tahr-he-tah pos-tahl*	una tarjeta postal

a parcel	*oon pah-ke-te*	un paquete
a telegram	*oon te-le-grah-mah*	un telegrama

I would like some stamps.
ki-sie-rah oo-nos se-lyos Quisiera unos sellos.
How much is the postage?
kwahn-to bah-le el ¿Cúanto vale el franqueo?
frahn-ke-o?
How much does it cost to
send this to …?
kwahn-to kwes-tah em-bi- ¿Cuánto cuesta enviar esto
ahr es-to ah …? a …?

an aerogram	*oon ah-e-ro-grah-mah*	un aerograma
air mail	*por bi-ah ah-e-re-ah*	por vía aérea
envelope	*so-bre*	sobre
mail box	*boo-thon*	buzón
parcel	*pah-ke-te*	paquete
registered mail	*ko-rre-o ther-ti-fi-kah-THo*	correo certificado
surface mail	*por bi-ah te-rres-tre/mah-ri-ti-mah*	por vía terrestre/marítima

Telephone
I want to ring …
kie-ro lyah-mahr ah … Quiero llamar a …
The number is …
el noo-me-ro es … El número es …

I want to speak for three minutes.

kie-ro ah-**blahr** tres mi-**noo**-tos

Quiero hablar tres minutos.

How much does a three-minute call cost?

kwahn-to kwes-tah/**bah**-le oo-nah lyah-**mah**-THah THe tres mi-**noo**-tos?

¿Cuánto cuesta/vale una llamada de tres minutos?

How much does each extra minute cost?

kwahn-to kwes-tah **cah**-THah mi-**noo**-to ah-**THi**-thi-o-**nahl**?

¿Cuánto cuesta cada minuto adicional?

I would like to speak to Mr Perez.

ki-**sie**-rah ah-**blahr** kon el se-**nyor** pe-**reth**

Quisiera hablar con el señor Pérez.

I want to make a reverse-charges phone call.

kie-ro ah-**ther** oo-nah lyah-**mah**-THah ah ko-bro rre-ber-ti-THo

Quiero hacer una llamada a cobro revertido.

It's engaged.

es-**tah** ko-moo-ni-**kahn**-do

Está comunicando.

I've been cut off.

me ahn kor-**tah**-THo (lah ko-moo-ni-kah-thion)

Me han cortado (la comunicación).

Sightseeing

Do you have a guidebook/
local map?
  tie-ne oo-nah gi-ah/oon
  plahn de lah thiu-THahTH?
¿Tiene una guía/un plan de
la ciudad?

What are the main attractions?
  kwah-les son lahs ah-trahk-
  thi-o-nes prin-thi-pah-les?
¿Cuáles son las atracciones
principales?

What is that?
  ke es e-so?
¿Qué es eso?

How old is it?
  es ahn-ti-gwo?/de kwahn-
  do es?
¿Es antiguo? ¿Dé cuándo
es?

Can I take photographs?
  pwe-THo to-mahr fo-tos?
¿Puedo tomar fotos?

What time does it open/close?
  ah ke o-rah ah-bren/thie-
  rrahn?
¿A qué hora abren/cierran?

ancient	*ahn-ti-gwo/-ah*	antiguo/a
archaeological	*ahr-ke-o-lo-hi-co/-ah*	arqueológico/a
beach	*plahy-ah*	playa
building	*e-THi-fi-thi-o*	edificio
castle	*kahs-ti-lyo*	castillo
cathedral	*kah-te-THrahl*	catedral
church	*i-gle-siah*	iglesia
concert hall	*te-ah-tro/sah-lah*	teatro/sala de
	THe kon-thier-tos	conciertos
library	*bi-bli-o-te-kah*	biblioteca
main square	*plah-thah mahy-or*	Plaza Mayor
market	*mer-kah-THo*	mercado

monastery	*mo-nahs-te-rio*	monasterio
monument	*mo-noo-men-to*	monumento
mosque	*meth-ki-tah*	mezquita
old city	*thiu-THahTH ahn-ti-gwah/bah-rrio bie-ho*	ciudad antigua/ barrio viejo
palace	*pah-lah-thio*	palacio
opera house	*lah o-pe-rah*	la Opera
ruins	*rroo-i-nahs*	ruinas
stadium	*es-tah-THio*	estadio
statues	*es-tah-twahs*	estatuas
synagogue	*si-nah-go-gah*	sinagoga
temple	*tem-plo*	templo
university	*oo-ni-ber-si-THahTH*	universidad

Entertainment

What's there to do in the evenings?
   ke se pwe-THe ah-ther por lah no-che?
¿Qué se puede hacer por la noche?

Are there any discos?
   ahy dis-ko-te-kahs?
¿Hay discotecas?

Are there places where you can hear local folk music?
   ahy loo-gah-res THon-de se pwe-THah o-ir moo-sik-ah fol-klo-ri-kah?
¿Hay lugares donde se pueda oír música folklórica?

How much is it to get in?
   kwahn-to kwes-tah lah en-trah-THah?
¿Cuánto cuesta la entrada?

cinema	*thi-ne*	cine
concert	*kon-thier-to*	concierto
discotheque	*dis-ko/dis-ko-te-kah*	disco/discoteca
theatre	*te-ah-tro*	teatro

In the Country
Weather

What's the weather like?
ko-mo es-tah el tiem-po? ¿Cómo está el tiempo?
The weather is fine/bad today.
ah-the bwen/mahl tiem-po Hace buen/mal tiempo hoy.
hoy

Will it be … tomorrow?
es-tah-rah/ah-rah/ah-brah ¿Estará/Hará/Habrá …
… mah-nyah-nah? mañana?

cloudy	*(es-tah-rah) noo-blah-THo*	(Estará) nublado
cold	*(ah-rah) fri-o*	(Hará) frío
foggy	*(ah-brah) ne-bli-nah/nie-blah*	(Habrá) neblina/niebla
frosty	*(ah-brah) es-kahr-chah*	(Habrá) escarcha
hot	*(ah-rah) kah-lor*	(Hará) calor
raining	*lyo-be-rah*	Lloverá
snowing	*ne-bah-rah/*	Nevará/
	(ah-brah) nie-be	(Habrá) nieve
sunny	*(ah-rah) sol*	(Hará) sol
windy	*(ah-rah) bien-to*	(Hará) viento

Camping

Am I allowed to camp here?
*es-**tah** per-mi-ti-THo
ah-kahm-**pahr** ah-**ki**?*

¿Está permitido acampar
aquí?

Is there a campsite nearby?
*ahy oon te-**rre**-no THe
kahm-ping **ther**-kah?*

¿Hay un terreno de camping
cerca?

backpack	*mo-**chi**-lah/mo-**rrahl***	mochila/morral
can opener	*ah-bre-**lah**-tahs*	abrelatas
compass	***broo**-hoo-lah*	brújula
crampons	*krahm-**po**-nes*	crampones
firewood	*le-nyah*	leña
gas cartridge	*kahr-**too**-cho THe gahs*	cartucho de gas
hammock	*ah-**mah**-kah*	hamaca
ice axe	*pi-ko/**pi**-kah*	pico/pica
mattress	*kol-**chon***	colchón
penknife	*nah-**bah**-hah*	navaja
rope	***kwer**-dah*	cuerda
tent	***tien**-dah (THe **kahm**-pah-nyah)*	tienda (de campaña)
tent pegs	*es-**tah**-kahs*	estacas
torch (flashlight)	*lin-**ter**-nah*	linterna
sleeping bag	***sah**-ko THe **THor**-mir*	saco de dormir
stove	*es-**too**-fah/ko-**thi**-nah*	estufa/cocina
water bottle	*kahn-tim-**plo**-rah*	cantimplora

Food

breakfast	*de-sahy-oo-no*	desayuno
lunch	*ahl-mwer-tho/ko-mi-THah*	almuerzo/comida
dinner	*the-nah*	cena

Table for ..., please.
 *oo-nah me-sah pah-rah ...,
 por fah-bor*

Una mesa para ..., por favor.

Can I see the menu please?
 *pwe-THo ber lah lis-tah/el
 me-noo por fah-bor?*

¿Puedo ver la lista/el menú,
por favor?

I would like the set lunch,
please.
 *ki-sie-rah el ahl-mwer-tho
 ah pre-thio fi-ho/ahl-mwer-
 tho ko-rrien-te por fah-bor*

Quisiera el almuerzo a
precio fijo/almuerzo
corriente, por favor.

What does it include?
 *ke es-tah in-kloo-i-THo
 ?/ke in-kluy-e?*

¿Qué está incluido?
¿Qué incluye?

Is service included in the bill?
 *el ser-bi-thio es-tah in-kloo-
 i-THo en lah kwen-tah?*

¿El servicio está incluido en
la cuenta?

Not too spicy please.
 *no mooy pi-kahn-te, por
 fah-bor*

No muy picante, por favor.

ashtray	*the-ni-the-ro*	cenicero
the bill	*lah kwen-tah*	la cuenta
a cup	*oo-nah tah-thah*	una taza
dessert	*pos-tre*	postre

a drink	*oo-nah be-bi-THah*	una bebida
a fork	*oon te-ne-THor*	un tenedor
fresh	*fres-ko/ah*	fresco/a
a glass	*oon bah-so (oo-nah ko-pah)*	un vaso (una copa for wine or spirits)
a knife	*oon ku-chi-lyo*	un cuchillo
a plate	*oon plah-to*	un plato
spicy	*pi-kahn-te*	picante
a spoon	*oo-nah koo-chah-rah*	una cuchara
stale	*pah-sah-THo/rrahn-thio*	pasado/rancio
stale (bread)	*(pahn) doo-ro*	(pan) duro
sweet	*dool-the*	dulce
teaspoon	*koo-chah-ri-tah*	cucharita
toothpick	*mon-dah-THien-tes/ pah-li-lyo*	mondadientes/ palillo

Vegetarian Meals

Vegetables are normally listed (and served) separately in Spanish menus, so you can always order them as separate courses. Look under *Legumbres* or *Entremeses* on the menu.

I am a vegetarian.
  soy be-he-tah-ri-ah-no/-ah   Soy vegetariano/a.
I don't eat meat.
  no ko-mo kahr-ne   No como carne.
I don't eat chicken, or fish, or ham.
  no ko-mo po-lyo, ni pes-kah-THo, ni hah-mon   No como pollo, ni pescado, ni jamón.

Judías verdes con salsa de tomate
   Green beans in tomato sauce.
Pisto manchego
   Stewed zucchini, peppers, tomatoes and onions.
Revuelto de huevos a la riojana
   Eggs scrambled in an onion and tomato sauce.
Tortilla de patata
   Fried potato and onion omelette. This is the basic tortilla (Spanish omelette), but other ingredients can be added: chorizo (sausage), ham, mushrooms, eggplant, prawns, peppers or tuna.

Staples & Condiments
Ali-oli
   Garlic mayonnaise served as an accompaniment to grilled meat or fish.
Arroz
   Rice.
Arroz con cangrejos
   Rice with crabmeat and onion.
Arroz con costra
   Rabbit and rice casserole with egg crust.
Arroz a la riojana
   Rice with tomato, green or red pepper, Spanish ham and chorizo sausage.

Soups
Caldo gallego
   White bean and potato soup with turnip greens and chorizo sausage.

Fabada asturiana
  Broad bean *(fava)* soup with Spanish sausages (chorizos, *morcillas)* and *serrano* ham.
Garbanzos con carne
  A chick-pea, pork, chorizo and vegetable thick soup that can be served as a main course.
Gazpacho
  A chilled soup made from tomato, onion, green pepper and garlic.
Olla podrida
  A soup/main course made with vegetables (chick-peas, carrots, potatoes, turnips), meats (pork, beef, chorizos) and broth, served with fried slices of bread.
Sopa de ajo
  Spicy garlic and bread soup.
Sopa al cuarto de hora
  Clam, shrimp, ham and rice soup, served with chopped hard-boiled egg.

Meat

Albóndigas de carne
  Meatballs in an onion and chicken stock sauce.
Callos a la madrileña
  Tripe stew with ham, chorizo, and sometimes calf's feet.
Cochifrito
  Fricassee of lamb cubes with a lemon and garlic sauce.
Cordero asado
  Roast lamb (often in white wine and garlic).
Chorizos al horno
  Spanish spicy sausages, fried in their own fat, and then baked in the oven.

Chuletas de cordero a la navarra
Lamb chops and chorizo sausage, baked with onion, garlic and tomato.

Filete de termera
Veal steak.

Habas a la catalana
A casserole of broad bean *(fava)* with chorizo sausage, parsley and mint.

Lomo de cerdo a la zaragozana
Pork loin chops with tomato sauce and black olives.

Paella
See the Seafood section, page 364.

Tortilla
See the Vegetarian Meals section, page 361.

Seafood

Almejas a la marinera
Clams in white wine with garlic, onions and parsley.

Bacalao al ajo arriero
Salt cod cooked in olive oil with tomatoes, onions and garlic.

Besugo al horno
Red snapper, baked with sliced potatoes in olive oil, onions and tomatoes.

Calamares en su tinta
Squid fried with onions, garlic and parsley, with a sauce made from the squid's ink.

Crema de cangrejos de Segovia
Freshwater crab and fish soup.

Changurro
Crabmeat with sherry and brandy, baked and served in individual ramekins.

SPANISH

Merluza/Mero en salsa verde
   Hake/Pollock cutlets fried in olive oil, with parsley and green
   pea sauce.

Merluza a la madrileña
   Tail piece of hake, baked in a wine, mustard, tomato and
   crushed black olive sauce.

Paella
   Spain's best-known dish: saffron rice with seafood, chicken
   pieces, chorizos and vegetables. In the Valencian paella the
   shellfish may be lobster, shrimps, prawns, clams and/or mussels. The Castilian paella is likely to have only clams, but veal,
   beef or pork cubes may be added as well as chicken. The
   vegetables are normally peas and peppers. The paella is
   traditionally cooked out-of-doors on wood fires.

Salpicón de mariscos
   Shrimp and lobster salad.

Truchas a la española
   Grilled trout with onion and parsley.

Truchas a la navarra
   Marinated trout, baked with red wine and herbs.

Zarzuela de mariscos
   A shellfish stew from Catalonia. The elaborate version will
   include lobster, shrimps, mussels, clams, scallops, *serrano*
   ham, ground almonds, tomato and white wine.

Poultry & Game

Cocido madrileño
   Boiled chicken, meats, chorizos and vegetables (usually
   chick-peas, potatoes, carrots and leeks).

Codornices a la cazadora
   Quail stew with onions, leeks, tomatoes, turnips and carrots.

Liebre a la cazadora
   A hare casserole in red wine and garlic.
Perdices estofadas
   Partridges braised in white wine with vegetables and garlic.
Pollo a la chilindrón
   Sautéed chicken, with green and red peppers, tomatoes, *serrano* ham, and green and black olives.
Pollo en pepitoria
   Casserole of chicken pieces braised in white wine, with ground almonds, garlic and saffron.

Desserts & Sweets
Bartolillos de Madrid
   Small pastry fritters with custard filling.
Bizcocho borracho
   Squares of sponge cake soaked in a syrup of sweet wine and cinnamon.
Brazo de gitano
   Sponge cake roll with rum cream filling.
Buñuelos de plátano
   Banana fritters.
Buñuelos de viento
   Pastry fritters sprinkled with sugar and cinnamon.
Churros madrileños
   Crisp-fried crullers, sprinkled with sugar (similar to doughnuts).
Flan de huevos
   Spanish version of creme caramel.
Flan de naranja
   Orange creme caramel.

Leche frita
    Custard squares fried in olive oil and sprinkled with sugar and
    cinnamon. Served hot or cold.
Mantecados de Astorga
    Plain or cinnamon muffins.
Natillas
    Soft custard served in individual dishes, topped with egg
    white or with a ladyfinger biscuit.

Drinks – Nonalcoholic

coffee	*café*
with milk	*café con leche*
iced	*café helado*
fruit juice	*zumo/jugo*
soft drinks	*refrescos*
almond	*horchata*
water	*agua*
mineral water	*agua mineral*
natural (no gas)	*sin gaz*
plain	*agua natural*
tea	*té*

Drinks – Alcoholic

beer	*cerveza*
sherry	*jerez*
wine	*vino*
red	*tinto*
red wine punch	*sangría*
rosé	*rosado*
sparkling	*espumoso*
white	*blanco*

Shopping

How much is it?

kwahn-to kwes-tah?	¿Cuánto cuesta?
kwahn-to bah-le?	¿Cuánto vale?

bookshop	*li-bre-ri-ah*	librería
camera shop	*tien-dah THe ahr-ti-koo-los fo-to-grah-fi-kos*	tienda de artículos fotográficos
clothing store	*tien-dah THe rro-pah/boo-tik*	tienda de ropa/boutique
delicatessen	*tien-dah THe em-boo-ti-THos/sahl-chi-che-ri-ah*	tienda de embutidos/salchichería
general store, shop	*tien-dah THe ah-li-men-tah-thion/ahl-mah-then*	tienda de alimen-tación/almacén
laundry	*lah-bahn-de-ri-ah*	lavandería
market	*mer-kah-THo*	mercado
newsagency/ stationers	*pah-pe-le-ri-ah*	papelería
pharmacy	*fahr-mah-thiah*	farmacia
shoeshop	*thah-pah-te-ri-ah*	zapatería
souvenir shop	*(tien-dah THe) rre-kwer-THos*	(tienda de) recuerdos
supermarket	*su-per-mer-kah-THo*	supermercado
vegetable shop	*ber-THoo-le-ri-ah/froo-te-ri-ah*	verdulería/frutería

I would like to buy …
ki-sie-rah kom-prahr …   Quisiera comprar …

Do you have others?
tie-ne o-tros?   ¿Tiene otros?

I don't like it.
no me goos-tah   No me gusta.

Can I look at it?
pwe-THo mi-rahr-lo/ah   ¿Puedo mirarlo/a?

I'm just looking.
so-lo es-toy mi-rahn-do   Sólo estoy mirando.

Can you write down the price?
pwe-THe es-kri-bir el   ¿Puede escribir el precio?
pre-thio?

Do you accept credit cards?
ah-thep-tahn tahr-he-tahs   ¿Aceptan tarjetas de crédito?
THe kre-THi-to?

Could you lower the price?
po-THri-ah bah-hahr oon   ¿Podría bajar un poco el
po-ko el pre-thio?   precio?

I don't have much money.
no ten-go moo-cho THi-ne-ro   No tengo mucho dinero.

Can I help you?
en ke pwe-THo ser-bir-le?   ¿En qué puedo servirle?

Will that be all?
ahl-go mahs?   ¿Algo más?

Would you like it wrapped?
se lo em-bwel-bo?   ¿Se lo envuelvo?

Sorry, this is the only one.
lo sien-to, es el oo-ni-ko ke   Lo siento, es el único que
te-ne-mos   tenemos.

How much/many do you
want?

  k**wahn**-to/s k**ie**-re?   ¿Cuánto/s quiere?

Souvenirs

bullfighting poster (with your name on it)	*oon pos-ter de to-ros (kon soo nom-bre den-tro)*	un póster de toros (con su nombre dentro)
earrings	*pen-dien-tes/ah-re-tes*	pendientes/aretes
fans	*ah-bah-ni-kos*	abanicos
handicraft	*ahr-te-sah-ni-ah*	artesanía
leather wine bottle	*bo-tahs de bi-no*	botas de vino
leathergoods	*ah-ti-koo-los de kwe-ro*	artículos de cuero
mantillas	*mahn-ti-lyahs*	mantillas
necklace	*ko-lyahr*	collar
nougat (Spanish)	*too-rron*	turrón
pottery	*ahl-fah-re-ri-ah/the-rah-mi-kah*	alfarería/cerámica
ring	*ah-ni-lyo/sor-ti-hah*	anillo/sortija
rug	*ahl-fom-brah/tah-pe-te*	alfombra, tapete
scarves	*pah-nywe-los*	pañuelos
statuettes (of bullfighters/ civil guards	*fi-goo-ri-lyahs de to-re-ros/gwahr-diahs THi-bi-les*	figurillas de toreros/guardias civiles

Clothing

clothing	**rro**-pah	ropa
coat	ah-**bri**-go	abrigo
dress	bes-**ti**-THo	vestido
jacket	chah-**ke**-tah	chaqueta
jumper (sweater)	her-**sey**/poo-lo-ber/ **swe**-ter	jersey/pullover/ suéter
shirt	kah-**mi**-sah	camisa
shoes	thah-**pah**-tos	zapatos
skirt	**fahl**-dah	falda
trousers	pahn-tah-lo-nes	pantalones

It doesn't fit.
  mo me **ke**-THah bien   No me queda bien.

It is …
  es …   Es …

too big	de-mah-si-**ah**-THo **grahn**-de	demasiado grande
too small	de-mah-si-**ah**-THo **pe**-ke-nyo	demasiado pequeño
too short	muy **kor**-to	muy corto
too long	muy **lahr**-go	muy largo
too tight	muy ah-pre-**tah**-THo	muy apretado
too loose	muy ol-**gah**-THo	muy holgado

Materials

cotton	ahl-go-**THon**	algodón
handmade	e-cho ah **mah**-no	hecho a mano
leather	**kwe**-ro	cuero

of brass	de lah-ton	de latón
of gold	de o-ro	de oro
of silver	de plah-tah	de plata
silk	se-THah	seda
wool	lah-nah	lana

Toiletries

comb	pey-ne	peine
condoms	pre-ser-bah-ti-bos/ kon-do-nes	preservativos/ condones
deodorant	de-so-THo-rahn-te	desodorante
hairbrush	the-pi-lyo (pah-rah el kah-be-lyo/pe-lo)	cepillo (para el cabello/pelo)
moisturising cream	kre-mah oo-mek-tahn-te	crema humectante
razor	nah-bah-hah THe ah-fey-tahr	navaja de afeitar
sanitary napkins	kom-pre-sahs i-hi-e-ni-kahs	compresas higiénicas
shampoo	chahm-poo	champú
shaving cream	kre-mah THe ah-fey-tahr	crema de afeitar
soap	hah-bon	jabón
sunblock cream	kre-mah pro-tek-to-rah kon-trah el sol	crema protectora contra el sol
tampons	tahm-po-nes	tampones
tissues	pah-nywe-los THe pah-pel	pañuelos de papel
toilet paper	pah-pel i-hi-e-ni-ko	papel higiénico
toothbrush	the-pi-lyo THe THien-tes	cepillo de dientes

toothpaste	*pahs-tah THen-ti-fri-kah*	pasta dentífrica

Stationery & Publications

map	**mah**-*pah*	mapa
newspaper	*pe-ri-o-THi-ko*	periódico
newspaper in English	*pe-ri-o-THi-ko en in-gles*	periódico en inglés
novels in English	*no-be-lahs en in-gles*	novelas en inglés
paper	*pah-pel*	papel
pen (ballpoint)	*bo-li-grah-fo*	bolígrafo
scissors	*ti-he-rahs*	tijeras

Photography

How much is it to process this film?

   kwahn-to kwes-tah rre-be-lahr es-te rro-lyo/es-tah pe-li-koo-lah? — ¿Cuánto cuesta revelar este rollo/esta película?

When will it be ready?

   kwahn-do es-tah-rah lis-to? — ¿Cuándo estará listo?

I'd like a film for this camera.

   kie-ro oon rro-lyo pah-rah es-tah kah-mah-rah fo-to-grah-fi-kah — Quiero un rollo para esta cámara fotográfica.

B&W (film)	**blahn**-*ko i ne-gro*	blanco y negro
camera	*kah-mah-rah fo-to-grah-fi-kah*	cámara (fotográfica)
colour (film)	*pe-li-koo-lah en ko-lo-res*	(película) en colores

film	*pe-li-koo-lah/**rro**-lyo fo-to-**grah**-fi-ko*	película/rollo (fotográfico)
flash	*bom-**bi**-lyah/flahsh*	bombilla/flash
lens	***len**-te*	lente
light meter	*me-THi-**THor** THe looth*	medidor de luz

Smoking

A packet of cigarettes, please.

*oon pah-**ke**-te THe thi-gah-**rri**-lyos, por fah-**bor*** — Un paquete de cigarrillos, por favor.

Are these cigarettes strong/mild?

*son fwer-tes o swah-bes es-tos thi-gah-**rri**-lyos?* — ¿Son fuertes o suaves estos cigarrillos?

Do you have a light?

tie-ne fwe-go? — ¿Tiene fuego?

cigarette papers	*pah-**pel** THe foo-**mahr***	papel de fumar
cigarettes	*thi-gah-**rri**-lyos*	cigarrillos
filtered	*kon **fil**-tro*	con filtro
lighter	*en-then-de-**THor**/me-**che**-ro*	encendedor/me-chero
matches	*fos-fo-ros/the-**ri**-lyahs*	fósforos/cerillas
menthol	*men-to-**lah**-THo*	mentolado
pipe	***pi**-pah*	pipa
tobacco (pipe)	*pi-kah-**THoo**-rah (**pah**-rah pi-pah)*	picadura (para pipa)

Colours

| black | ***ne**-gro/ah* | negro/a |

blue	*ah-**thool***	azul
brown	*mah-**rron**/ko-**lor** kah-**fe***	marrón/color café
green	*ber-**THe***	verde
pink	*rro-**sah**-THo/-ah*	rosado/a
red	*rro-ho/-ah*	rojo/a
white	***blahn**-ko/-ah*	blanco/a
yellow	*ah-mah-**ri**-lyo/-ah*	amarillo/a

Sizes & Comparisons

small	*pe-**ke**-nyo/-ah, **chi**-ko/-ah*	pequeño/a, chico/a
big	***grahn**-de*	grande
heavy	*pe-**sah**-THo/-ah*	pesado/a
light	*le-be, li-**he**-ro/-ah, li-bi-**ah**-no/-ah*	leve, ligero/a, liviano/a
more	*mahs*	más
less	***me**-nos*	menos
too much/many	*de-mah-si-**ah**-THo/s*	demasiado/s
many	***moo**-chos*	muchos
enough	*bahs-**tahn**-te/su-fi-**thien**-te*	bastante/suficiente
also	*tahm-**bien***	también
a little bit	*oon po-ko/oon po-**ki**-to*	un poco/un poquito

Health

Where is …?
| ***don**-de es-**tah** …?* | ¿Dónde está …? |
| the doctor | *el dok-**tor**/el me-**THi**-ko* | el doctor/el médico |

the hospital	*el os-pi-tahl*	el hospital
the chemist	*lah fahr-mah-thiah*	la farmacia
the dentist	*el den-tis-tah*	el dentista

I am sick.
   es-toy en-fer-mo/-ah   Estoy enfermo/a.

My friend is sick.
   mi ah-mi-go/-ah es-tah   Mi amigo/a está enfermo/a.
   en-fer-mo/-ah

Could I see a female doctor?
   me po-THri-ah ah-ten-der   ¿Me podría atender una
   oo-nah THok-to-rah   doctora?

What's the matter?
   de ke se ke-hah?   ¿De qué se queja?

Where does it hurt?
   don-de le THwe-le?   ¿Dónde le duele?

It hurts here.
   me THwe-le ah-ki   Me duele aquí.

My … hurts.
   me THwe-le   Me duele … (sg)

Parts of the Body

ankle	*el to-bi-lyo*	el tobillo
arm	*el brah-tho*	el brazo
back	*lah es-pahl-dah*	la espalda
blood	*sahn-gre*	sangre
bone	*el we-so*	el hueso
chest	*el pe-cho*	el pecho
ear	*lah o-re-hah*	la oreja
eye	*el o-ho*	el ojo

finger	*el de-THo*	el dedo
foot	*el pie*	el pie
hand	*lah mah-no*	la mano
head	*lah kah-be-thah*	la cabeza
heart	*el ko-rah-thon*	el corazón
leg	*lah pier-nah*	la pierna
mouth	*lah bo-kah*	la boca
nose	*lah nah-rith*	la nariz
ribs	*lahs kos-ti-lyahs*	las costillas
skin	*lah piel*	la piel
spine	*lah ko-loom-nah (ber-te-brahl)*	la columna (vertebral)
teeth	*los THien-tes*	los dientes
throat	*lah gahr-gahn-tah*	la garganta

Ailments

I have …
   ***ten*-go …**   Tengo …

an allergy	*ah-ler-hiah*	alergia
anaemia	*ah-ne-miah*	anemia
a blister	*oo-nah ahm-po-lyah*	una ampolla
a burn	*oo-nah ke-mah-THoo-rah*	una quemadura
a cold	*oon res-fri-ah-THo/ kah-tah-rro*	un resfriado/ catarro
constipation	*es-tre-nyi-mien-to*	estreñimiento
a cough	*tos*	tos
diarrhoea	*di-ah-rre-ah*	diarrea
fever	*fie-bre*	fiebre
glandular fever	*mo-no-noo-kle-o-sis*	mononucleosis

a headache	*do-lor THe kah-be-thah*	dolor de cabeza
indigestion	*in-di-hes-tion*	indigestión
an inflammation	*oo-nah in-flah-mah-thion*	una inflamación
influenza	*gri-pe*	gripe
lice	*pio-hos*	piojos
low/high blood pressure	*pre-sion bah-hah/ahl-tah*	presión baja/alta
sore throat	*do-lor THe gahr-gahn-tah*	dolor de garganta
sprain	*oo-nah tor-the-THoo-rah*	una torcedura
a stomachache	*do-lor THe es-to-mah-go*	dolor de estómago
sunburn	*oo-nah ke-mah-THoo-rah THe sol*	una quemadura de sol
a venereal disease	*oo-nah en-fer-me-THahTH be-ne-re-ah*	una enfermedad venérea
worms	*goo-sah-nos/lom-bri-thes*	gusanos/lombrices

Some Useful Words & Phrases

I'm …
soy … Soy …

diabetic	*THi-ah-be-ti-ko/-ah*	diabético/a
epileptic	*e-pi-lep-ti-ko/-ah*	epiléptico/a
asthmatic	*ahz-mah-ti-ko/-ah*	asmático/a

I'm allergic to antibiotics/penicillin
*soy ah-**ler**-hi-ko/-ah ah los ahn-ti-bi-o-ti-kos/lah pe-ni-**thi**-**li**-nah*

Soy alérgico/a a los antibióticos/la penicilina.

I'm pregnant.
*es-**toy** em-bah-rah-**thah**-THah/en-**thin**-tah*

Estoy embarazada/encinta.

I'm on the pill.
*to-mo lah **pil**-do-rah ahn-ti-kon-thep-**ti**-bah*

Tomo la píldora anticonceptiva.

I haven't had my period for … months.
*ah-the … me-ses ke no me **bie**-ne/**lye**-gah lah **rre**-glah*

Hace … meses que no me viene/llega la regla.

I have been vaccinated.
*es-**toy** bah-ku-**nah**-THo/-ah*

Estoy vacunado/a.

I have my own syringe.
*ten-go mi **pro**-piah he-**rin**-gah*

Tengo mi propia jeringa.

I feel better/worse.
*me **sien**-to me-**hor**/pe-**or***

Me siento mejor/peor.

accident	*ahk-thi-**THen**-te*	accidente
addiction	***bi**-thio/dro-**gàh**-THik-**thion**/de-pen-**den**-thiah*	vicio/drogadicción/dependencia
antibiotics	*ahn-ti-bi-o-ti-kos*	antibióticos
antiseptic	*ahn-ti-**sep**-ti-ko*	antiséptico
bandage	*ben-**dah**-he*	vendaje
bite (insect)	*pi-kah-**THoo**-rah*	picadura

bite (dog)	*mor-THe-**THoo**-rah*	mordedura
blood pressure	*pre-**sion** ahr-te-ri-**ahl***	presión arterial
blood test	*ah-**nah**-li-sis THe **sahn**-gre*	análisis de sangre
contraceptive	*ahn-ti-kon-thep-**ti**-bo*	anticonceptivo
injection	*in-yek-**thion***	inyección
injury	***dah**-nyo*	daño
itch	*ko-me-**thon**/pi-kah-**thon***	comezón/picazón
menstruation	*men-stroo-ah-**thi**-on/**rre**-glah*	menstruación/regla
oxygen	*ok-**si**-he-no*	oxígeno
vitamins	*bi-**tah**-mi-nahs*	vitaminas
wound	*e-**ri**-THah*	herida

At the Chemist

I need medication for …
   *ne-the-**si**-to oon me-THi-kah-**men**-to pah-rah …*   Necesito un medicamento para …

I have a prescription.
   ***ten**-go rre-**the**-tah me-**THi**-kah*   Tengo receta médica.

At the Dentist

I have a toothache.
   *me **THwe**-le oo-nah **mwe**-lah*   Me duele una muela.

I've lost a filling.
   *se me kahy-o oon em-**pahs**-te*   Se me cayó un empaste.

I've broken a tooth.
  *se me rrom-pi-o oon **dien**-te* Se me rompió un diente.
My gums hurt.
  *me **THwe**-len lahs
  en-**thi**-ahs* Me duelen las encías.
I don't want it extracted.
  *no **kie**-ro ke me lo
  ah-**rrahn**-ke* No quiero que me lo
  arranque.
Please give me an anaesthetic.
  *por fah-**bor** THe-me oon
  ah-nes-te-si-ko* Por favor, deme un
  anestésico.

Time & Dates

What date is it today?
  *ke **THi**-ah es oy/ah **kwahn**-
  tos es-**tah**-mos?* ¿Qué día es hoy?/
  ¿A cuántos estamos?
What time is it?
  ke o-rah es/ke o-rahs son? ¿Qué hora es? ¿Qué horas
  son?

It is one o'clock.
  es lah oo-nah Es la una.
It is (two o'clock).
  son lahs (dos) Son las (dos).

in the morning	*de lah mah-**nyah**-nah*	de la mañana
in the afternoon	*de lah **tahr**-THe*	de la tarde
in the evening	*de lah **no**-che*	de la noche

Days of the Week

Monday	*loo-nes*	lunes
Tuesday	*mahr-tes*	martes
Wednesday	*mier-ko-les*	miércoles
Thursday	*hwe-bes*	jueves
Friday	*bier-nes*	viernes
Saturday	*sah-bah-THo*	sábado
Sunday	*do-min-go*	domingo

Months

January	*e-ne-ro*	enero
February	*fe-bre-ro*	febrero
March	*mahr-tho*	marzo
April	*ah-bril*	abril
May	*mahy-o*	mayo
June	*hoo-nio*	junio
July	*hoo-lio*	julio
August	*ah-gos-to*	agosto
September	*se-tiem-bre/*	setiembre/
	sep-tiem-bre	sep-tiembre
October	*ok-tu-bre*	octubre
November	*no-biem-bre*	noviembre
December	*di-thiem-bre*	diciembre

Seasons

summer	*be-rah-no*	verano
autumn	*o-to-nyo*	otoño
winter	*in-bier-no*	invierno
spring	*pri-mah-be-rah*	primavera

Present

today	*oy*	hoy
this morning	*es-tah mah-nyah-nah*	esta mañana
this afternoon	*es-tah tahr-THe*	esta tarde
tonight	*es-tah no-che*	esta noche
this week/year	*es-tah se-mah-nah/es-te ah-nyo*	esta semana/este año
now	*ah-o-rah*	ahora

Past

yesterday	*ahy-er*	ayer
day before yesterday	*ahn-te-ahy-er*	anteayer
yesterday morning	*ahy-er por lah mah-nyah-nah*	ayer por la mañana
yesterday afternoon/evening	*ahy-er por lah tahr-THe/no-che*	ayer por la tarde/noche
last night	*ah-no-che*	anoche
last week/year	*lah se-mah-nah pah-sah-THah/el ah-nyo pah-sah-THo*	la semana pasada/el año pasado

Future

tomorrow	*mah-nyah-nah*	mañana
day after tomorrow	*pah-sah-THo mah-nyah-nah*	pasado mañana
tomorrow morning	*mah-nyah-nah por lah mah-nyah-nah*	mañana por la mañana

tomorrow afternoon/evening	*mah-nyah-nah por lah tahr-THe/no-che*	mañana por la tarde/noche
next week	*lah se-mah-nah ke bie-ne*	la semana que viene
next year	*el ah-nyo ke bie-ne*	el año que viene

During the Day

afternoon	*tahr-THe*	tarde
dawn, very early morning	*mah-THroo-gah-THah*	madrugada
day	*di-ah*	día
early	*tem-prah-no*	temprano
midnight	*me-THiah-no-che*	medianoche
morning	*mah-nyah-nah*	mañana
night	*no-che*	noche
noon	*me-THio-THi-ah*	mediodía
sundown	*pwes-tah THel sol/-ah-tahr-THe-ther*	puesta del sol/atardecer
sunrise	*ah-mah-ne-ther*	amanecer

Numbers & Amounts

0	*the-ro*	cero
1	*oo-no/oo-nah*	uno, una
2	*dos*	dos
3	*tres*	tres
4	*kwah-tro*	cuatro
5	*thin-ko*	cinco
6	*seis*	seis
7	*sie-te*	siete
8	*o-cho*	ocho

9	*nwe-be*	nueve
10	*dieth*	diez
11	*on-the*	once
12	*do-the*	doce
13	*tre-the*	trece
14	*kah-tor-the*	catorce
15	*kin-the*	quince
16	*die-thi-seis*	dieciséis
17	*die-thi-sie-te*	diecisiete
18	*die-thi-o-cho*	dieciocho
19	*die-thi-nwe-be*	diecinueve
20	*bein-te*	veinte
30	*trein-tah*	treinta
40	*kwah-ren-tah*	cuarenta
50	*thin-kwen-tah*	cincuenta
60	*se-sen-tah*	sesenta
70	*se-ten-tah*	setenta
80	*o-chen-tah*	ochenta
90	*no-ben-tah*	noventa
100	*thien/thien-to*	cien/ciento
1000	*mil*	mil
one million	*oon mi-lyon*	un millón
1st	*pri-me-ro*	primero (1ro)
2nd	*se-goon-do*	segundo (2do)
3rd	*ter-the-ro*	tercero (3ro)
¼	*oon kwahr-to*	un cuarto
⅓	*oon ter-thio*	un tercio
½	*me-THio/ah*	medio/a
¾	*tres kwahr-tos*	tres cuartos

Some Useful Words

a little (amount)	*oon po-ki-to*	un poquito
double	*el do-ble*	(el) doble
a dozen	*oo-nah THo-the-nah*	una docena
Enough!	*bahs-tah*	¡Basta!
few	*(oo-nos) po-kos*	(unos) pocos (m)
	(oo-nahs) po-kahs	(unas) pocas (f)
less	*me-nos*	menos
many	*moo-chos/ahs*	muchos/as
more	*mahs*	más
once	*oo-nah beth*	una vez
a pair	*oon pahr*	un par
percent	*por thien-to*	por ciento
some	*ahl-goo-nos/ahs*	algunos/as
too much	*de-mah-si-ah-THo*	demasiado
twice	*dos be-thes*	dos veces

Abbreviations

A.C. *or* d.de.J.C.	AD
a.de J.C.	BC
Ayto	Town Hall
C/Av., Avda./Pza.	St, Rd/Ave/Square
CE	EC
(Administración General de) Correos	GPO
C.I.	ID
Cia	Co. (company)
Depto./Sede	Dept/HQ
IVA	VAT
NN.UU.	UN

N./S.	Nth/Sth
PVP	RRP (recommended retail price)
R.U.	UK
SIDA	AIDS
Sr./Sra./Srta.	Mr/Mrs/Ms
Talgo	inter-city train
EE.UU.	USA

Index

Basque *10*

Food 15
Greetings & Civilities 13
Pronunciation........................12
Small Talk.............................. 14
Specific Dishes 16

Catalan *18*

Food 22
Greetings & Civilities 20
Pronunciation........................19
Small Talk.............................. 20
Useful Phrases...................... 22

Dutch *26*

Abbreviations........................96
Accommodation.....................52
Age.......................................31
Ailments................................88
Air...44
Around Town..........................58
Bank, at the 60
Booking Tickets 43
Breakfast 68
Bus.......................................45
Camping................................65
Car..49
Car Problems.........................51
Chemist, at the 90
Clothing 83
Colours 86
Condiments, Spices &
    Garnish.............................76
Cooking, methods of 77
Country, in the 65
Dairy Products.......................69
Days of the Week 91
Dentist, at the 90
Dessert, Biscuits & Sweets .. 78
Directions 42
Drinks 79
Emergencies......................... 38
Entertainment....................... 64
Entrées................................. 70
Family 33
Feelings 35
Food 66
Forms of Address................. 30
Fruit...................................... 77
Game Food 72
Garnish 76
Getting Around 41
Greetings & Civilities 29
Health................................... 87
    Useful Words & Phrases... 89
Hotel, at the 53
Indonesian Food 75
Language Difficulties............. 35
Lunch 68
Materials 83
Meat...................................... 70

Meeting People 30
Methods of Cooking 77
Metro 47
Months 92
Nationalities 31
Numbers & Amounts 94
Occupations 32
One-Pan Dishes 73
Paperwork 40
Parts of the Body 87
Photography 85
Post Office, at the 61
Poultry & Game 72
Pronunciation 27
Religion 33
Requests & Complaints 56
Seafood 71
Seasons 92
Shopping 80

Sightseeing 63
Signs 37
Sizes & Comparisons 86
Small Talk 30
Smoking 85
Snacks 74
Souvenirs 82
Stationery & Publications 84
Taxi 47
Telephone 61
Tickets, booking 43
Time & Dates 91
Toiletries 84
Top Useful Phrases 29
Train 46
Vegetables 72
Vegetarian Meals 68
Weather 65

French 98

Abbreviations 169
Accommodation 125
Age 104
Ailments 160
Air 117
Around Town 133
Bank, at the 134
Booking Tickets 116
Breakfast 142
Bus 118
Camping 140
Car 123
Car Problems 125
Chemist, at the 163
Clothing 155
Colours 158
Country, in the 139
Days of the Week 165

Delicatessen, in the 143
Dentist, at the 163
Desserts 150
Directions 114
Drinks 151
Emergencies 110
Entertainment 138
Family 106
Feelings 107
Food 141
Forms of Address 103
Fruit & Nuts 150
Getting Around 114
Greetings & Civilities 102
Health 159
    Useful Words & Phrases . 162
Hotel, at the 126
Language Difficulties 108

Materials 155
Meat & Poultry 144
Meeting People 103
Menus, see Sample Menu ....
Metro 120
Months 165
Nationalities 104
Numbers & Amounts 167
Nuts 150
Occupations 104
Paperwork 113
Parts of the Body 160
Photography 157
Poultry 144
Post Office, at the 135
Pronunciation 100
Religion 105
Requests & Complaints 130
Sample Menu: One 147
Sample Menu: Two 148
Sample Menu: Three 149
Seafood 145

Seasons 165
Shopping 152
Sightseeing 137
Signs 110
Sizes & Comparisons 158
Small Talk 103
Smoking 157
Snacks 143
Souvenirs 154
Starters 144
Stationery & Publications 156
Taxi 121
Telephone 136
Tickets, booking 116
Time & Dates 164
Toiletries 156
Top Useful Phrases 102
Train 119
Typical Dishes 146
Vegetables 145
Vegetarian Meals 142
Weather 139

German 172

Abbreviations 240
Accommodation 201
Age 178
Ailments 232
Air 193
Appetisers & Snacks 219
Around Town 208
Bank, at the 209
Booking Tickets 191
Breakfast 219
Bus 194
Camping 215
Car 198
Car Problems 200
Chemist, at the 234

Clothing 226
Colours 230
Cooking, methods of 222
Country, in the 214
Days of the Week 235
Dentist, at the 234
Dessert & Pastries 222
Directions 190
Drinks 223
Emergencies 185
Entertainment 214
Family 180
Feelings 182
Food 216
Forms of Address 177

Getting Around......................189
Greetings & Civilities 176
Health..................................230
   Useful Words & Phrases .233
Hotel, at the 202
Language Difficulties 183
Materials.............................227
Meat & Seafood...................220
Meeting People....................177
Methods of Cooking.............222
Metro 196
Months................................236
Nationalities........................178
Numbers & Amounts............238
Occupations........................178
Paperwork 188
Parts of the Body.................231
Photography 228
Post Office, at the 210
Pronunciation......................173
Religion...............................180
Requests & Complaints 205
Seafood 220

Seasons..............................236
Shopping.............................224
Sightseeing 212
Signs...................................184
Sizes & Comparisons..........230
Small Talk............................177
Smoking..............................229
Snacks................................219
Soups..................................220
Souvenirs............................226
Staples & Condiments 219
Stationery & Publications....228
Taxi.....................................196
Telephone 211
Tickets, booking 191
Time & Dates 235
Toiletries..............................227
Top Useful Phrases.............176
Train....................................195
Vegetables 221
Vegetarian Meals 218
Weather...............................214

Irish 242

At the Restaurant.................248
Greetings & Civilities 245
Irish Words Commonly
   Heard in English..............249

Pronunciation 244
Signs...................................249
Small Talk............................246
Useful Phrases....................247

Portuguese 252

Abbreviations.......................311
Accommodation....................277
Age......................................259
Ailments..............................304
Around Town........................282
Bank, at the 283
Booking Tickets 270
Bus......................................272

Camping..............................287
Car......................................275
Car Problems.......................277
Chemist, at the 307
Clothing...............................299
Colours................................303
Country, in the 287
Days of the Week.................308

Dentist, at the 307
Desserts 295
Directions............................269
Drinks 296
Emergencies........................264
Family 260
Feelings...............................261
Food 288
Forms of Address 258
Fruit 294
Getting Around....................268
Greetings & Civilities 257
Health 303
　Useful Words & Phrases 305
Hotel, at the 278
Language Difficulties 262
Materials...............................300
Meat......................................290
Meeting People....................258
Metro 274
Months..................................308
Nationalities.........................258
Numbers & Amounts............310
Occupations.........................259
Paperwork............................267
Parts of the Body 304

Photography..........................301
Post Office, at the 284
Pronunciation 253
Religion 260
Seafood.................................292
Seasons 309
Shopping...............................297
Sightseeing 286
Signs......................................264
Sizes & Comparisons...........303
Small Talk 258
Smoking.................................302
Soups & Staples 289
Souvenirs..............................298
Stationery & Publications.....301
Sweets & Desserts...............295
Taxi..274
Telephone 285
Tickets, booking 270
Time & Dates 307
Toiletries...............................300
Top Useful Phrases 257
Train 273
Vegetables 293
Vegetarian Meals 289
Weather.................................287

Spanish *314*

Abbreviations.......................385
Accommodation....................343
Age 320
Ailments...............................376
Air 334
Around Town.........................350
Bank, at the 351
Booking Tickets 332
Bus 335
Camping 358
Car 340

Car Problems 342
Chemist, at the 379
Clothing.................................370
Colours..................................373
Condiments...........................361
Days of the Week..................381
Dentist, at the 379
Desserts & Sweets...............365
Directions..............................331
Drinks 366
Emergencies.........................326

Entertainment 356
Family 322
Feelings 323
Food 359
Forms of Address 319
Game Food 364
Getting Around 330
Greetings & Civilities 318
Health 374
   Useful Words & Phrases . 377
Hotel, at the 343
In the Country 357
Language Difficulties 324
Materials 370
Meat 362
Meeting People 319
Metro 337
Months 381
Nationalities 320
Numbers & Amounts 383
Occupations 320
Paperwork 329
Parts of the Body 375
Photography 372
Post Office, at the 352

Poultry & Game 364
Pronunciation 315
Religion 321
Requests & Complaints 347
Seafood 363
Seasons 381
Shopping 367
Sightseeing 355
Signs 325
Sizes & Comparisons 374
Small Talk 319
Smoking 373
Soups 361
Souvenirs 369
Staples & Condiments 361
Stationery & Publications 372
Taxi 337
Telephone 353
Tickets, booking 332
Time & Dates 380
Toiletries 371
Top Useful Phrases 318
Train 336
Vegetarian Meals 360
Weather 357

Language Survival Kits

Complete your travel experience with a Lonely Planet phrasebook. Developed for the independent traveller, the phrasebooks enable you to communicate confidently in any practical situation – and get to know the local people and their culture.

Skipping lengthy details on where to get your drycleaning ironed, information in the phrasebooks covers bargaining, customs and protocol, how to address people and introduce yourself, explanations of local ways of telling the time, dealing with bureaucracy and bargaining, plus plenty of ways to share your interests and learn from locals.

Australian
Introduction to Australian English, Aboriginal and Torres Strait languages.
Arabic (Egyptian)
Arabic (Moroccan)
Brazilian
Burmese
Cantonese
Central Europe
Covers Czech, French, German, Hungarian, Italian and Slovak.
Eastern Europe
Covers Bulgarian, Czech, Hungarian, Polish, Romanian and Slovak.
Fijian
Hindi/Urdu
Indonesian
Japanese
Korean
Mandarin
Mediterranean Europe
Covers Albanian, Greek, Italian, Macedonian, Maltese, Serbian & Croatian and Slovene.

Nepali
Pidgin
Pilipino
Quechua
Russian
Scandinavian Europe
Covers Danish, Finnish, Icelandic, Norwegian and Swedish.
Spanish (Latin American)
Sri Lanka
Swahili
Thai
Thai Hill Tribes
Tibet
Turkish
Vietnamese
Western Europe
Useful words and phrases in Basque, Catalan, Dutch, French, German, Irish, Portugese and Spanish (Castilian).

Lonely Planet Audio Packs

The best way to learn a language is to hear it spoken in context. Set within a dramatic narrative, with local music and local speakers, is a wide range of words and phrases for the independent traveller – to help you talk to people you meet, make your way around more easily, and enjoy your stay.

Each pack includes a phrasebook and CD or cassette, and comes in an attractive, useful cloth bag. These bags are made by local communities using traditional methods, through Community Aid Abroad projects with the support of Lonely Planet.

Forthcoming Language Survival Kits
Greek, the USA (American English and dialects, Native American languages and Hawaiian), Baltic States (Estonian, Latvian and Lithuanian), Lao, Mongolian, Bengali, Sinhalese, Hebrew, Ukrainian

Forthcoming Audio Packs
Indonesian, Thai, Vietnamese, Mandarin, Cantonese

LONELY PLANET PUBLICATIONS
Australia: PO Box 617, Hawthorn, Victoria 3122
USA: 155 Filbert Street, Suite 251, Oakland CA 94607-2538
UK: 10 Barley Mow Passage, Chiswick, London W4 4PH
France: 71 bis, rue du Cardinal Lemoine – 75005 Paris

PLANET TALK

Lonely Planet's FREE quarterly newsletter

We love hearing from you and think you'd like to hear from us.

When...is the right time to see reindeer in Finland?
Where...can you hear the best palm-wine music in Ghana?
How...do you get from Asunción to Areguá by steam train?
What...should you leave behind to avoid hassles with customs in Iran?

For the answer to these and
many other questions read
PLANET TALK.

Every issue is packed with up-to-date travel news and advice including:

- *a letter from Lonely Planet founders Tony and Maureen Wheeler*
- *travel diary from a Lonely Planet author - find out what it's really like out on the road*
- *feature article on an important and topical travel issue*
- *a selection of recent letters from our readers*
- *the latest travel news from all over the world*
- *details on Lonely Planet's new and forthcoming releases*

To join our mailing list contact any Lonely Planet office.

LONELY PLANET PUBLICATIONS
Australia: PO Box 617, Hawthorn, Victoria 3122 (tel: 03-819 1877)
USA: 155 Filbert Street, Suite 251, Oakland, CA 94607 (tel: 510-893 8555)
UK: 10 Barley Mow Passage, Chiswick, London W4 4PH (tel: 0181-742 3161)
FRANCE: 71 bis, rue du Cardinal Lemoine – 75005 Paris (tel: 1-46 34 00 58)

Also available Lonely Planet T-Shirts. 100% heavy weight cotton (S, M, L, XL)